In this study, Mark Parker proposes that literary magazines should be an object of study in their own right. He argues that magazines such as the *London Magazine*, *Blackwood's Edinburgh Magazine*, and the *New Monthly Magazine*, offered an innovative and collaborative space for writers and their work – indeed, magazines became one of the preeminent literary forms of the 1820s and 1830s. Examining the dynamic relationship between literature and culture which evolved within this context, *Literary Magazines and British Romanticism* claims that writing in such a setting enters into a variety of alliances with other contributions and with ongoing institutional concerns that give subtle inflection to its meaning. The book provides the only extended treatment of Lamb's Elia essays, Hazlitt's Table-Talk essays, "Noctes Ambrosianae," and Carlyle's *Sartor Resartus* in their original contexts, and should be of interest to scholars of cultural and literary studies as well as Romanticists.

MARK PARKER is Professor of English at Randolph-Macon College in Ashland, Virginia. He has published widely on Romantic literature in *Studies in Romanticism*, *Studies in English Literature*, and *Harvard Studies in English*.

CAMBRIDGE STUDIES IN ROMANTICISM 45

LITERARY MAGAZINES AND BRITISH ROMANTICISM

CAMBRIDGE STUDIES IN ROMANTICISM

This series aims to foster the best new work in one of the most challenging fields within English literary studies. From the early 1780s to the early 1830s a formidable array of talented men and women took to literary composition, not just in poetry, which some of them famously transformed, but in many modes of writing. The expansion of publishing created new opportunities for writers, and the political stakes of what they wrote were raised again by what Wordsworth called those "great national events" that were "almost daily taking place": the French Revolution, the Napoleonic and American wars, urbanization, industrialization, religious revival, an expanded empire abroad, and the reform movement at home. This was an enormous ambition, even when it pretended otherwise. The relations between science, philosophy, religion, and literature were reworked in texts such as *Frankenstein* and *Biographia Literaria*; gender relations in *A Vindication of the Rights of Woman* and *Don Juan*; journalism by Cobbett and Hazlitt; poetic form, content, and style by the Lake School and the Cockney School. Outside Shakespeare studies, probably no body of writing has produced such a wealth of response or done so much to shape the responses of modern criticism. This indeed is the period that saw the emergence of those notions of "literature" and of literary history, especially national literary history, on which modern scholarship in English has been founded.

The categories produced by Romanticism have also been challenged by recent historicist arguments. The task of the series is to engage both with a challenging corpus of Romantic writings and with the changing field of criticism they have helped to shape. As with other literary series published by Cambridge, this one will represent the work of both younger and more established scholars, on either side of the Atlantic and elsewhere.

For a complete list of titles published see end of book

LITERARY MAGAZINES AND BRITISH ROMANTICISM

MARK PARKER

CAMBRIDGE
UNIVERSITY PRESS

PUBLISHED BY THE PRESS SYNDICATE OF THE UNIVERSITY OF CAMBRIDGE
The Pitt Building, Trumpington Street, Cambridge, United Kingdom

CAMBRIDGE UNIVERSITY PRESS
The Edinburgh Building, Cambridge CB2 2RU, UK
40 West 20th Street, New York, NY 10011-4211, USA
10 Stamford Road, Oakleigh, VIC 3166, Australia
Ruiz de Alarcón 13, 28014 Madrid, Spain
Dock House, The Waterfront, Cape Town 8001, South Africa

http://www.cambridge.org

First published 2000

Printed in the United Kingdom at the University Press, Cambridge

Typeset in Monotype Baskerville 11/12½ in QuarkXPress™   [SE]

A catalogue record for this book is available from the British Library

Library of Congress cataloguing in publication data

Parker, Mark Louis.
Literary magazines and British Romanticism, 1820–1834 / Mark Parker.
p.   cm. – (Cambridge studies in Romanticism)
Includes bibliographical references and index.
ISBN 0 521 78192 2 (hardback)
1. English literature – 19th century – History and criticism.   2.
Periodicals – Publishing – Great Britain – History – 19th century.   3. Authors and
publishers – Great Britain – History – 19th century.   4. Literature publishing – Great
Britain – History – 19th century.   5. English periodicals – History – 19th century.   6.
Romanticism – Great Britain.   I. Title.   II. Series.

PR468.P37 P37 2001
820'.8'0145 – dc21   00-041399

ISBN 0 521 78192 2 hardback

To my parents, Hollis and Miriam

Contents

Acknowledgments

I was especially fortunate in the advice and encouragement given by David Perkins when I wrote the first part of this book in 1989. Jerome McGann helped me to shape and to reconceive this project from nearly the beginning. When I returned to school each fall after a summer of writing, two of my colleagues at Randolph-Macon College, Amy Goodwin and Tom Peyser, offered thoughtful comments on successive chapters of the manuscript. My chair, Dal Wooten, helped me to find the time to write and the will to pursue a long project. Peter Manning, who read the manuscript in its last stages, gave me a clearer sense of the coherence and the implications of the project. And finally, I thank my wife Deborah for her patience as a listener and intelligence as a reader. I hope that she profited as much from talking about my research as I did from discussing hers.

I am grateful to the Craigie family, from whose support of summer research at Randolph-Macon I have benefited greatly, and to the Rashkind family, whose support for sabbatical travel allowed me to do research abroad.

Earlier versions of parts of chapter 1 appeared in *Studies in Romanticism* and *Studies in English Literature*. I am grateful to the editors of these journals for permission to reprint.

Introduction: the study of literary magazines

This book seeks to do three things: to demonstrate that literary magazines should be an object of study in their own right, to argue that they are the preeminent literary form of the 1820s and 1830s in Britain, and to explore the ways in which literary magazines begin to frame a discussion of Romanticism. To do so, I have taken five instances from the four most prominent magazines of the time: the *London Magazine* from 1820 to 1821, the *New Monthly* from 1821 to 1825, *Blackwood's Edinburgh Magazine* from 1822 to 1825, and *Fraser's Magazine* from 1833 to 1834. The first two of these instances are more traditionally author-centered, treating Charles Lamb's Elia essays and William Hazlitt's Table-Talk essays in the *London*. The third comes from the pages of *Blackwood's*, whose "Noctes Ambrosianae" constitutes one of the great experiments within the form of the magazine. The fourth takes up the *New Monthly*, perhaps the most consciously and purposefully homogeneous of the great magazines. The final instance, the run of *Fraser's* containing Thomas Carlyle's *Sartor Resartus*, signals the limit to this period of intense creativity in magazine production and writing. In most considerations of this literature, the essay or poem is to the magazine as figure is to ground in the plastic arts; it is my hope that by dissolving the figures of Elia and the author of Table-Talk into the ground of Scott's *London*, by examining the shifting relation of figure to ground in the *New Monthly* and the playful reversals of such notions in "Noctes," and by observing the emergence of Carlyle's *Sartor* from the ground of magazine writing generally, we can begin to appreciate the importance of the magazine in the literary history of the period we have come to call Romantic.

Such an analysis requires the development of two key terms, context and politics. Context is the more difficult term, as it can mean the immediate environment of the other contributions in a given number of a magazine, the tenor or feel of a particular magazine, magazines and periodical literature more generally, or the wider social world within which magazines move. Context can also be produced by the relations between editor and contributor: overtly in the commissioning of a particular article or essay, in negotiations about the product, and through editorial changes; covertly in the silent adjustments contributors might make in fitting their work to a specific magazine. All of these versions of context are necessary to a study of literary magazines, but, as they are invoked at different times and with different force, their application varies considerably. The work of politics in literary magazines is less various and more subtle. Magazines such as *Blackwood's*, the *London*, the *New Monthly*, and *Fraser's* are conventionally categorized as Tory, Whig, or apolitical, but these tags tell us remarkably little. The literary magazines of this study offer surprisingly clear and self-conscious meditations on politics considered in the largest sense, as having to do with the nation as a whole. Considered together, these meditations provide a coherent and progressive argument about the way in which politics might be conceived and discussed.

The present chapter is offered as an introduction to the study of literary magazines. It specifically addresses those of the late Romantic period in England, but I believe that it raises critical issues basic to the study of literary magazines generally. The real difficulty in pursuing this project has been the lack of an existing conceptual framework for the study of literary magazines, or even a reliable description of the materials. This has forced a more inductive approach than might be taken in other kinds of studies, which can situate themselves among or against many recent good critical books. I am mindful that literary history has no self-evident and implicit meaning: it is not an empirical process, nor a recitation of facts. Nevertheless, it relies on empirical evidence, which it is the work of theory or interpretation to employ or set aside. At this point in the study of periodicals, the more we proceed inductively, the better, so long as we consider "induction" and "empiricism" as relative, not absolute states. The choice of the years between 1820 and 1834 and four middle-class magazines might seem eccentric, given the proliferation of magazine and periodical work in terms of new titles, of circulation numbers, and of audiences during that period and through the rest of the century. But I intend to show that a confluence of social, cultural, and literary factors make this early period in the history of literary magazines the most experimental, the most self-conscious, and, at least for the student of periodicals, one of the most telling.

As they have become more complex, magazines and periodicals have been less an object of study than an adjunct to literary investigation. Periodicals that are essentially single essays, such as Addison and Steele's

Tatler and *Spectator*, Johnson's *Rambler*, and Goldsmith's *Citizen of the World*, receive close attention. But when periodicals take on a more modern form – collaborations of many hands with an editor – they are treated largely as an archive from which scholars draw evidence to use in other arguments. Typically, scholars cite negative reviews in magazines to establish the newness or revolutionary qualities of Romantic writing (the familiar rehearsal of Francis Jeffrey's response to Wordsworth's *Excursion*, "This will never do," might stand as the type of this critical move). More often magazines are simply ignored in critical discussions. Few treatments of De Quincey's "Confessions of an English Opium Eater," for example, do more than mention the *London*, although that magazine, which had made a point of recounting and analyzing unusual psychological experiences, had much to do with preparing for the initial, unexpected success of this work. And while such compilations of magazine material as *The Romantics Reviewed*[1] have made reception histories easier to trace and the critical mood of the period easier to apprehend, scholars still tend to view magazines and periodicals merely as collections of discrete articles, as a system for delivering individual literary works or critical opinion that is itself disposable.

This critical tendency is unfortunate. What is lost in reading individual contributions outside the orbit of the periodical is not simply an immediate context for the work but a mode of emergence which radically affects the meaning of a particular essay, review, poem, or novel. A writer's intentions are only part of the meaning of the work in a periodical: a work in such a setting enters a variety of relations with other articles and ongoing institutional concerns that give subtle inflection to its meaning. This irreducible rhetoricity takes many forms: appeals to what often goes without saying in a particular magazine or review, innuendo familiar to its circle of readers, exaggeration discernible only by reference to the standard line of the periodical. The periodical does not simply stand in secondary relation to the literary work it contains; a dynamic relation among contributions informs and creates meaning.

Recapturing the world of the magazine involves substantial difficulties. To begin with, the sheer abundance of magazine writing, even in so small a part of the nineteenth century as this study proposes, is daunting. Michael Wolff's estimate that between twenty-five and fifty million articles appeared in Victorian periodicals is disturbing for its inexactness as well as its magnitude.[2] The concept of "information overload" is a commonplace to us, but Hazlitt and De Quincey wrote essays premised upon it. Of course, we might balance this rebarbative aspect of periodical research against Carlyle's matter-of-fact claim that, upon receiving the back issues of the *Edinburgh Review* (not an unusual gift from a publisher to a new contributor), he read them straight through, or the ambitious project set out by James Mill and his son John to review the first twenty-two years of the *Edinburgh Review* for the first few numbers of the *Westminster Review*. Such feats, however, are likely to provide faint inspiration for the modern researcher.

Moreover, the complexity of periodicals makes them formidable. To read a magazine such as *Blackwood's* or the *London* is to be plunged into a world of diurnal reference and innuendo largely lost to us. Nearly all periodicals in the 1820s trade in "personality," or rancorous personal attack, and by nature such writing is elusive and topical. What goes without saying, especially in magazines, has heightened importance at a time of stringent libel laws and active state censorship. In addition, each magazine labors to develop a specialized frame of reference, in which certain names or topics can trigger the reader's recollection of earlier material. For instance, the mere mention of "Leigh Hunt" in *Blackwood's* suggests some bullyragging to follow: it allows the reader to anticipate a certain kind of carnivalesque entertainment. "Hunt" functions as a master trope, which not only characterizes other writers and situations but embodies a particular view of the literary world. Moreover, not all such uses of charged language are so easily recoverable: perhaps the more decisive term of belletristic denigration in *Blackwood's* is "Tims," an idiosyncratic nickname for Patmore that has more subtle connotations of effete and ineffectual writing.

In fact, almost no aspect of periodical study is unproblematic. Almost all Romantic magazines (and all those taken up in this study) present their contributions anonymously or under a pseudonym. Scholarly efforts, which have been directed at attribution, have been extended and codified by the *Wellesley Index to Victorian Periodicals*.[3] This monumental work of many years and many hands would seem, at first glance, to ease some of the difficulties for students of magazines by providing the means for a classification which affords powerful ways of discriminating among individual contributions. Of course, one might have reservations about this kind of author-centered methodology, just as one might, from a more traditional perspective, have some doubts about the relative uncertainty of some of the attributions. But more problematic is the way in which the form of the magazine itself undermines either an exclusively author-centered or an exclusively poststructural approach. It is a critical commonplace that reviewers write with the force of the magazine or review behind them, that Gifford or Lockhart, in attacking Keats, write with the weight of the *Quarterly* or *Blackwood's* behind them. Yet it is also a critical commonplace that editors routinely changed and at times substantially rewrote contributions. Moreover, we know that contributors wrote for particular periodicals, shaping their remarks for the particular tenor of a magazine or review. Their intentions, apparently, would be to produce something like the "discourse" of poststructuralism. Therefore we have a range of modalities within periodicals, from relative authorial autonomy to collaborations between editor and contributor. In between we have elusive hybrids: collaborations before the fact, in which the contributor tunes his remarks to the key of the magazine; works of many hands, such as Hazlitt's continuation of John Scott's "Living Authors" after Scott's death; and deliberate submission of fragments to be sutured together by the editor, such as *Blackwood's* "Noctes Ambrosianae." An author-centered approach leaves us vulnerable to the deconstruction of agency inherent in contributions by multiple hands; if we consider periodicals as "discourse," we run afoul of the intentionality of this consciously anonymous production.

These two critical approaches are set out in contemporary assessments of periodicals by Hazlitt and James Mill, the former writing for the well-established *Edinburgh Review* and the latter in the first number of the radical *Westminster*. A comparison of these two accounts by two working writers has much to tell us about the advantages and drawbacks of each.

Hazlitt's 1823 "The Periodical Press" begins with a question: whether periodical criticism is good for literature. His response, once he has named Wordsworth and Scott as proof that writers can write well despite the immediate judgment of periodicals, is to turn his attention to periodical writing itself:

we will content ourselves with announcing a truism on the subject, which, like many other truisms, is pregnant with deep thought, – *viz. That periodical criticism is favourable – to periodical criticism.* It contributes to its own improvement – and its cultivation proves not only that it suits the spirit of the times, but it advances it. It certainly never flourished more than at present. It never struck its roots so deep, nor spread its branches so widely and luxuriantly. Is not the proposal of this very question a proof of its progressive refinement? and what, it may be asked, can be desired more than to have the perfection of one thing at any one time?[4]

The question posed by Hazlitt echoes through the Romantic period; it is connected with the decline of the epic and the "burden of the past" perceived by so many writers of the age.[5] Hazlitt's answer, under his characteristically smart magazine contributor's opening, is a surprising one: he implies that periodical writing is itself something of a literary genre, and that, at this moment in the sweep of literary history, in the rise and fall of genres and kinds of literature, the periodical has taken precedence. Hazlitt then focuses on the situation of the periodical writer:

Literary immortality is now let on short leases, and we must be contented to succeed by rotation . . .We exist in the bustle of the world, and cannot escape from the notice of our contemporaries. We must please to live, and therefore should live to please. We must look to the public for support. Instead of solemn testimonies from the learned, we require the smiles of the fair and the polite. If princes scowl upon us, the broad shining face of the people may turn to us with a favourable aspect. Is not this life (too) sweet? Would we change it for the former if we could? But the great point is, that *we cannot!* Therefore, let Reviews flourish – let Magazines increase and multiply – let the Daily and Weekly Newspapers live for ever! ("The Periodical Press," p. 358)

This is a complicated passage, both in its sensitivity to its historical moment and in its rhetoric. On the one hand, Hazlitt gives an insider's view of the historical shift from literary production under a patronage system to production based on a market. But Hazlitt also indulges in a not uncharacteristic touch of Coriolanian spleen at this change. His distrust of the reading public and his uneasiness at being judged by the "fair and polite" instead of the "learned" are evident. He further complicates the passage with a glancing quotation of the Duke Senior in Shakespeare's *As You Like It* – an exile who has bought philosophical insight and resignation with the loss of power and position.[6]

Like the Duke, however, Hazlitt manages to find sweet uses in adversity. Anticipating De Quincey's argument in his 1848 essay "Literature of Knowledge and Literature of Power," Hazlitt sets out the present task for intellectuals:

To dig to the bottom of a subject through so many generations of authors, is now impossible: the concrete mass is too voluminous and vast to be obtained in any single head; and therefore we must have essences and samples as substitutes for it. We have collected a superabundance of raw materials: the grand *desideratum* now is, to fashion and render them portable. Knowledge is no longer confined to the few; the object therefore is, to make it accessible and attractive to the many. The *Monarchism* of literature is at an end; the cells of learning are thrown open, and let in the light of universal day. (p. 358)

Hazlitt then turns to various periodicals, commenting unsystematically, idiosyncratically, and at times mysteriously on the tenor of and often the personalities behind each. The strength of his article lies in its clarification of the situation of the periodical writer, considered historically: the effects of the shift from patron to market audience, of the newly professional status of writers, and of the new status of the periodical as a genre or kind of literature. Throughout, Hazlitt is alive to the nuance and innuendo particular to the periodical world, as one might expect of a writer who had been immersed in its invective, its public squabbles, and its attendant legal actions.

When Hazlitt turns to individual magazines, however, the limitations of his insider's view are apparent. His stated topic was "The Periodical Press," but what follow are brief characterizations of individual magazines, most of which turn on the perceived disposition of the editor or some prominent contributor. So strong is Hazlitt's bias toward personalities that the clarity of his remarks suffers, at least for readers unfamiliar with the contemporary periodical scene. In his discussion of magazines, for instance, *Blackwood's* is not mentioned by name, except as one "extremity of the series" (p. 369). It does not figure at all in his treatment of leading magazines. Only later, when he addresses the scurrility rife in periodical discourse, does Hazlitt turn to *Blackwood's*, and here too not by name. There are several reasons for this elusive treatment: the Whig *Edinburgh*, for which Hazlitt is writing, had been involved in a running dispute with the Tory *Blackwood's*, and its editor, Francis Jeffrey, was often ridiculed personally in the pages of the latter. (His size was a common target: in a witty reworking of Walter Scott's nickname, "The Great Unknown," he was dubbed "the small known.") Hazlitt himself had been caught up in *Blackwood's* "Cockney School" attacks (among other things, he had been called "a pimple," and he had taken legal action against the magazine for libel). Hazlitt's analysis of the periodical world derives its power and insight from his engaged position as periodical writer, but that very experience entangles him with the current scene and precludes sustained reflection upon it. "The Periodical Press," enmeshed as it is in the working world of the periodical writer, cannot step outside it for long.

James Mill's 1824 "Periodical Literature" could not be more different. Mill's article – forty pages of dense quotation and analysis – is sober where Hazlitt is playful, and it counters Hazlitt's rhetorical flights with an austere and measured prose. Mill takes the stance of an outsider, one who brings to bear "a regular and systematic course of criticism"[7] to the largely unexamined world of periodical writing. His main point is to demonstrate that the political affiliation of the *Edinburgh Review* motivates its characteristic contradictions. As one might expect, Mill uses a Benthamite chain of reasoning, beginning with axiomatic statements and moving inexorably toward conclusions. The article opens with a powerful attack on both Whig and Tory politics: behind their seeming antagonism lies a shared interest in retaining the *status quo*. Rather than reform, the Whigs simply want the financial benefits that the governing Tories command. Although representing an exclusively aristocratic interest, they are forced to address another audience, the middle class, in hopes of regaining political influence. This forces them into a double pleading, characterized by recourse to vague language, championing of superficial reform, and what Mill calls the "see-saw" – the opportunistic embrace of both sides of an argument. Throughout the article, Mill considers the *Edinburgh Review* solely as a monolithic discourse. He respects neither the bounds of individual articles nor the possible distinctions of authorship; the "motives which must govern the class," not those which "actuate individuals" ("Periodical Literature," p. 217), are Mill's concern. Hazlitt's analysis turns upon the lived situation of periodical literature – what the audience demands, what constrains the writer, what the present situation enforces – and the aesthetic aspects of this kind of writing. Mill's analysis is above all a critique of ideology: critical, disinterested, dismissive of individual cases and personal agency.[8]

But just as Hazlitt's strength, his intimate knowledge of the nuance and innuendo of periodical writing, limits his analysis, Mill's penchant for abstraction creates systematic blindnesses within his work. In the axiomatic stage of his analysis, he posits that the *Edinburgh Review* is "addressed to the aristocratical classes" (p. 210). Such a formulation, as an insider like Hazlitt would surely know and as Mill's own analysis later implies, is much too simple. If the review is addressed to aristocrats, what Mill describes as the characteristic voice of the *Edinburgh Review* and the Whig constituency, a "double pleading" to the aristocratic opposition and the middle classes, is surely out of place. Throughout the Regency, the *Edinburgh Review* boasted circulations of 12,000–14,000, and these remained high over the next decade as well. Such penetration of the market goes well beyond the two hundred or so aristocratic families (according to Mill's own count) that have or aspire to political power in Britain. Even if one figures in what Mill terms the "props" and "servants" of the aristocracy – the church and the legal professions, each of whom "receives its share of the profits of misrule" (p. 214) – it is unclear what the point of the *Edinburgh Review*'s "double pleading" might be. Aristocrats and their "props" would presumably need no persuading to protect their own interests. In critiquing an ideology, Mill overlooks the complexities of both author and audience – the rhetorical situation implicit in the form of the magazine. Hazlitt is alive to the intricacies of voicing in periodical writing; Mill is virtually tone-deaf. Where Hazlitt recognizes the personal agency that pervades periodical writing, the bustling, individualist spirit of this sector of the ascendent professional middle class, Mill speaks impersonally of classes of men and their inevitable interests.

The best recent scholarly treatments of magazines closely follow the two approaches set out by Mill and Hazlitt. Jon Klancher takes Mill's more abstract line in the second chapter of *The Making of English Reading Audiences, 1790–1832*, and Peter Murphy in "Impersonation and Authorship in Romantic Britain" recalls Hazlitt's more situational and concrete position.[9] Each account displays the strengths and limitations that characterize its predecessor.

Klancher, like Mill, begins with an analytic thesis about the audience formed by middle class journals such as *Blackwood's* and the *New Monthly*. Such discourse, he argues, constitutes a "representation in which the British middle class could become more acutely conscious of itself" (*Making of English Reading Audiences*, p. 49). He supports this claim by providing a typology of the means used by particular magazines to achieve this self-consciousness. *Blackwood's*, for example, celebrates "the power of mind itself" (p. 55) and "the ultimately contentless activity of the mind's self-discovery" (p. 60). This "positive hermeneutic" (p. 60) is balanced and opposed by the "negative hermeneutic" of the *New Monthly*, which seeks to make "its middle-class audience the adroit manager of all sign systems in which it might be ensnared" (p. 62). The rhetoric that characterizes *Blackwood's* reaches beyond signs, while that of the *New Monthly* empties signs of meaning, but both magazines programmatically seek to develop the self-consciousness of their readers.

The strengths of such a critique are readily apparent. Few readers would counter Klancher's basic assertion that middle-class magazines and journals of the period are tireless promoters of intellect and mind, and his account of the various "hermeneutics" developed in such periodicals is trenchant and informative – perhaps all the more so as the analysis and study of non- fictional prose has lagged behind other scholarship of the Romantic period. But, as in the case of Mill, Klancher's argument omits much of the specifics of reading such magazines as *Blackwood's* and the *New Monthly*. Klancher's focus on this particular "transauthorial discourse" (p. 52) comes at the expense of other features of magazines, notably the complexities of the relation between magazine and reader. The particular "hermeneutics" he cites are present in the pages of the magazines, but they compete with other ways of understanding the world explicit and implicit in other articles. For instance, the "full-blown ideology of the power of mind" (p. 55) traced by Klancher is complicated in *Blackwood's* by the looming figure of Christopher North, who revels in intellectual pursuits but celebrates the purely physical pleasures as well. (One might note that when John Wilson takes up the "Noctes Ambrosianae" in 1825 he routinely balances mind, in the figure of De Quincey, with body, in the figure of the Ettrick Shepherd.) The "ideology of mind," like many other concerns taken up by magazines, is in play, and as such its importance is subject to interpretation by readers and intervention by contributors and editors.

Secondly, Klancher's analysis, like Mill's, considers the basic unit of analysis to be the periodical considered in its entirety (at least over the period his analysis sets out) and at once. The discourse of *Blackwood's* is not only "transauthorial" but, at least within the period under discussion, timeless as well. Hence perhaps the basic feature of a periodical, its periodicity, disappears, along with the particularly agile historicity often displayed in a succession of numbers. The "negative hermeneutic" of the *New Monthly*, for instance, does not have the same value or meaning over time in the magazine. Its application is by turns liberating and depressing, and it is capable of enforcing a heightened sense of engagement with the social world as well as withdrawal from it. In essence, Klancher has chosen semiology over rhetoric in his analysis. Consequently, while his consideration of reading audiences is sensitive to larger historical shifts, his treatment of periodicals, this most diachronic of literary forms, is unexpectedly synchronic.

Murphy's method, like Hazlitt's, turns from the consideration of magazines as a static archive of authorless "discourse" to an intricate account of the agency of individual contributors and the occasions on which they acted. If Klancher's critique sets out the innuendo of periodical discourse, Murphy's essay is concerned with the inflections found in the magazines of Romantic Britain. Focusing on the quarrel between John Gibson Lockhart, a prominent *Blackwood's* contributor and John Scott, editor of the rival *London Magazine*, Murphy offers what he terms "a parable about writing and reference" ("Impersonation," p. 626). Murphy notes the highly self-conscious nature of the use of pseudonym and personality (that is, rancorous personal attack) in *Blackwood's* – that what contributors to the magazine "say" often undercuts their status as a speaker. He suggests that this borders on being "a strange sort of tactical warfare, aimed at destroying the world of public discourse" (p. 633). In examining a typical *Blackwood's* "quiz" (a witty, punning, often vicious reference to persons or events) he concludes that "[t]he *Blackwood's* experiments force us to acknowledge that the published self is a curiously unstable thing, almost impossible to control and almost impossible to bring home to some person with a body" (p. 635). The duel between John Scott and Jonathan Christie that resulted from Scott's public denunciations of Lockhart then becomes a "parable" of the instabilities and ironies of representation.

Like Hazlitt, Murphy is sensitive to the specificities of utterance and occasion in magazines. The "parable" that he traces in the Scott–Lockhart–Christie affair is only legible to readers steeped in the working world of the magazine. As one might expect, this heightened sensitivity to historicity and the agency of individuals is purchased at some cost: it precludes, or at least postpones, larger consideration of the place of the magazine in its culture.

The difficulty presented by the sharp disparity between the systematic criticism of Mill and Klancher and the edifying approach of Hazlitt and Murphy can partly be answered by thinking of literary magazines in more broadly cultural terms, as attempts to organize the spectrum of cultural production at a time marked, according to Raymond Williams, by "the emergence of *culture* as an abstraction and absolute."[10] Where culture had once been a process, a kind of training, in the Romantic period it was increasingly becoming, both in and through the agency of the magazine, a thing in itself. Hence the task in the study of literary magazines is to investigate both the place of the magazine in culture and the place of culture within the magazine. As a purely methodological resolution, I propose in the chapters that follow to treat the run – as opposed to the entire periodical, as Mill proposes, and the author, as Hazlitt would have it – as the basic unit of study. The run, or a limited succession of numbers, will be defined in terms of a particular work or aspect of the magazine. The *London* will be examined in terms of the cultural program of John Scott's brief editorial regime, *Blackwood's* in terms of the collaborative series "Noctes Ambrosianae," the *New Monthly* through the early work of Horace Smith and Cyrus Redding, and *Fraser's* through Carlyle's *Sartor Resartus*. The treatment in each chapter will involve a kind of dialectic between an analysis of the cultural work of magazines and a description of the place of culture in the magazine.

This method of inquiry will, to borrow Mill's phrase, involve a sort of "see-saw": a continual tacking back and forth from the very particular and detailed approach of Hazlitt to the abstractions of Mill. But I think this method especially well suited for magazines, which exist in many configurations, with variations in intention and aims, in projected audience, in contributors, and in effects – often within a particular magazine and sometimes within a given number. Hazlitt's approach runs the risk of never coming to a point, of enmeshing the reader in a continual stream of anecdote and isolated fact; Mill's bold abstractions tend to dismiss the experience of reading magazines.[11]

If a dialectic of sorts is indicated in the study of magazines, we might begin from the pole of abstraction. On one aspect of periodical writing Mill and Hazlitt agree, both embracing it apodictically: that this literature must please immediately to have success. Hazlitt displays a sardonic ambivalence toward this iron law of periodical writing: "we must please to live, and therefore should live to please." The dispassionate Mill draws a series of logical conclusions from it. Since "it must aim at that immediate applause which is bestowed only for immediate pleasure; for gratification administered to the mind in its present state; for encouragement of the favourite idea, flattery of the reigning prejudice" ("Periodical Literature," p. 210), periodical literature is not a good means of enlightening the reading public. Mill notes that a book might gain an audience over time, despite its initial fortune, but that periodicals afford no such possibility. Hazlitt, while agreeing with Mill about magazines and reviews, feels that the entire literary profession, not just the periodical sector, has become market-driven. In other words, both writers insist that periodicals and periodical writing are first and foremost commodities.

This aspect of periodicals – especially magazines as opposed to the more established reviews – puts them in sharp contrast with earlier writing of the Romantic period. Poets such as Blake, Wordsworth, and Coleridge register a protest against industrialization and materialism, and they manage to skirt these forces in their productive lives as well – Blake by a principled refusal to enter the commercial publishing world; Wordsworth and Coleridge through timely, if not lavish, benefits from patronage, both private and governmental. Periodical writers of the 1820s operate in a system of production that has been, in the terminology of economists, rationalized. Payments to contributors are made by the sheet, that is, per sixteen pages of the periodical, in a fairly tight range across the industry. Favored contributors, such as Charles Lamb, might receive sixteen guineas per sheet; regular contributors twelve. Thomas Campbell's contract with Henry Colburn to edit the *New Monthly* stipulated only the number and kind of article – six of prose and six of poetry – he was expected to provide.[12] Moreover, this mode of production is referred to openly within the pages of the magazine: it is not occluded, as is often the case in later novels produced under the commodity system. At no point in the magazine world of the 1820s and 1830s could an article take the demystifying stance toward its mode of production that Gissing's *New Grub Street* could toward the three-decker; there is little space for the high-flown rhetoric of aesthetic idealism in the working world of magazines and reviews.

Moreover, the format of the magazine offers a suggestive parallel to what Adam Smith famously considered the motive force of the Industrial Revolution: the concept of division of labor. A quick look at the table of contents of almost any magazine of the period shows how much specialization had begun to creep into the medium. Part of this derives from the professionalization of the middle classes, in which differentiation and segmentation of occupation were crucial to achieving status. But the practice goes deeper than simply professional self-interest. We can see this ideology at work in the contradictory way that Hazlitt invokes the concept in "The Periodical Press." Hazlitt, after arguing that progress in the arts has resulted in a diffusion of artistic effort and noting that at present "Politics blend with poetry, painting with literature," concludes that "[a]ll the greatest things are done by the division of labour – by the intense concentration of a number of minds, each on a single and chosen object" (p. 354). Hazlitt provides two examples, Rembrandt and Michelangelo, the latter of which, in his own analysis, does not support his claim. That a writer like Hazlitt, not to mention an editor like Jeffrey, would let such a unconvincing presentation stand, testifies eloquently to the ideological force of the concept.

That division of labor or specialization was a given in reviews and magazines of late Romanticism is easy to document: it informs the discussions of a wide range of intellectual phenomena.[13] This ideological commitment makes periodicals, considered historically, progressive, as opposed to other media with other conceptions of the breadth of knowledge that a public intellectual should possess. Moreover, this ideological formation is in stark contrast with that of the rest of the century, which regarded such divisions as ominous and troubling, and in which the figure of the "Victorian Sage," the polymath who could speak authoritatively on many subjects and thereby alleviate these anxieties, was put at a premium.[14]

While the text as commodity and the division of labor in the mode of production are generally apparent in periodicals of the Romantic period, these features are intensified in magazines. If the literature of the previous century – and much of that written in the first twenty years of the nineteenth century – sought "to instruct and to delight," so do magazines of the late Romantic period, but with some renegotiation of the terms. The nature of instruction has changed. Where Samuel Johnson might note, with the authority of an entire literary tradition behind him, that "mankind need more to be reminded than instructed," Hazlitt sees "a superabundance of raw materials" and a pressing need "to fashion and render them portable" ("The Periodical Press," 358). And delight has become far less ineffable a category, since, as James Mill puts it, "Every motive, therefore, which prompts to the production of any thing periodical, prompts to the study of immediate effect, of unpostponed popularity, of the applause of the moment" ("Periodical Literature," 207). Hence magazines represent, through their formal properties, a characteristically modern experience of their world, at least for the middle-class readership they address.

The basic formal features of periodicals, commodification and division of intellectual labor, have determinate effects for readers. The most important of these are the dialogism within the magazine (more specifically the heteroglossia of language), both in terms of the run and the individual number, and the dialectic in the form between what Umberto Eco has termed "open" and "closed" tendencies.[15] In some ways, these features are two sides of the same coin: "dialogism" being more descriptive of the means of expression than the terms "open" and "closed," which look to the ends. Heteroglossia, as developed by Bahktin, concerns language on the level of the utterance. The concept assumes that language is made up of languages, each of which is the product (and in turn producer) of the experience of a social group. As Bakhtin writes in "Discourse in the Novel," the stratification of language takes place along the lines of "social dialects, characteristic group behaviour, professional jargons, generic languages, languages of generations and age groups, tendentious languages, languages of the authorities, of various circles and of passing fashions, languages that serve the specific sociopolitical purposes of the day, even of the hour."[16] Ultimately, each of these languages has its own way of understanding and representing the world.

While the contributors to literary magazines come from a rather small slice of British society, which restricts the heteroglossia of magazines in important ways,[17] the division of intellectual labor nevertheless sets up its own internal dynamic among the competing languages of middle-class Britain – languages of aesthetics, of religious life, of economic life, or of the leisured gentleman. This struggle, recorded vividly in magazines, insures that a magazine carries a great variety of potential meanings, none of which can be said to be dominant.

The resulting ambiguity, in terms of the overall effect of a publication, is perhaps better approached in terms of "open" and "closed" form.[18] A magazine, considered abstractly, presents readers with a field of possibilities and leaves it in large part to them to decide what approach to take or what conclusions to take away. In fact, compared with a novel or other kinds of written discourse, a magazine does little to enforce the most basic rules for closure, such as a prescribed order of perusal. Given the looseness of the reading protocols for magazines, one could imagine any number of idiosyncratic and contradictory experiences across their audiences – an unparalleled openness within the form. Yet evidence of such readerly freedom does not appear in the historical record, which would lead us to investigate the devices employed within the magazine to temper the centrifugal tendency of openness. A few of these are formal, such as the activity of a strong editor who arranges contributions to enforce certain strains of discourse within the magazine and who addresses, from a self-proclaimed seat of authority, some of the running rifts among contributors and various languages. Moreover, for regular readers of a magazine, idiosyncratic interpretations might sharply decline over time: as one reads more numbers of a magazine, even in snatches, a set of expectations might take shape to give more determinate shape to response. But perhaps most decisive in the conflict between open and closed effects is the work of ideology: the desire of the reader to have not so much the experience of openness as the opportunity for it. The closure of periodicals, the stable world they evoke, is in part a function of their readers' preference for choice on the abstract level – their pleasure in not availing themselves of the choices offered by this conspicuously open form. Apparent freedom is part of the pleasure of the magazine.

In terms of form, the magazine in the last decade of the Romantic period mirrors the transformation of Britain in the first twenty-five years of the nineteenth century. As the new industrial order rationalizes older modes of production and recasts older social attitudes, so too does the magazine, and as such it represents the middle-class revolution that characterizes this stage of capitalism. But it is also, as we shall see, the site of considerable resistance to the changes dictated by newer modes of production, and it is a medium through which some of the harsher aspects of this new world could be mystified as well. While the magazine represents this new order abstractly in terms of its form, it also provides, on the level of content, a forum where the terms of the middle-class order could be negotiated and promulgated.

In turning to an experience-near account of literary magazines from 1820 to 1834, we must begin with the history that impinges upon the moment. Britain was, as one historian puts it, "unprepared for peace" in 1815.[19] The war ended surprisingly quickly, and the adjustments that followed were painful. The Corn Laws were enacted, to much distress and amid much protest, before Napoleon's surrender. The next year was a bad one: poor harvests, a glut of labor, and the collapse of the immense war industry to the detriment of shipbuilding, coal-mining, and iron production.[20] From Waterloo through 1819, reform interests, having learned much from their defeats in the early 1790s and in 1811–12, formed the large Political Unions, which generally prepared their members for the responsibilities of suffrage. By 1818–19 these massive organizations of workmen met to carry resolutions, make petitions, and resolve to act peacefully. From our perspective, the moment of reform was a brief one. The 1819 Peterloo Massacre, at which a peaceful crowd was dispersed by a yeoman guard wielding sabers and several members of the crowd killed, prompted an anxious government to pass the Six Acts. The so-called Cato Street conspiracy of February 1820, in which Arthur Thistlewood was arrested in a plot to blow up the Cabinet, marked the end of such reform and revolutionary movements. But to those alive in 1820, at least those in the aristocracy and the middle classes, the times seemed dangerous.

Clearly one class was acting consciously in terms of its interest during the tumult of the post-war period: the landowning aristocracy. They moved decisively in 1814, passing the Corn Laws to ensure rents inflated by the wartime economy, and in 1819, with the Six Acts. But the period 1816–20 marks, for most historians, the moment at which the other classes formed a distinctive consciousness. For the working class, this consciousness is clear: begun in simple opposition to the aristocracy and middle classes, it had fairly direct aims and aspirations. The orientation of the middle classes during this formative period, however, is a matter of debate among historians. Two schools of thought have developed: one argues that the middle class aligned itself, at least until the 1832 Reform Bill, with the insurgent working class against what was perceived as a corrupt and decadent aristocracy; the other considers the middle class as already working with the aristocracy.[21] While one would expect accounts of a class "coming to consciousness" to be complex, both theories accept a significant split within the middle classes, between those members conforming to what the historian Harold Perkin usefully terms the "entrepreneurial" and "professional" ideals.[22]

The "entrepreneurial" ideal is fairly easy to sketch, as it largely approximates the portrait of the expansionist bourgeoisie provided by Karl Marx in the first section of *The Communist Manifesto*. It insists on the primacy of the capitalist, who awakes slumbering capital or property and by his efforts provides wages for workmen. The "professional" ideal, the product of the industrial revolution and some shrewd self-policing, is more complicated. Members of this group, such as doctors, lawyers, or architects, are neither capitalists nor landowners, although they readily identify with one or the other as their interest leads them. The members of the professional middle class justified themselves and their demands on the rest of society through arguments based on merit and what might be called the ideology of the examination – a commitment to testing, certification, and professional standards. What characterizes the members of this class is "their comparative aloofness from the struggle for income" (Perkin, *Origins*, pp. 256–7), that is, their indirect relations to the market, and, more broadly, their ambiguous relation to the economic base. Significantly, most theorists of economics and class come from the ranks of the professional middle class.

Perkin calls the professional order the "forgotten class," by which he means that their analyses of society often did not take into account their own anomalous situation. This group poses something of a problem for commentators on both class and economics. For instance, Marx's consideration of this class in the last chapter of *Capital* is revealing: his analysis, which simply adds more "classes" for doctors and lawyers and similar professions, undercuts the powerful simplicity of his analysis, his tripartite division of society.[23] This sector of the middle class expanded greatly in the 1820s, as lawyers, doctors, and architects began to control their own accreditation through professional organizations and groups. It is from this class, as the century wore on, that disinterested analysis was expected. (One might say that through spokesmen such as both Mills and Arnold they managed to project their ideals on Victorian society effectively.) More importantly, this sector became more and more alienated from the entrepreneurial wing of the middle class, in part because of its different relation to market forces, and in part because of its aspirations toward genteel status.

The analysis stressing collusion between aristocratic and middle-class interests downplays the effect of Perkin's entrepreneurial sector, arguing that such activity was already typical of aristocrats. Advocates of this theory stress the aggressive "agricultural entrepreneurship" of landowners, as well as heavy investment in "government funds, speculative stocks like the South Sea Company, and turnpike trusts" (Perkin, *Origins*, p. 302). Lawrence and Jeanne C. Fawtier Stone, in explaining the long ascendancy of the aristocracy in England, characterize the middle class in this way:

What makes the rise of this middling sort so crucial is their attitude towards their social superiors. Instead of resenting them, they eagerly sought to imitate them, aspiring to gentility by copying the education, manners, and behaviour of the gentry. They sent their children to boarding-schools to learn social graces, they withdrew their wives from work to put them in the parlour to drink tea, they patronized the theatres, the music-rooms, the print shops, and the circulating libraries, and they read the newspapers, the magazines, and the novels. Their attitude thus provided the glue which bound together the top half or more of the nation by means of an homogenized culture of gentility that left elite hegemony unaffected. (*An Open Elite?*, p. 291)

Clearly this describes Perkin's professional class; where the Stones' analysis differs from that of Perkin is in the importance it assigns to the entrepreneurial sector of the middle class.

Fortunately, we need not choose between these alternatives in order to profit from them. For in a sense, they are both right: what is apparent in this tumultuous period, in which the social contract is being renegotiated, is that much of the middle-class behaved largely in the way the Stones suggest. The alliance between the middle classes and the aristocracy, in essence, is codified by the 1832 Reform Bill, which addresses some of the corruption issues raised by the reform movement, but largely leaves the extension of suffrage to later bills. Although both the entrepreneurial and professional ideals are in play in middle-class economic life, the private life of this class is, as the Stones insist, imitative of the aristocracy. Literary magazines address this sector (or, in Perkin's analysis, the professional sector) of the middle class. Moreover, such magazines draw their contributors and their editors almost exclusively from this sector. Hence the concerns and aspirations of this class are the basis for an experience-near account of literary magazines. For whatever the professed attitude a contributor to the *London* or the *New Monthly* takes toward the aristocracy as a class, the pull of gentility (or, put in its ubiquitous magazine vernacular, "respectability") aligns the writer with it.

The aspiration toward gentility characteristic of the middle class generally is particularly trying for contributors to literary magazines. Some writers might achieve this status, such as Thomas Campbell, the leisured editor of the *New Monthly*, or John Wilson, who performed a variety of roles for *Blackwood's* (which he shrewdly combined with a University Chair to which his literary work had helped him). Others, such as Hazlitt and Thomas De Quincey, lived a hand-to-mouth existence reminiscent of Grub Street, regularly working under acute financial duress. Such struggles could be painfully obvious, as in the case of Charles Lamb, whose Elia essays often represent (or betray) anxieties about status. As a clerk in the India House whose father was a servant, reminiscences concerning "Poor Relations," financial privation during the early years of his career, or his parents evoke all Lamb's sensitivity and nuance as an essayist. His mystification of his father's occupation in "The Benchers of the Old Temple" might be taken as the extreme case: Elia aligns him through quotations with Lear's faithful and forthright retainer Kent, thereby suggesting that his father's worldly status was a kind of disguise.[24] A more cruel example of the struggle for gentility would be the routine use of James Hogg, the Ettrick Shepherd, for spectacular purposes in *Blackwood's*. However resolutely the historical figure Hogg moved toward gentility, publishing his poems to some acclaim, dining at the tables of the country gentry, setting himself up as a gentleman farmer, and regaling visitors to his home with hearty (and financially ruinous) entertainment, his fellow contributors delighted in chaffing him with an urbane humor that insisted on his provinciality, rude manners, and primitive charm. That they occasionally pause to wonder at his natural wit and poetic imagination in no way alters the anxieties attendant upon this presentation.

In fact the case of Hogg is far more suggestive than that of Lamb. While Elia may evoke, through his recollections, anxieties about gentility common to many in the middle class, the treatment of Hogg presents these anxieties in action. In *Blackwood's*, the representation of Hogg is a defensive mechanism: in a world marked by the struggle for gentility, one of the weapons of class warfare is just such exclusionary activity. In denying the claims of Hogg to gentility, his middle-class detractors, the journalistic corps of *Blackwood's*, shore up their own claims to such status by assuming the role of social arbiter. Such regulative and exclusive energy pervades the entire "Cockney School" episode, in which various *Blackwood's* writers – initially and prominently John Gibson Lockhart – mix aesthetic criticism of a group of London-based artists with personal attack. Whether they take up Leigh Hunt, Robert Benjamin Haydon, Keats, or Hazlitt, *Blackwood's* contributors seize upon lapses in taste and refinement. As in the case of Hogg, the humor can be cruel, and it often focuses on the physical characteristics or circumstances of the victim, whether it be the insistence upon Hunt's effeminacy and lubricity, ridicule of Keats's life as an apothecary's apprentice, or the reduction of Hazlitt to "an overgrown pimple, sore to the touch."[25]

It would be a mistake to treat the eruption of such anxieties as unusual in the world of literary magazines. "The Cockney School" was the leading article in the first number of *Blackwood's* over which Lockhart and Wilson had control in April 1817, and similar outbursts feature regularly through 1824, perhaps culminating in the grotesque transformation of "pimpled" Hazlitt, who had just published an account of his affair with a servant girl in *Liber Amoris*, into the "Cockney Adonis." While writers in magazines such as the *London* or the *New Monthly* eschew such gross caricature, similar energies circulate in their writings. John Scott, in surveying the unrest of 1820, is far more likely to characterize popular reform agitation as a trespass on a middle class privilege than to examine the merits of the case. Literary magazines of the 1820s and 1830s are entangled in the struggle for gentility that is characteristic of the middle-class, at times representing it and at times enforcing it harshly. Moreover, the contributors themselves are caught up in the same forces.

Hence the world of literary magazines is a kind of arena, where what is often at stake, for both reader and contributor, is one's image. This antagonism is further encouraged by the obvious marketability of such displays. The notoriety of the April 1817 number of *Blackwood's*, which, in addition to Lockhart's "Cockney School," ran an ill-mannered attack by John Wilson on Coleridge (Wilson had recently been Coleridge's guest) and included the infamously personal "Chaldee Manuscript," produced an immediate and gratifying spike in circulation. What the *London's* John Scott, in a forgiving vein, called the "merry ruffianism"[26] of *Blackwood's* was enforced by the dynamics of the market as well.

The circumstances of the Scott–Christie duel of February 1821 provide the most notorious example of the struggle for gentility that pervades the world of magazines. Historians have long cited the adoption of the aristocratic ritual of dueling as evidence of the middle class's "cultural mimicry."[27] Judges and juries, even in the first half of the nineteenth century, would not convict in cases of death by dueling, and in 1812 the Lord Chief Justice, in high aristocratic fashion, complained that "really it was high time to stop this spurious chivalry of the counting-house and the counter."[28] Spurious or not, this remnant of feudal times cost John Scott his life, and the literary scene of the 1820s lost a talented editor and a gifted critic.

The *London Magazine* was begun in January 1820, as a conscious rival to *Blackwood's*. The similarity between the two magazines is striking. Each number contains 128 pages of double columns, an economical but certainly not an elegant or easy-to-read format. The typeface is identical in each. While the general line of each magazine differs sharply – the *London* was consciously urban, smart, and politically sophisticated; *Blackwood's* reveled in a proud provinciality and reactionary politics – many of the articles from one could easily have emerged in the other. Despite his apparently Cockney proclivities, the *London's* Elia was much admired by Christopher North, the pseudonymous editor of *Blackwood's*, and one of the *London's* great successes, De Quincey's "Confessions of an English Opium Eater," was promised, but never delivered, to *Blackwood's*. Both magazines provide a medley of literary reviews, articles on aesthetics, and humorous pieces. An experienced editor, John Scott clearly recognized the value of the spritely format developed by *Blackwood's*, and he hoped that a literary magazine along the lines of his northern rival but based in London and representing London would be profitable.

During the first half of 1820, the *London* won a respectable audience, though considerably smaller than that of *Blackwood's*. Scott defended some of the "Cockneys" from the "merry ruffianism" of his northern rival, but he did so not as an advocate but as a careful and sensitive judge of their merits and faults. Although each magazine took jostling notice of the other, both kept up the bonhomie of worthy competitors. On the success of Scott's "Lion's Head" – a feature shared with *Blackwood's*, like so many in the *London* – which included notes to contributors and general light remarks, *Blackwood's* discontinued the original with good-humored admiration for its competitor. When Scott announced a northern journey in the pages of his magazine, he angled after a dinner invitation from the *Blackwood's* crowd.

This palmy era ended in November 1821, when Scott attacked *Blackwood's* directly in a slashing article. Taking Hamlet's quip "They do but poison in jest" as his epigraph (which, viewed in terms of the magazine's ever-present anxieties over gentility, suggestively aligns him with the dispossessed prince of Elsinore), Scott inveighs against the rival magazine's use of multiple pseudonyms by the same writer. Scott finds this practice, which creates the illusion of contradicting voices, especially reprehensible when used to praise and damn a literary work by turns, as had been done in treatments of Wordsworth and Coleridge. Taking the high line, Scott solemnly intones that "The honour of the literature of the present day we consider now at stake" (*London Magazine* 2, 515). Scott finds "pungency" to be the salient feature of *Blackwood's*: "like that of the trash they sell in the common liquor-shops under the name of brandy – which is seasoned with burning poison to recommend it to the diseased tribe of drabs and dustmen" (pp. 511–12). As ever in these magazines, attacks on gentility are the staple of invective, and Scott's rejoinders to *Blackwood's* achieve a "pungency" of their own. Scott followed this assault in the December number with "The Mohawk Magazine," which repeats earlier charges with just enough variation to warrant another article.

The historical record does not provide the specific reasons behind Scott's change of attitude toward *Blackwood's*. Scholars have looked to his northern journey, concerning which little information survives, for clues to his motives.[29] Surely the journey would have provided ample opportunity for Scott to discover the backstage antics of the magazine his namesake, Walter Scott, privately referred to as the "mother of mischief."[30] The high jinks of Wilson, Lockhart, and Maginn were an open secret in Edinburgh literary circles. But this search for specific occasion undervalues other clues to Scott's motives. Despite the praise subsequently heaped upon the *London* by scholars and critics, the magazine had not been an unqualified success. Circulation numbers of the period are not reliable, coming as they mostly do from obviously self-interested mentions in the magazines themselves or from memoirs written long after the fact, but Scott's concern had not made much money, and its monthly figures, while respectable and rising, remained between 1,100 and 2,000. Scott knew the value of controversy in providing a spur to sales. *Blackwood's*, of course, had begun by courting sensation and outright notoriety, creating sales so plump that its publisher was perfectly willing to absorb the payment of libel claims as a cost of doing business. And Scott himself had managed a similar *coup* as editor of the weekly

Champion. In 1816, after his separation from his wife, Byron had an unwilling Murray print fifty copies of "Fare Thee Well," a poem he intended to circulate privately in hopes of mitigating the effects of his wife's friends' rumor-mongering about his behavior. Scott obtained a copy and published it with scathing commentary on what he considered Byron's ungentlemanly behavior toward "the weak and defenceless party."[31] Finally, one can argue that the occasion for the November attack on *Blackwood's* was partly the need to fill out the number: Hazlitt did not turn in his usual drama review, nor did he produce a Table-Talk. If this is the case, then some of the repetition – unusual for Scott – in his critique of *Blackwood's* is understandable, as well as the scattershot treatment of the shortcomings of Hunt, Shelley, and Byron that seem included only to fill out the article.

Hence a number of causes, among them the indignation Scott projects in the article, are at work here. But the next stage, the round of accusations and counter-accusations that precede the actual duel, provides a measure of the struggle for gentility so central to middle-class life in the 1820s. In the January 1821 number, Scott named Lockhart as the editor of *Blackwood's* and thereby brought the responsibility for what he considered the magazine's "organized plan of fraud, calumny, and cupidity" (*London Magazine* 3, 77) to Lockhart's door. These were something like fighting words, and Lockhart's response, as well as the reactions of Scott, was something like a preparation for a duel.

The subsequent exchanges, with the exception of the final arrangements between Scott and Christie that led to an appointment at Chalk Farm, are both hyper-punctilious and hypocritical. The language employed by the litigants and their supporters is often curious – an antiquated and strained amalgam of revenge tragedy and aristocratic hauteur. William Maginn, a *Blackwood's* contributor who had ironically written some of the squibs Scott attributed to Lockhart, urged strong measures, noting that the *London* was "very insolent." Thomas De Quincey wrote to his neighbor and friend John Wilson that he was "burning for vengeance" and, in something of Sir Andrew Aguecheek's strain of eloquence, confessed "I do so loathe the vile whining canting hypocrisy of the fellow." Christie's odd turn of phrase in a letter to Lockhart urging a duel smacks of Elizabethan discourse: "I think you must do more with him than kill the zinc-eating spider."[32] Lockhart's first extant reaction, in a reply to Christie, is all posture. In his best laird of the manor tone, Lockhart confesses to have been so caught up in "running down hares and stiking salmon" that he "did not hear of it for many weeks." The second article undermined this defense, moving Lockhart to these sentiments: "The second distressed me very much, not on account of myself, but of [Walter] Scott, of whose hitherto unprofaned name such base use was made in it – although, if any insult could move a man's rage, without doubt the allusions to my marriage, wife etc, were well entitled to do so."[33] Scott's third mention, in the January "Lion's Head," provoked Lockhart to notice the slights to his honor: "I find myself charged with distinctness in a sort which neither present engagement, or any thought for the future, can induce me, or could induce any man, to overlook."[34] Lockhart's umbrage here is largely contrived. Walter Scott had been mildly censured by John Scott for condoning the actions of *Blackwood's*, but he also emerges in the same articles as the only healthy influence on an otherwise sickly and depraved literary scene. Moreover, the allusion to Lockhart's wife did not go beyond the simple naming of Lockhart's relation to Walter Scott, his father-in-law. And if the charge made by Scott in January, that Lockhart was the editor of *Blackwood's*, were false, it is only because the truth was unusually complex. Lockhart had undoubtedly performed editorial duties, and he had colluded with others in some of the mystifications that Scott named. Wilson, Lockhart, and Blackwood had all done the editing over time. The informality of the editorial situation had been convenient: Blackwood, who held final editorial control, repeatedly complained when faced with libel suits that he could do nothing with his editors. Ultimately, Lockhart employed the same equivocation in his exchanges with Scott.

The negotiations, taken up by Christie on Lockhart's behalf, present a confusion of punctilio, as each side maneuvered for the maximum advantage without fighting. Scott insisted as a precondition for the duel that Lockhart identify himself as editor of *Blackwood's* (or, later in the negotiations, that he clarify his relation to the magazine), and he stood his ground on this reasonable point. Lockhart refused to provide this information, preferring to "post" Scott – that is, to send him a letter directly accusing him of cowardice. If either man had wanted to fight, the means lay at their disposal. But for all the tension of the exchange, an equilibrium had been achieved: once Scott had settled on his precondition, and once Lockhart had resolved not to meet it, both men could bluster away. Moreover, at this point, the supporters of both men seemed satisfied that their man had bested his opponent. Lockhart, who had come to London to demonstrate his readiness, felt sufficiently vindicated and returned home. Scott, who had seized upon an error by Christie in publishing an account of Lockhart's actions, felt he had evidence of his opponent's bad faith and disinclination for a duel. Both gentlemen printed and circulated "Statements" that supported their status as "gentlemen," and each used the newspapers to further their claims.

Subsequent events show how easily arrangements to "walk out" could be made – if one of the litigants showed determination. Christie took umbrage at Scott's insinuations concerning his part in the transactions, and he bluffly called him to account. Scott must have known that delay with Christie would undermine the credibility of his carefully constructed persona: his standing in the Lockhart affair hinged upon his willingness to fight. The two met at Chalk Farm that night. Christie, perhaps because he saw the entire affair as pro forma, did not aim at Scott in the first exchange. In an entirely unnecessary second exchange of shots, Scott was mortally wounded. The words between the wounded Scott and Christie resonate with homosocial platitudes. Christie, taking his opponent's hand, said: "I would rather that I was in your situation and that you were in mine." Scott's reply shows the degree to which the struggle for gentility permeated the entire affair: "I beg you all to bear in remembrance that every thing has been fair and honourable."[35] After the ultimate demonstration of gentility, the recourse to pistols, Scott ritually cancels the basis for the dispute and, mindful of the inevitable legal proceedings to follow, moves to protect his fellow gentleman, who shot him, from the law. The subsequent regrets of Christie and Lockhart complete the familiar trajectory of this middle-class story-line.

Only outcomes can help in determining the intentions of the principals. Christie was willing and ready to "walk out" with Scott, although he purposely fired away from his opponent in the first exchange of shots. Scott was willing to fight if faced with the loss of his reputation. Lockhart was willing to engage in a spectacular defense of his gentility, and, like Scott, he probably could have been drawn onto the field by a determined opponent. It might be more exact to say that Lockhart and Scott were willing to risk death for their reputations, which is not quite the same thing as being ready and willing to fight for their honor. In fact, the main difficulty in understanding the Scott–Lockhart–Christie affair lies in the manifest unfamiliarity of the principals with the dueling code. The negotiations took place in an atmosphere charged with aristocratic pretension, not with the assurance that might come from an abiding knowledge of the protocols of this feudal custom. We might recall that Byron, whose way of life drew him into many scrapes, managed to live his entire life without dueling simply by choosing seconds who knew their business.

To speak of dueling for middle-class professionals such as Lockhart and Scott is itself an arrogation of sorts. Neither had any lived relation to the already outmoded feudal code behind the trial by combat. Although Andrew Lang labors mightily – and possibly with tongue-in-cheek – over a possibly aristocratic genealogy in his biography of Lockhart, his subject had no more claim to exalted rank than many, many Scots would have had at the time. Lockhart's father was a respectable minister, and Lockhart grew up on the edges of gentility. He received no patrimony. His education was gotten through scholarships, and, when he returned to Edinburgh from Oxford at nineteen to make his way as a lawyer, he had no influential friends to ease his way. He spent three years in financial distress until he took up writing for *Blackwood's*. Scott's father was an upholsterer. If we recall the circumstances of the litigants' friends, it is with amazement that we read their bloody-minded encouragements. De Quincey's father was a wine-merchant, Lamb's a servant, and Maginn's a teacher.[36] And the aristocratic pretensions of Lockhart's father-in-law Walter Scott, who refused to speak to his brother after he did not meet a challenge, require little comment. Shots were fired in the Scott–Christie–Lockhart affair, but they were not, as Scott himself and some critics have claimed, over the honor of literature.[37] What was at stake were the aspirations and idealized selves of the litigants.

Gripping as the experience-near account of the duel might be, the tack toward Mill's abstract approach provides its own powerful reading of these events. From the experience-distant perspective, the duel provides a measure of the power of the social forces bound up in literary magazines. Played out publically – in the *London*, in "Statements," and in newspapers – for a considerable audience, the duel takes to extremes the struggle for gentility and the tendency of the middle class to mimic the aristocracy. The self-mystifications of the process are also visible. Scott's attack on what he considered the abuse of pseudonyms by *Blackwood's* contributors was carried out under the aegis of honorable behavior and truth, but it was also an attack on a practice that distinguished a rival magazine from other publications and contributed greatly to its success in a crowded field. Scott seemed determined to force Lockhart into an embarrassing confession of shady practices within *Blackwood's*. Moreover, the attack itself was made within the *London*, which stood to gain from a successful exposure of the imposture and deceit of a formidable rival. Hence the pretensions of each litigant are bound up intricately with competition for a share of a market.

Ultimately, the duel is both a part of and a representation of the world of literary magazines. The uncertain, and at times awkward, struggles of Lockhart and Scott for gentility are those of their audience, exaggerated. Just as the mystified punctilio of dueling and reputation partly eludes the combatants, for the middle-class reading audience literature and polite learning generally present an unfamiliar code. If dueling and middle-class pretensions are entangled in the extreme case of the Scott–Lockhart–Christie affair, literature and middle-class pretensions are bound up in the everyday life of the literary magazine. In a moment marked by expensive books, a collapsing market for books, and, despite the abundance of gift books and annuals, a perceived dearth of poetry, literary magazines largely become literature for the middle-class reading audience. Such magazines deliver literature, providing original essays and poems directly and relatively cheaply to their audience, and, through extensive quotation in reviews, they disseminate it indirectly. They produce the official discourse on literature, through reviews and running commentary throughout their pages. And ultimately, literary magazines themselves aspire to be literature. *Blackwood's* self-consciously offers itself as a "classical entertainment."[38] Campbell's *New Monthly*, like so much literature in the nineteenth century, imagines itself as a "calm spot"[39] held resolutely against the encroachment of party feeling and entanglements with the world of everyday affairs. The *London*, in words that conspicuously recall the advice of Hamlet to the players, sets its sights on representing the city: "to convey the very 'image, form, and pressure' of that '*mighty heart,*' whose vast pulsations circulate life, strength, and spirits, throughout this great Empire."[40] Other aristocratic signs and protocols, such as political privilege, feudal sports, travel, or a classical education, could not be so easily obtained, but the gentility provided by "Literature" was within reach. If literature has an outsize presence in this period for the growing middle class, it is partly because a taste for literature is relatively easy to develop – thanks largely to the instance of literary magazines. Literary magazines, at least those written for the British middle class in the 1820s and 1830s, register the restraining force of material circumstances as well as the pull of aspirations beyond them.

The energies, both social and personal, that circulate in literary magazines are considerable – more often than not, uncontainable – and the practical demands of monthly production are considerable. These ventures often fail to cohere, becoming instead a hodgepodge of weak tendencies. But several early magazines brilliantly resolved these difficulties, providing not only numbers that are clear and purposeful but runs that sustain well-articulated points of view, sharply delineated conflicts, or successive arguments among various contributors. The following chapters examine such moments in early literary magazines. To do justice to the complexity of the form, I have tried to emphasize different elements of literary magazines in each chapter. The first two chapters examine the relation of an individual contributor to the editor or editorial presence in the magazine. The aim in each is twofold: to recover the original place of an author's work that has been lost in subsequent literary history, and to follow the shaping hand of a strong editor, in this case, John Scott. Chapter 1 traces the early history of Lamb's Elia essays in the *London*, in which the editor takes up Lamb's essays into his own political and artistic plans, and chapter 2 takes up the more troubled relation of Hazlitt to Scott and to the *London* after Scott's death. The latter chapter's account of the magazine's uncertain reconfiguration under John Taylor and Thomas Hood also provides a measure of the difficulties involved in magazine publication.

John Scott's practice epitomizes what a vigorous and determined editor can do, and I will recall his editorial procedures throughout the rest of the book. My use of Scott in these later discussions, however, is purely expository; he is not, in any sense, proposed as a model editor or norm. His *London* illustrates a particular kind of magazine practice, as do the other magazines in this study, and he remains subordinate to the larger discussion of the interplay between and among individual authors and the resonance produced by context.

The next two chapters, while still attending to individuals and their collaborative acts, shift the focus to a more formal analysis of the magazine. The example of Scott's *London* demonstrates that literary magazines can be productively approached as a genre, but such a treatment is most useful when applied to the 1822–25 run of *Blackwood's* and the new series of the *New Monthly*. Chapter 3 examines *Blackwood's* as an experiment in and a meta-commentary on magazine publication, and chapter 4 takes up the calculated political reticence of Campbell's *New Monthly*. Each magazine, like the *London*, presents and ultimately embodies a fully articulated theory of recent literature.

The final chapter of this study takes up the relation of Carlyle's *Sartor Resartus* and *Fraser's*, both of which have elements of nostalgia, and both of which are haunted by the imaginative verve of past writers or magazines. In this collaboration, we can see the contributor begin to emerge from the control of the editor. John Scott put the work of Lamb and

Hazlitt to work for the *London,* Campbell excluded material that did not suit his "calm spot," and the *Blackwood's* crew go to extraordinary lengths to create an editorial presence – in each case the magazine subordinates individual contributions to itself. Carlyle brilliantly reverses this procedure by consciously incorporating the frame of *Fraser's,* and in doing so, he effectively closes the initial and most innovative stage of British periodical literature of the nineteenth century.

The study of literary history, like the study of history itself, is not simply the study of what the literary world or the larger world is like. It is also a study of what people thought the world was like and how they acted upon this conception. Nowhere is the range of such responses so wide as in literary magazines.

CHAPTER ONE

Ideology and editing: the political context of the Elia essays

Mario Praz presents a singular picture of Charles Lamb in *The Hero in Eclipse* – as a man whose essays trace his determined probing of the wounds given him by nascent capitalism, whose ideals are aristocratic but whose place as a clerk is socially ambiguous, and whose "Biedermeier" aesthetic is marked by an "ability to express the quintessence of bourgeois feeling."[1] This tendentious assessment has not been taken up by later critics, who have preferred immanent or at least more formal approaches to the essays of Elia. But beneath the somewhat programmatic thrust of Praz's remark lies an important yet unregarded aspect of Lamb: the social and political context of his essays.

Book-length studies have traced Lamb's development as a craftsman, examined his creation of a "neutral ground" that permits the exercise of negative capability, presented a reading of the essays from a phenomenological perspective, and provided a deconstructive account of Lamb's examination of the authorial voice and his exploration of time and eternity.[2] Three early articles have considered the essays as prose poems and applied new critical techniques to them.[3] Later studies have focused on his use of irony and the psychological burdens inherent in his relation with Coleridge.[4] None of the scholarship on Lamb makes more than passing reference to the monthly publication of the essays; it can be said to take as its text not the essays as they first appeared in the *London Magazine*, but as they later appeared in the 1823 collection *Elia* and the 1833 *The Last Essays of Elia*. This scholarly orientation amounts to a covert editorial decision. Analysis of the *Elia* and *The Last Essays* conceals the links between the essays and their most immediate context, the material surrounding them in the *London Magazine*. Treating the essays in such isolation tends to produce interpretations oriented toward immanent, formal, or autobiographical readings which emphasize the personal and the escapist elements of the essays.

Political contexts are difficult to reconstruct, and in the case of Lamb such an undertaking is daunting. Despite a somewhat polemical, politicized youth, in which he was notorious enough to be paired with the dangerous, "Jacobin" Charles Lloyd in an *Anti-Jacobin* cartoon, Lamb seemed to settle into silence.[5] His essays, like Austen's novels, are marked by an apparent avoidance of politics. His letters contain jocular or ambiguously ironic comments about his lack of interest in such matters. But the circumstances of the essays, their monthly publication in the *London Magazine*, provide a measure of their underlying politics. The magazine's editor, John Scott, had clear political opinions, and the use to which he put the Elia essays in the *London Magazine* allows us to gauge the ways in which these essays ramify into the social and the political – how they embody a symbolic act through which social contradictions are presented and explored. If, as Jerome McGann has argued in "Keats and the Historical Method," the intentions of the author are "codified in the author's choice of time, place and form of publication," then attention to Scott's use and placement of the essays in the *London Magazine* becomes crucial in redressing the formal and autobiographical orientation of the criticism of Lamb.[6]

Critical accounts of John Scott's editorship praise his apolitical stance. Josephine Bauer is typical of many commentators when she cites approvingly Scott's determination to keep the magazine free of political affiliation and his refusal to let politics and political ideas sway his critical judgment.[7] Walter Graham, in his pithy account of English literary periodicals, praises the critical tenor of the *London Magazine* without mention of its politics.[8] Such accounts attest to the persistence of the critical tradition which Scott himself helped to create, one which Burke and Coleridge inaugurate, writers like Scott take up in the 1820s, Victorians like Arnold amplify, T.S. Eliot rediscovers and codifies, and the New Criticism makes ubiquitous. This tradition obscures the political coding of Scott's critical remarks and editorial practices.

As it was for many in his generation, the French Revolution was the dominant political event for Scott. And like many others in his class, he endorsed the interpretation of it provided by Burke in *Reflections*. Scott echoes Burke's attack on the revolution's ideology: its simplification of individual psychology, preference for abstraction, celebration of system and theory, contempt for tradition, cosmopolitanism, and sexual license. So too does Scott echo Burke's praise of the concepts of "presumption," which grants preference to existing institutions, and "prescription," which seeks to legitimate presumption by arguing that long possession justifies claims of property and title. Scott handles Burke's concept of "wisdom without reflection," that product of English society and institutions by which individuals act a truth they only dimly perceive, reverentially.[9]

But Burke's interpretation of the revolution in France did not come to Scott directly. During the post-war crises of 1815–19 Burke's ideas received powerful restatement and significant modification by Coleridge in *The Statesman's Manual, A Lay Sermon, Biographia Literaria*, and his "rifacciamento" of *The Friend*. In them Coleridge attempts to ground Burke's remarks philosophically, to trace them to "principles" and "ideas." And by them Coleridge attempts to become a second Burke, to interpret the post-war unrest with the same prescience and prophetic power with which Burke surveyed the revolutionary moment of the early 1790s. In addition, Coleridge begins the transfer of Burke's political analysis into literary criticism, a move that Scott continues and which will gather force in later versions by Arnold and Eliot.

Coleridge's debt to Burke in *The Statesman's Manual* is manifold. Early in the essay he announces that the only "antidote to that restless craving for the wonders of the day" and the only "means for deriving resignation from general discontent" are to "be sought in the collation of the present with the past, in the habit of thoughtfully assimilating the events of our own age to those of the time before us."[10] Significantly, this appeal is followed by a critique of the French Revolution along Burkean lines. The rhetorical strategy is obvious: as Burke warned his audience in 1790, so will Coleridge warn the "Higher Classes of Society" in 1816. Later Coleridge provides his own version of the Burkean concept of "wisdom without reflection, and above it":

At the annunciation of principles, of ideas, the soul of man awakes, and starts up, as an exile in a far distant land at the unexpected sounds of his native language, when after long years of absence, and almost of oblivion, he is suddenly addressed in his own mother-tongue . . . How else can we explain the fact so honorable to Great Britain, that the poorest among us will contend with as much enthusiasm as the richest for the rights of property? These rights are the spheres and necessary conditions of free agency. But free agency contains the idea of the free will; and in this he intuitively knows the sublimity, and the infinite hopes, fears, and capabilities of his own nature. (*Collected Works*, vol. vi, pp. 24–5)

Burke's insistence on the unity of thought and feeling informs the entire passage.[11]

Of course Coleridge refines the tradition as he takes it up. Unlike Burke, he is inclined to give a cautious opening to reason and theory. And although he shows the same leanings toward "presumption" and "prescription," he tends to conceive of this legacy in a different way:

I would far rather see the English people at large believe somewhat too much than merely just enough, if the latter is to be produced, or must be accompanied, by a contempt or neglect of the faith and intellect of their forefathers. For not to say what yet is most certain, that a people cannot believe just enough, and that there are errors which no wise man will treat with rudeness, while there is a probability that they may be the refraction of some great truth as yet below the horizon. (*Collected Works*, vol. VI, p. 87)

Burke would explain his tolerance of such "errors" by arguing that the limits of individual reason preclude a clear view of the advantages and disadvantages of tradition. Coleridge, more sanguine about the efficacy of reason, applies a symbolic hermeneutic, seeking a refracted truth in error. But this is not, in its spirit, un-Burkean. This typically Coleridgean assertion of the interdependence of reason and faith is an extension of Burke's basic belief in the unity of thought and feeling. The difference lies in whether the truth behind error is available to human reason.

In the introduction to *A Lay Sermon* Coleridge again emphasizes the Burkean concept of "wisdom without reflection":

Few are sufficiently aware how much reason most of us have, even as common moral livers, to thank God for being ENGLISHMEN. It would furnish grounds both for humility towards Providence and for increased attachment to our country, if each individual could but see and feel, how large a part of his innocence he owes to his birth, breeding, and residence in Great Britain. The administration of the laws; the almost continual preaching of moral prudence; the number and respectability of our sects; the pressure of our ranks on each other . . . the vast depth, expansion and systematic movements of our trade; and the consequent inter-dependence, the arterial or nerve-like net-work of property . . . and lastly, the naturalness of doing as others do: – these and the like influences, peculiar, some in the kind and all in the degree, to this privileged island, are the buttresses, on which our foundationless well-doing is upheld, even as a house of cards, the architecture of our infancy, in which each is supported by all. (*Collected Works*, vol. VI, pp. 126–7)

Although earlier Coleridge enjoins the reader to make an earnest "endeavor to walk in the Light of your own knowledge" (p. 121), he is well aware of the automatic pilot provided by Burke's "second nature." The jingoistic celebration of nation which pervades Burke's rhetoric is also present in Coleridge's account of "foundationless well-doing." In the *Biographia Literaria* Coleridge continues to trumpet nationalism, maintaining that the rhetorical excesses of both parties during the war had taught the country "to prize and honor the spirit of nationality as the best safeguard of national independence, and this again as the absolute pre-requisite of individual rights."[12] But, as in *A Lay Sermon*, Coleridge couples this kind of remark with the insistence that such feelings "are worthy of regard only as far as they are representatives of their fixed opinions" (*Biographia Literaria*, vol. I, p. 190). While recognizing that the idea or principle must work subconsciously, producing "foundationless well-doing" in the larger populace, Coleridge urges a policing activity on the "higher and middle classes" (later it will be the function of his clerisy), who, as their duty, must seek the idea behind this activity. In doing so Coleridge expands on Burke's desire for unity of thought and feeling by making an almost Kantian turn in which experience, the "wisdom without reflection," is assumed to be conditioned by certain principles.

The 1818 republication of *The Friend* continues this line of argument.[13] In it Coleridge makes some apparently un-Burkean remarks: "For the meanest of men has his Theory: and to think at all is to theorize" (*Collected Works*, vol. IV, part I, p. 189). But it must be recalled that such celebrations of system are reserved for certain kinds of thinking, for the operations of what Coleridge calls "Reason." Much of life passes, and indeed must pass, in the realm of what Coleridge calls "Understanding," and Coleridge's practice here is thoroughly Burkean. Institutions, in a characteristically Burkean passage, are legitimated by expedience (p. 176).

It is important to keep Coleridge's relation to Burke clear. From 1816 to 1818 Coleridge is intent upon countering popular radicalism, much as Burke sought to counter the threat posed by revolutionary France. Characteristically, Coleridge cannot be satisfied with repeating the claims of others; he must place them in his own system. Thus he incorporates Burke's ideas within an almost Platonic scheme in which Burke's cherished "wisdom without reflection" is the everyday guise of the principles and ideas beneath. Coleridge maintains this conception in *On the Constitution of the Church and State*, simply shifting the philosophic burden from the higher and middle classes to his clerisy. In the post-war context, this aggressive reinterpretation allows Coleridge to have it both ways – he can use the authority of tradition in countering radicalism, and, by explaining the tradition, at the same time present himself as something of a panoptic thinker who hails the "great truth as yet below the horizon."

For Scott the historical moment of the *London Magazine* must have seemed to confirm Coleridge's concerns in *A Lay Sermon*. In 1819 Scott was on the Continent, collecting material for another work along the lines of his *Visit to Paris in 1815*, when the publisher Robert Baldwin contacted him about starting a London-based magazine to compete with the established Scottish journals. This new magazine was conceived and begun during the last throes of the radical movement, and the immediate political context of much of Scott's preparatory correspondence with Baldwin was the Peterloo Massacre. A letter to Baldwin dated 8 November 1819 reveals a highly political Scott staking out his position in the proposed magazine. Arguing against Baldwin's misgivings about assuming a political slant, Scott echoes Burkean sentiments. However his position might anger violent factions and the ministerial party, "chances are" they will "chime with the unexpressed feelings of thousands." His appeal to a Regency silent majority is based on his trust in the "wisdom without reflection" lauded by Burke. In a similar vein, Scott argues for the political context not only of literature, but of everyday life: "If it were said that a Literary work has nothing to do with Politics, – the answer would be, that a Magazine has much to do with Politics – that English Literature is closely connected with Politics – as are English trade, English amusements, Manners, thought, and happiness."[14] That manners have a political dimension is a key Burkean claim in his *First Letter on a Regicide Peace*:

Manners are of more importance than laws. Upon them, in a great measure, the laws depend. The law touches us but here and there, and now and then. Manners are what vex or soothe, corrupt or purify, exalt or debase, barbarize or refine us, by a constant, steady, uniform, insensible operation, like that of the air we breathe in. They give their whole form and colour to our lives. According to their quality, they aid morals, they supply them, or they totally destroy them. (*Writings and Speeches*, vol. IX, p. 242)

More important, however, is the ground of Scott's claim about the ubiquity of politics. His stress on the unity of social institutions and their action on the individual parallels Burke's insistence on the unity of thought and feeling as well as his connection of the psychology of the individual to the whole of society.[13]

For Scott, the ministerial reaction to the Peterloo Massacre was nearly as bad as the unrest itself. Alienated from both sides, like both Burke and Coleridge before him, Scott fell back on his trust in his version of Burke's "wisdom without reflection" and Coleridge's "foundationless well-doing": "An instinctive feeling of the fit and decent, superior to argument and therefore out of the reach of sophistry, – quicker than reason, and therefore not liable to be surprised" (*London Magazine* 1 [1820], 176). However ineffectual, this is certainly a recognizable political stance. The events of 1820 only deepened Scott's opposition to popular movements, his anger at ministerial cynicism, and his disgust at the opposition's opportunism. Caroline's return from Italy to claim her place as Queen and her subsequent trial for adultery provide, at least in Scott's eyes, ample occasion for everyone to reveal their worst instincts. Scott's disappointment at the maneuverings of each political faction is only rivaled by his anxieties over the unrest in England: "We have no interest now to lavish on secondary subjects of debate, for we have become familiar with the language of life and death, and live in the near approach of an inevitable crisis" (*London Magazine* 2 [1820], 100). Coleridge's fears of 1816 had been realized just as surely as Burke's fears in the *Reflections*.

Coleridge's importance to Scott can be measured by the warmth with which he implores his publisher Baldwin to hire Coleridge as a contributor to the *London Magazine*: "I would again impress upon *you the necessity of securing him.*"[16] Scott's solicitation goes beyond simple staffing problems. In seeking out Coleridge, he seeks to invest the proposed magazine with a well known political commentator. Coleridge's reply to Baldwin, in which he pleaded a prior commitment to *Blackwood's*, must have been a blow to Scott.[17]

But perhaps a better indication of Scott's commitment to a Burkean– Coleridgean literary culture are his remarks on Godwin in the August 1820 number of the *London Magazine*. Godwin had long since become a favorite whipping boy for conservative writers. By 1820 Scott must have known that there was little life left in the subject. Thus at first glance his inclusion of Godwin in his "Living Authors" series along with Walter Scott, Wordsworth, and Byron is puzzling. But the immediate context of popular unrest justifies this re-examination of the thinker whose name was most commonly equated with radical politics. Just as Coleridge wondered in 1816 "[w]hether the spirit of jacobinism, which the writings of Burke exorcised from the higher and from the literary classes, may not like the ghost in Hamlet, be heard moving and mining in the underground chambers with an activity the more dangerous because less noisy," so did Scott in 1820 feel the need to put the spectre of radical politics to rest.[18] He presents Godwin as a famous convert to be applauded for his ultimate recognition of conservative doctrine.

Scott applies a Burkean measure to Godwin's politics, but he does so without the viscerally nationalistic tone taken up in *Reflections*. His treatment of Godwin recalls Coleridge's consideration of Rousseau's thought in *The Friend* more than Burke's attack on the *philosophes*. The effect of Godwin's work is to "wither the heart," and Scott expands upon the causes of this:

In his philosophical treatise, as in his novels, he considers man in patches and parcels rather than in the totality of his nature; he argues on one fact, rather than on that combination that constitutes truth; – satisfied with having discovered a weakness, he does not trouble himself to enquire whether it be not inextricably connected with some vital principle or source of welfare, which must perish under its remedy. (*London Magazine* 2, 166)

Here Scott eloquently updates Burke's strictures against "system," mechanistic psychology, and shortsighted reform with Coleridgean moderation. When he moves to the novels themselves, Scott criticizes their lack of social benefit; they are based on an erroneous system which causes the reader to "rise with the heartache from his works" (p. 163): "This plan includes but little of comfort or consolation; little, we are afraid, of derivable benefit to either the mind or the manners of people in general" (p. 167). Scott praises Godwin's later works, which are more likely to "repress presumptuous dissent, and angry opposition, than to provoke them" (p. 166).

In a September 1820 review of *Lamia* Scott cautions Keats for a similar inattention to "the varieties of human nature" and the "deep, internal, and inextricable connection between the pains and penalties of human nature, and its hopes and enjoyments" (*London Magazine* 2, 315). He sees an "extravagant school-boy vituperation" in Keats's treatment of the merchant brothers in "Isabella." After contrasting it with Boccaccio's characterization, he turns to Elia as an example of an author with a more complex vision: "That most beautiful Paper . . . on the 'ledger men,' of the South Sea House, is an elegant reproof of such short-sighted views of character; such idle hostilities against the realities of life." Elia, a less "systematic" thinker than Keats, is praised for presenting "so clear and fair an impression from facts" (p. 317). To call such remarks apolitical, as many critics have, would be to mistake the tradition in which Scott operates, one in which a highly articulated Burkean–Coleridgean culture gives a subtle political resonance to critical discourse.

Scott furthered his political and social views by either pairing articles or by weaving a kind of running commentary into articles throughout an entire number. The political effectiveness of this might be questioned, especially if one takes as normative the hamfisted methods of most of his competitors. But since Scott wrote many of the articles himself, and since many of the contributors knew each other well, this practice was feasible, and often resulted in persuasive, indirect expression of Scott's politics.

Scott's monthly "Historical and Critical Summary of Intelligence" provides a reference point for the apparent diversity of the magazine. Read with an eye to whatever this section contains, the articles of a given number often take on a different cast; what may seem eccentric in either focus or tone becomes relevant to catching "the spirit of things" as Scott sensed it. The July 1820 number is an example. Its table of contents might suggest that the magazine is a pleasant miscellany, but there are subtle resonances among the articles. In the "Historical and Critical Summary of Intelligence" Scott takes up the ministerial response to Caroline's return from Italy to take her place as Queen. He is concerned that such actions will tarnish the King's image, and that this will in turn "interpose a gulph between the past and the future, and break up the glorious associations that are now linked to her [the Queen's] name" (*London Magazine* 2, 101). Scott counsels silence and caution at so shocking a scandal: "this is not a moment for tampering carelessly with the sentiments of respect for the splendid fictions of what is called, and what may really be, state-necessity" (p. 102). This crisis provides a meaning for the apparently trivial review of "The History of Madame Krudener, A Religious Enthusiast," as well as for this review's survey of the conditions and dispositions of Europe's sovereigns immediately prior to Madame Krudener's vogue in court. The review's intricate analysis of the political climate of 1814 (most monarchies harbored liberal, reformist intentions, but could not put them into effect; the blame for this is not simply owing to their inaction, but also to "the unreasonableness of popular demand, and the disgusting intemperance of its self-elected organs") continues, by analogy, the apocalyptic warnings of the "Summary." Then, as now, governments could founder by not paying close attention to the wear and tear on the "splendid fictions" of the monarchy. Scott continues in this vein in his monthly "Collector" contribution, which reviews Samuel Johnson's account of the coronation of George III, noting that Johnson's style, which Scott terms "big writing," leaves the modern reader cold, but speculating that it was in fact "a sly sentiment of irony" (*London Magazine* 2 [1820], 57). The lesson here, evidently, is that the "splendid fictions" need not be taken seriously by the sophisticated reader of the magazine, however much they require maintenance and adherence among others. Scott follows this article with a review of Mathews's *Diary of an Invalid*, which occasions yet more praise of the old customs, notably the "durability of prejudice and bias" which guides the populace to proper action. He quotes approvingly Mathews's praise of "female virtue," which provides for "the happiness of our homes" as well as, ultimately, for the national character upon which England prides itself. In a stunningly Beidermeier reduction of the Romantic eternal feminine, Mathews concludes that "all the best virtues of manhood" are produced by "maternal precepts and maternal example" (p. 64). In an obvious reference to Caroline's difficulties, Scott remarks that "the necessity for giving all publicity to such observations, is but too apparent" (p. 64).

This ongoing analysis of custom culminates later in the number, when Scott reviews Arthur Taylor's *The Glory of Regality: An Historical Treatise of the Anointing and Crowning of the Kings and Queens of England*. Here the near reactionary views he expressed earlier are somewhat tempered, and the subject receives a compressed but credible historical treatment. Medieval coronations, and the monarchy in general, were supported and legitimated by real signs, which "had so obvious a counterpart in reality, that it could not but strike on the imaginations of those present, as an imposing symbol of the courage, prowess, zeal, and fidelity of the adherents to the new prince" (p. 81). Time has made such customs obsolete and ridiculous, and the extreme literal-mindedness of the current public renders them dangerous. Scott appeals anxiously for the production of a credible, uplifting ceremony, one which will be appropriate for the current government. This apt formulation of the manufacture of consent, when read in the context of the numerous references to the government's legitimation crisis, makes for a fairly pragmatic conclusion on Scott's part, and it draws together the strands of this discussion throughout the number. Thus the July *London* introduces a problem, analyzes it, and enforces a conclusion through the juxtaposition of texts.

The initial number of the *London* also exemplifies this cumulative effect. The January 1820 number begins with the "Prospectus," in which the editor gives free range to his patriotism and nationalism. In the next article, "General Reflections, Suggested by Italy," a description of the Alps is followed by a meditation on national events, the "instruments of a great design" which insure "a slow progressive order of development" (*London Magazine* 1, 2). An examination of the work of Walter Scott in the first of the "Living Authors" series allows John Scott to trace these concerns further: Bailie Nicol Jarvie of *Rob Roy* is the type of traditional religious feeling, and Scott's characters are generally praised for their delineation of the national character. The next entry, a review of "The Memoirs of Mr. Hardy Vaux," laments the commonplace tenor of contemporary society: since "the materials of romance are eradicated" (p. 24), one finds the stuff of patriotic feeling only in the past. The following essay, "The Influence of Religious and Patriotic Feeling on Literature," continues this meditation on change and national character, asserting that great works of literature are dependent upon deep religious and patriotic feeling, and it effectively concludes the discussion with the pithy generalization that "every change in established ideas which removes from a people their great points of rallying and union, is a real evil" (p. 41).

Scott's editorial hand can also be seen in pairings of articles, such as his back to back reviews of Shelley's *The Cenci* and Maria Edgeworth's *Memoirs of the Late R. L. Edgeworth* in the May 1820 number. The review of Shelley begins with a general criticism of the tendency of his thought. For Scott, Shelley exemplifies the sickly constitution of the age: he sees the world through his prejudices and system, and he "seeks gratification in conjuring up, or presenting the image or idea of something abhorrent to feelings of the general standard" (*London Magazine* 1, 46). *The Cenci* combines these tendencies. In it Shelley turns from the usual vices "to cull some morbid or maniac sin of rare and doubtful occurence, and sometimes to found *a system* of practical purity and peace on violations which it is disgraceful even to contemplate" (p. 548). Scott finds Shelley's "Preface," which interprets Cenci's incestuous passion as a manifestation of his implacable hatred of his daughter, incoherent: it is "against common sense, irrational, absurd, nonsensical" (p. 549). Since he cannot accept Cenci's action as anything other than that of a madman, Scott's negative reaction to the play is in perfect accord with his principle that literature should represent human nature: Cenci is not representative, therefore he should not be the subject of drama. Later in the review, however, Scott provides another key to his reaction, one more directly political. Scott seems particularly disturbed that Shelley so clearly connects unthinkable crimes with authority. He seems anxious lest this association might, in the revolutionary social climate of 1820, be taken as the norm. This danger is heightened by the power of the play: despite the unthinkable horror of the subject, it is almost redeemed by the "uncommon force of poetical sentiment, and very considerable purity of poetical style" (p. 550).

After this manifestation of concern for the "splendid fictions" of authority, Scott turns to Maria Edgeworth's *Memoirs*, a choice calculated to continue the scrutiny of father–daughter relations begun in the review of *The Cenci*. Although he doubts the utility and tact of criticism in such instances as this, in which a daughter dutifully praises her father, he wonders if such interested appraisals as Maria Edgeworth's can be accurate. In asking if a daughter can judge her father with objectivity, Scott comments subtly on Shelley's Beatrice. He implies that Beatrice's actions prejudice her case against her father – a murderer's accusation is unacceptable. Scott praises Maria Edgeworth's talent lavishly, showing great perspicacity in his consideration of her praise for her father's specific corrections of her literary taste and style. Ultimately Scott judges her account more dutiful than accurate: he credits her own talent more than her claims of dependency. He then turns to praise Edgeworth's management of his children, his cultivation of his daughter's talent, and his exemplary social and domestic virtue. Scott concludes with an instance of the father's concern for justice: when a punishment seemed capricious to him, he intervened with letters and inquiries which overturned the verdict. This kind of care and activity, Scott asserts, makes for a contented society; such vigorous maintenance of the "splendid fictions" of authority would deflect any rebellious tendency on the part of the people. Taken as a whole, the review balances Shelley's portrait of corrupt authority and filial relations in *The Cenci*. Maria Edgeworth's *Memoirs* provides the representation of nature altogether lacking in Shelley's play, which, despite his abundant genius, "does not teach the human heart, but insults it" (p. 550).

These styles of presentation are powerful rhetorical tools: Scott's political and social arguments have an indirection that amounts to an almost subliminal persuasion. Scott cannot, of course, control the ordering and content of the articles absolutely. The requirements of monthly publication and the variety of contributors involved limit him, and readers may not, despite Scott's careful attention, read the articles consecutively. But by heightening the resonances and echoes among the essays and by drawing out the political implications of other essays in his own contributions, Scott did what he could with the means at hand, producing, if not a figure in the carpet, at least an occasional design.

Scott's subtle but palpable politics figure prominently in his handling of the Elia essays. The domestic, personal, and ultimately escapist aspects of the Elia essays respond to a need Scott had articulated in his *London* from its opening number. Faced with the contradictions of a degraded public sphere, Scott felt powerless to address particular issues or to effect reform. The warm, domestic recollections of Elia suit this intolerable political present. In Scott's hands the essays become soothing displacements. His editorial decisions ensure that the Elia essays, like the other essays in the *London*, emerge within a context that makes Elia's recollections representative of feelings held by an entire class of political observer. Scott saw a political dimension in the essays and put them to political use in his magazine.

Recent critics, notably Jerome McGann, have commented on the tendency of Romantic writers to produce a literature "marked by extreme forms of displacement and poetic conceptualization whereby the actual human issues with which the poetry is concerned are resituated in a variety of idealized localities."[19] Clearly, such displacements are just what attracts Scott to the Elia essays. Unlike many later readers and critics, Scott is not caught up in what McGann has called the Romantic Ideology, "an uncritical absorption in Romanticism's own self-representations" (*Romantic Ideology*, p. 1); he is fully conscious of the displacement he finds in the essays, and he recognizes the value that such a posture offers at a specific historical moment. Scott's handling of the essays shows that there is a contemporary tradition of reading the displacement in Romantic works, and such readings suggest that the hermeneutics of suspicion deployed by New Historians may be, at least in some cases, misplaced. The conscious seeking by editor, writer, and reader in the later Romantic period for the consolations of displacement is an eloquent testimony to the pressures and frustrations of a reactionary social and political climate.

We can follow Scott in the act of interpreting the first Elia essay, August 1820's "The South Sea House." Scott's "Historical and Critical Summary" continues its vexed reporting on the would-be Queen's trial in the usual terms of crisis, warning that the country is in a "high state of fermentation" (*London Magazine* 2, 216). Scott's editorial column, the "Lion's Head," actively seeks diversion from these political problems, finding some consolation in the fact that the trial has not cooled the ardor of the populace for sporting events. Scott reads the abundant interest in these activities (always a useful means of managing the lower classes) as a comforting sign of the times: "the Prize-ring is our security, that the energies of the nation will not be wholly smothered in that slough of slander and obscenity, now forming for the public annoyance, under the superintendance of the Crown and the two Houses of Parliament!" (p. 122). Reynolds's review of *Sporting Anecdotes* later in the number continues this comforting interpretation of a "sign of the times." Taken out of context, recommending the prize-ring as an anti-dote to the distress produced by Caroline's trial seems pathetically mis-guided. But from within a Burkean–Coleridgean framework, Scott reads this particular diversionary tactic as a sign that Burke's "wisdom without reflection" still survives.[20] Scott feels, and sees in others, an intense desire for escape. It is to this need that Lamb's first essay offers an eloquent answer.

"The South Sea House" begins with a description of the antiquated, deserted edifice – the empty shell of a great commercial enterprise "where dollars and pieces of eight ounce lay, an 'unsunned heap, ' for Mammon to have solaced his solitary heart withal" (p. 142). Significantly, this lament for the vibrant life of yesterday admits of other, less nostalgic, considerations: the firm was involved in a "Bubble" of speculation, a "tremendous hoax" which present investors look back upon with "incredulous admiration" and "hopeless ambition of rivalry" (p. 142). Given the past "fret and fever of speculation" and the present turbulence of the commercial houses nearby, its desuetude becomes a symbol of escape: Elia, as he evokes it, finds "charm in thy quiet: – a cessation – a coolness from business." This relief is paralleled, even intensified, by Elia's recollection of his own activity there as clerk. He thinks of massive account books at which he toiled, but "can look upon these defunct dragons with complacency." The respite from the pressures of business is both public and personal. From the safe distance of the present, Elia recalls and describes the other clerks, remarking in each case how each managed to escape his lot. Elia sketches the cashier Evans, in whom the small salary of the South Sea House produces a "hypochondry" in which he imagines himself a defaulter. "Melancholy as a gib-cat over his counter all the forenoon," performing his accounts with "tremulous fingers," he is slowly transformed during the day, "his tristful visage" reaching his "the meridian of its animation" during the hour of tea and visiting. Only then does he expand into the "dear old bachelor" whose visits animate the homes of several families. Evans's financial stress is shared by his deputy, Thomas Tame, and he too manages a compensatory escape. Though impoverished, he and his wife claim descent from nobility "by some labyrinth of relationship" (p. 143), and this consciousness of breeding becomes a means of finding a slim contentment:

This was the thought – the sentiment – the bright solitary star of your lives, – ye mild and happy pair, – which cheered you in the night of intellect, and in the obscurity of your station! this was to you instead of riches, instead of rank, instead of glittering attainments: and it was worth them all together. You insulted none with it; but, while you wore it as a piece of defensive armour only, no insult likewise could reach you through it. (p. 144)

These portraits of humiliations transmuted are followed by more absolute methods of escape. John Tipp manifests a complete separation of home and office; Elia presents him as a consummate actor playing the role of accountant.[21] Henry Man finds relief in writing. Plumer transforms his illegitimacy into a pretension toward blue-blood. Elia recalls M–, significantly singing "that song sung by Amiens to the banished Duke, which proclaims the winter wind more lenient than for a man to be ungrateful" (pp. 145–6). Elia's reveries concern less the matter-of-fact conditions of the lives of his co-workers than the complex mechanisms of sublimation they employ against real humiliations. The essay is a study in alienation overcome by eccentric defenses.[22]

The attraction of this kind of whimsical evasion for Scott needs little explanation. The essay takes the reader from the unacceptable present to an idealized past. The sublimations and compensations of the clerks are, for Scott, triumphs. His allusion to this essay in his review of Keats's *Lamia* in the next number emphatically praises Lamb's "fair and clear impression from facts" – that is, the essay provides an adequate response to problems which are, in Scott's mind, intractable. It does no good to resist or complain about one's lot, be it the wear and tear of a marginal job or a distasteful political situation. At this particular political moment, evasion is the path to happiness.

Scott returns – albeit indirectly – to this point later in the number. His "Living Authors, No. 3" takes up Godwin's work and thought. While praising Godwin's tenacity and perspicacity in pursuing political and social abuses, Scott nevertheless finds his political criticisms pointless. Clearly, Godwin cannot provide what Elia does so abundantly – relief and comfort. Unlike Elia, he fails to see the whole man or the whole of the situation:

For the harmony of union he seems to have little feeling: to the softening and reacting springs of conduct; the modifying influences; the preserving, and redeeming guards and checks; in short, to all that lessens dead weight, and breaks collision in the moral machinery of the world, he is almost insensible. He delights in simple principles, and undivided forces. (*London Magazine* 2, 163)

For Scott, the slightness and the whimsical grace of Elia's contributions – their superficial irrelevance to social and political conditions – are a reflex of their historical moment, and their complicated play of nostalgia and reminiscence a cogent resolution of social and political contradiction.

As the situation of the Queen worsened, so did Scott's mood in the "Lion's Head"; the 1820 October number provides more anxious commentary than convivial growls. Scott reports that the Regent's credibility has sunk very low indeed: even the French – the constant butt of Scott's wit – consider his claims hypocritical. This marks a new danger to civil order: "Whether the English manners and national character will ever recover from the shock they have received, is doubtful; and the blow given to them may be a fatal one to the Monarchy" (*London Magazine* 2, 364). Scott's response, as one might expect, is to weight the magazine with articles that indirectly promote a respect for tradition, continuity, and the past. Elia's "Oxford in the Vacation," which directly follows the "Lion's Head," eloquently furthers these aims. As in his previous essay, Elia displays the recognition of the "realities of life" so central to Scott's politics. Elia returns to the topic of his clerking occupation, terming it a necessary "relaxation" from his literary pursuits. His levity, however, is not easily maintained; the very real constraints of clerking are apparent in Elia's discussion. He acknowledges the truth of the impression given the reader from the previous essay, that Elia is "a notched and cropped scrivener – one that sucks his sustenance, as certain sick people are said to do, through a quill" (p. 365). Although Elia's depiction suggests contentment or at least resignation, one cannot fail to see that these are the triumph of will over circumstance. We are surely close here to the "subtext of desperation" one critic has seen in the essays.[23] The essay offers two interpretations of Elia's working life. The whimsical charm of Elia's contention that "the very parings of a counting-house are, in some sort, the setting up of an author" (p. 365) predominates in the essay, but the grinding reality reflected in Lamb's letters – in which he famously described himself as "chained to my desk" – is also present.

More attractive to Scott would have been Elia's other remedies. This is not an essay about drudgery; it concerns the escape from drudgery. Arbitrary, whimsical charm becomes, for Scott, a readable code. Through it, Elia skirts the dangerous shoals of the working day and then sets a course for the open waters of holidays and vacation expeditions. Again, Scott's criticisms of Godwin provide a context for his preference of Elia. One of Godwin's shortcomings as a thinker, in Scott's opinion, was his failure to consider the inextricability of good and evil. Elia's mingling of the two makes his essay less sentimental than deeply philo-sophical. Seeing man, as Scott insists, "in the totality of his nature" pro-duces a consoling recognition of a "picturesque variety of phenomena" that displaces real and present pain (p. 166). Essential to his triumph over the vicissitudes of the work day is Elia's subtle mingling of the occupa-tions of clerk and scholar. Red letter days are "bright visitations to both," and they allow him the opportunity to "play the gentleman, enact the student" on a visit to Oxford. Scott must have caught the reference to Lamb's keen educational disappointments in such remarks as "To such a one as myself, who has been defrauded in his young years of the sweet food of academic institution, nowhere is so pleasant, to while away a few idle weeks at, as one or other of the Universities" (p. 366). But to say, as one critic does, that the whimsical charm of such moments rises "from the abyss," while perhaps true for Charles Lamb, misses what Scott and his contemporaries saw in it.[24] To a reader like Scott, whose disposition is more accepting of society's checks and limitations on the individual, the essay presents a reconciliation based on a buoyant embrace of com-plexity and contradiction, the "impression from facts" for which he praises Elia in the Keats review.

The essay's progress toward the penetralia of antiquarian and schol-arly feeling – embodied in the discovery of George Dyer absorbed in backbreaking, unappreciated literary work in "a nook at Oriel" – allows Elia a moment of reflection on the past:

Antiquity! thou wondrous charm, what art thou? that, being nothing, are every thing! When thou wert, thou wert not antiquity – then thou wert nothing, but hadst a remoter antiquity, as thou called'st it, to look back to with blind vener-ation; thou thyself being thyself flat, jejune, modern! What mystery lurks in this retroversion? or what Januses are we, that cannot look forward with the same idolatry with which we for ever revert! the mighty future is nothing, being every thing! the past is every thing, being nothing! (p. 366)

Such sentiments mesh with Scott's political and social perspectives nicely, registering simultaneously the allure of the past and the unaccept-ibility of the present. Nor would Elia's recognition of the "mystery" involved in the past's attraction prove problematic for the editor – his pragmatic view of the past can easily assimilate questions about the arbi-trary nature of a tradition. Scott was far less interested in the past as it was than in the past as it presented itself for use. Elia's preference for print over manuscripts, which he states in a footnote to the essay, echoes this acceptance of tradition as final: "There is something to me repug-nant, at any time, in written hand. The text never seems determinate.

Print settles it" (p. 367). Elia's antiquarianism tends toward use, not the recovery of absolute origin.

Scott continues this strategy of avoiding the present by means of a backward glance at an idealized past in the number's next articles, "Old Stories" and Proctor's imitation of Elia, "The Cider Cellar." By means of editorial intervention and his own contributions as writer, Scott returns throughout the number to the topic of the past. However, Scott is most forthright (predictably) in his review of Walter Scott's *The Abbot*. The review, after a quick dismissal of the novel as a comparative failure, moves to a consideration of Walter Scott's future direction as novelist:

We have heard it said for him, that he still had the past, the present, and the future: – of the present, we would advise him to beware: we do not see very well what he could do with the future – it is a comfortless prospect, and our sympathies recoil from it. But the past is human nature itself, removed to its far point of sight, and its suggestions are endless. (p. 428)

This social and political outlook ratifies Elia's whimsical antiquarianism as a welcome, even essential escape.

The November 1820 number of the *London* continues in much the same pessimistic vein, as Scott's sense of crisis over Caroline's trial deepens. His "Lion's Head" as well as the "Historical and Critical Summary" both move gloomily over the political situation. At first glance the lead article in the number seems to take, as did the articles of the previous number, another tack. "The Literature of the Nursery" surveys current trends in children's books and finds them uniformly appalling: "Innovation has made fearful progress in the child's library; and to no purpose, we verily think, but a bad one" (*London Magazine* 2, 479). Scott laments the passing of the oral tradition of nursery songs, now all printed. When they can be read "one may be . . . sure that they have lost their empire in their proper sphere." Similar depredations have been made on children's books: the old-fashioned style of illustration has given way to what Scott terms "flashy" modern techniques. Modern illustration, although more exact, does not encourage the "sense of mystery conveyed by the undefined" (p. 482) that the admittedly poor representations of the past did. Over-colorful prints teach children to prefer illustration to nature, and the results of such education are predictable for a social critic like Scott: "A sickly, bad taste in mature age is the natural result of these overcharged displays to youth: they affect the whole train of thinking and feeling throughout afterlife; for nature can

never have her due and delightful effect on any mind that is not allowed
to grow up in just allegiance to her power" (p. 483). Such personal shortcomings have national effects as well. Such education in youth accus-
toms mature minds to run to excess – the public interest in the details of
the investigation of the Queen being a case in point.[25]

Scott continues this line of argument in a subtle way by allowing Elia
to take it up. Rather than bludgeoning his readership with his interpretation, he suggests it by careful placement of essays. Lamb's "Christ's
Hospital Five and Thirty Years Ago" follows Scott's denunciation of
modern innovation. What Scott presented theoretically, Elia's recollections embody practically. The essay presents a remarkable admixture of
pleasure and pain, of sympathy and sadism. Bad food, punishments,
enforced whole-day leaves, bitter cold, arbitrary discipline, thieving
cooks, and the fantastic pampering of a concealed animal form the basis
of this essay, which claims to be a correction of the misrepresentations
in another essay, one by Charles Lamb. The fact that the ideal past is
evoked in the form of a correction of a too favorable account suggests
much about the dynamic of displacement: "ideal" is what satisfies the
desire for the ideal at a particular moment. The greyness of the recollection echoes Scott's strictures on childhood education in the previous
article without directly calling attention to them.

Scott emphasizes this loss of the proper educational tradition by par-
alleling it with other losses. The next article, "Old Stories, No. III,"
returns to the Middle Ages to praise its manners and loyalty indirectly
but no less clearly. This story's return to the past, as the returns in Scott's
evaluation of nursery stories and in Elia's depiction of the good old ways
of childhood education, stresses the bonds of the social order. Scott
manages to capitalize on the character he has given this number in a
later article, his famous attack on *Blackwood's Magazine*. That the success
of *Blackwood's* is a product of "sickly, bad taste" is evident in his reference
to its articles' "pungency . . . like that of the trash they sell in the common
liquor-shops under the name of brandy – which is seasoned with
burning poison to recommend it to the diseased taste of drabs and
dustmen" (pp. 511–12).

Scott's most felicitous pairing of essays, however, is his last one. In the
February 1821 number, he follows one of his most cogent assessments of
the political scene in England, "The Signs of the Times," with one of
Elia's finest essays, "Mrs. Battle's Opinions on Whist." Scott, in a characteristically Burkean–Coleridgean key, sees the restoration of tradition
as the only hope for the current political crisis:

we must have rank and title again seen forward, and adventurous, and triumphant, in behalf of Justice, and Truth, and Morals, and Independence . . . We
must look again to our natural political guardians. At some recent county meet-
ings, the people have shown a disposition to do so, and we hail the first symp-
toms of this return to their old confidence, as indications of a cheering nature,
streaking the general gloom of our political horizon. (*London Magazine* 3, 161)

His essay functions as a prosy gloss to Elia's play of recollection,
emotion, and sentiment. Lamb presents a purely formal world of struggle, the card game, in which human instincts for gaming are safely
roused and satisfied. The "temporary illusion" of the card table represents a little world of durable, lasting play enmity. Rank, order, and
degree are here givens, they are not subject to vertiginous speculation.
Here rank holds to its ceremonial functions; no unseemly private details
undermine authority and precedence. A strict rationalist, Mrs. Battle
questions the arbitrary elements in cards. Preferring that things be
settled absolutely, she finds naming trumps by turning a card disagreeable. But Elia meets this contradiction with an ingenious bit of special
pleading for the charms of what he terms "variety." The arbitrary features of the rules to and the look of the game are not to be discounted:

All these might be dispensed with; and, with their naked names upon the drab
pasteboard, the game might go on very well, picture-less. But the beauty of
cards would be extinguished for ever. Stripped of all that is imaginative in them,
they must degenerate into mere gambling. – Imagine a dull deal board, or drum
head, to spread them on, instead of that nice verdant carpet (next to nature's),
fittest arena for those courtly combatants to play their gallant jousts and tour-
neys in! (p. 163)

Mrs. Battle's reaction – "The old lady, with a smile, confessed the sound-
ness of my logic" (p. 163) – testifies to the efficacy of the Elian resolution
of contradiction in the kingdom of cards. His argument forms an
obvious parallel to Scott's earlier discussions of the value of viable ceremony in maintaining the "splendid fictions" of the monarchy. The
essay ends with a glimpse of an even more private world: Mrs. Battle's
card parties give way to the more secluded pleasures of "sick whist"
between Bridget and Elia. The meditative, recessive turn of the essay, so
often seen as autobiographic and idiosyncratic, takes on a wider application as both commentary on as well as relief from the contemporary
political scene. Scott's bracketing of the two essays is a subtle reminder
of the subterranean workings of politics in the essays: Elia's ironic displacement of political struggle to the little world of cards solves or at
least fends off a political problem by symbolic means.

To clarify the interpretive difference provided by this context, we might briefly recall Donald Reiman's New Critical treatment of "Mrs. Battle's Opinions." Reiman finds the essay expressive of a more time-less concern: "the elevation of sports and games as symbols or parallels of human life's serious occupations" ("Thematic Unity," p. 474). While this does not exclude political considerations, it admits them in an abstract, ahistorical way – not at all with the particular urgency felt by Scott in 1820 and 1821. Ultimately, Reiman finds value in Elia's crea-tion of "a symbol-world through which he could explore universal human problems in a truly imaginative way" (p. 478). Such an assess-ment, while perfectly consonant with the textual tradition inaugurated by the 1823 and 1833 collections of the essays, all but erases the origi-nal scene of reception, in which "universal" human problems took the form of a frightening (at least to the readers of the *London*) popular cyn-icism about monarchal prerogatives and claims to respect. It also dis-regards the more ominous features of Elia's special pleading for the arbitrary rankings of cards. Elia, while unconvinced himself, convinces Mrs. Battle of the beauty of the *status quo* in the world of cards; simi-larly, Scott, while aware of the manifest shortcomings of the royal family, would be happy to restore popular "old confidence" in these "natural political guardians." Equally intriguing is the appeal to art – here painting – in Elia's persuasion of Mrs. Battle. A glance at John Scott's reviews of the Waverley novels provides a suggestive parallel: he rarely omits consideration of Walter Scott's art as an instrument for maintaining the "splendid fictions" of the monarchy and of society in general.

John Scott's editorship ended with his death in February of 1821, but we can deduce much from the interpretations he gave the first Elia essays.[26] Scott's bibliographic coding allows us to reconstruct a context which suggests that, at least for some of the first readers, the personal and auto-biographical aspects of the Elia essays explored by later critics have a social and political component, one not so much to be teased out by a critical social reading such as that of Praz, but one available as a kind of editorial packaging. From this perspective the Elia essays are a conscious reaction to particular historical pressures; Elia's famous evasion of such issues is a gesture that contemporaries could read. Thus the strategies of personal consolation explored by such critics as Barnett, Frank, Randel, and McFarland can be read as public strategies for resolving the contra-dictions and pressures of the current political crises.

Three consequences follow from this analysis. First, by turning our eyes from the putative originary moment in which Lamb produced the essays to Scott's productive linking of them to a specific historical situation, we uncover a wealth of information about the reception of not only Lamb's essays but Romantic works generally. Janusz Sławiński, in a compact account of the reorientation forced on literary history by various reception theories, has located a tension between the historian's expansive project and the narrow range of documents available: "The literary historian obviously tries in various ways to break through the individualism and one-time, incidental nature of such testimonies to discover the underlying standards of literary reception. Sometimes he succeeds, and with interesting results. The problem, however, is that these underlying standards still do not reach beyond the expert level."[27] Scott's editorial activities offer a more reliable measure of these underlying standards of reception. Scott's market-wise decisions, especially when read against his own "expert" readings in numerous essays and reviews, are invaluable to a reception history that wishes to map responses other than those of eminent readers.

Secondly, we are encouraged to entertain a new conception of what constitutes the text of the Elia essays. Scott's editorial procedures are not simply a frame for Lamb's work; they are an expansion of the work itself, a part of the text as it was first received. In redrawing the boundary between Elia and the *London* itself, we must adopt a more complex notion of the morphology of the work, as well as a more complex sense of the textuality of such magazines. There are two moments and two texts for the Elia essays: one constituted by the 1823 and 1833 collections and subsequently enshrined by an idealist textual tradition; the other the product of the individual numbers and the very different textuality of the *London*.[28]

This textual situation brings us to the third consequence of such an analysis of the Elia essays: the implications for literary history. The two moments, two texts, and two textualities of the essays produce different readings. The historical specificities apparent in the Scott/Lamb *London* text tend, in *Elia* and the *Last Essays of Elia*, to fade into more timeless concerns – concerns articulated very well in the New Critical interpretations of Haven, Reiman, Mulcahy, and Frank. Read in a collection, the essays prove more amenable to parallels with the poetry of Wordsworth and Coleridge. In this format the view of the essays as embodying an attenuated, domesticated Romanticism becomes more valid. Nor does Pater's ecstatic praise of Lamb seem particularly far-fetched in a context shorn of the crises and political anxieties of 1820. Hence a literary history must consider this double strain in the reception of the Elia essays: a dominant idealist tradition inaugurated by the collections, and a largely neglected tradition bound up with the equally neglected question of the role of literary magazines in literary history.

The 100 years that follow Lamb's death in 1834 demonstrate the productivity of the Elia essays – that is, their capacity to support new readings over time. Once detached from their complex and politically charged moment in the *London*, the essays are fitted to a variety of aesthetic programs and social purposes, until, at the centennial year of 1934, Lamb's reputation collapses. The critical fortunes of Elia make up a cautionary tale, in which the critical move that allows the rehabilitation of Lamb and productive rereadings of the essays ultimately leads to an impoverished tradition.

The vigorous suppression of Lamb's politics makes his reputation in the nineteenth century possible. This battle is waged on two fronts by an unlikely coalition between his memorialists and commentators on the political right. During his lifetime Lamb had received unfortunate characterization in the periodical press – notably in Gilray's caricature for the *Anti-Jacobin*, in which Lamb and Lloyd were portrayed as a toad and a frog – and he had endured the charge of atheism, which was tantamount to an accusation of Jacobinism, from Southey in the *Quarterly*. His literary executors, publisher Edward Moxon (virtually his son-in-law), editor of the letters Thomas Talfourd, and biographer Brian Waller Proctor (Barry Cornwall), countered this characterization with understandable exaggeration. Talfourd's 1837 selection of the letters, in a discussion of Lamb's friendship with Godwin, dismisses any radicalism on the part of Lamb: "Indifferent altogether to the politics of the age."[29] The desire to banish politics from discussion of Lamb leads Proctor to a tortured, if not contradictory statement in his 1866 biography: "Lamb's writings had no reference whatever to political subjects; they were, on the contrary, as the first writings of a young man generally are, serious, – even religious."[30] De Quincey, in his 1838 "Recollections of Charles Lamb," dismisses the entire subject: "Politics – what cared he for politics?"[31]

Such expressions, the product of friendly interest in the reputation of Lamb, are seconded by the politically interested efforts of periodical writers on the right. Even before Lamb was Elia, a *Blackwood's* writer, in an 1818 review of his *Works*, sought to detach Lamb from the taint of radical politics and the pernicious influence of his companions Hazlitt and Hunt: "He never utters any of that dull or stupid prosing that weighs down the dying Edinburgh Review, – never any of those utterly foolish paradoxes which Hazlitt insidiously insinuates into periodical publications, – never any of those flagitious phillipics against morality and social order that come weekly raving from the irascible Hunt."[32] In 1835 William Maginn sought to claim Lamb for the far right in *Fraser's*, declaring that Lamb was neither Jacobin nor Cockney, and that the famous attack on him in the *Anti-Jacobin* was unjustified.[33]

The complications of his historical moment removed, Elia was now ready to become a Victorian icon. There are three phases in this formation. First, Lamb gains the reputation of a "contracted genius" with an unusually complete power of expression. Later, when the public silence about Mary Lamb's madness and matricide is broken with her death, mid-century Victorian critics fashion Lamb's life into an emblem of heroic suffering, self-renunciation, and hard-won domestic contentment – an emblem best summed up by Thackeray's apocryphal quip about "St. Charles." Finally, this consensus stifles reconsideration of Lamb's work, setting the stage for a reversal of critical opinion and the collapse of his reputation.

Hartley Coleridge's 1835 essay for the *Quarterly*, a belated review of the 1833 *Last Essays of Elia*, sounds the keynote of Lamb's early posthumous reception.[34] Coleridge begins by insisting that the essayist is "one of nature's curiosities, and amongst her richest and rarest" ("The Last Essays of Elia," p. 58), and he continues this line of miniature imagery throughout. For Coleridge, Lamb's essays resist critical analysis because of their unusual expressive power: "He was all-compact – inner and outer man in perfect fusion, – all the powers of the mind, – the sensations of the body, interpenetrating each other. His genius was talent, and his talent genius; his imagination and fancy one and indivisible; the finest scalpel of the metaphysician could not have separated them" (p. 59). Coleridge insists upon this view of Lamb as a peculiar, even singular case: "He has a small, well-situated parterre on Parnassus, belonging exclusively to himself. He is not amongst the highest, but then he is alone and aloof from all others" (p. 69). The reviews that follow Talfourd's 1837 edition of the letters echo these sentiments. Bulwer, in an 1837 *Westminster Review* essay, contrasts Lamb's completeness, at least within the narrow range of his expression, with the incomplete appearance of works by other writers of his generation. Glancing at Coleridge, Bulwer notes the finish of Lamb's essays: "we do not obtain his mind by bits and fragments."[35] De Quincey, in his 1838 "Recollections of Charles Lamb," concludes with this consideration of Lamb's artistry: "Every literature possesses, besides its great national gallery, a cabinet of minor pieces, not less perfect in their polish, possibly more so. In reality, the characteristic of this class is elaborate perfection – the point of inferiority is not in the finishing, but in the compass and power of the original creation" (p. 89). Such remarks provide the plinth on which the statue of "St. Charles" is placed. Lamb is praised, curiously, as his work is effectively removed from critical consideration. Perfect, on his elegant "parterre on Parnassus," he awaits the laurels of his Victorian reputation.

While Mary Lamb was alive, periodical writers and reviewers kept up a respectful silence about her madness. But after her death in 1847, these events formed the basis for Charles Lamb's Victorian reputation. George Henry Lewes, with his usual journalistic dexterity, managed to tell the story first in the *British Quarterly Review*, prompting Lamb's literary executors, Moxon and Talfourd, to publish *Final Memorials*, which included letters touching on these painful subjects. Lewes's essay takes a sternly Victorian turn in handling the Lambs' tragedy: "Like a brave, suffering, unselfish man, he, at twenty-one, renounced the dream of love for the stern austerity of duty."[36] Later in the essay Lewes declares, "it is his whole life which we call heroic" and, in one of the first of many psychological readings of Lamb's work, insists that the "extremity of his suffering" ("Charles Lamb," p. 308) explained Lamb's taste for the "horrors" of old English drama. William Henry Smith, in an 1848 review of Talfourd's *Memorials* for *Blackwood's*, dwells on the burdens of Lamb's care for his sister. B. W. Proctor's 1866 biography of Lamb narrows this focus. For Proctor, Lamb's life "is a history with one event predominant" (*Charles Lamb*, p. 12), and everything in his account recalls the reader to the enormity of Lamb's self-sacrifice and brotherly duty. Proctor concludes with a forceful moralization, which was approvingly extracted by reviewers of his book:

Charles Lamb was born almost in penury, and he was taught by charity. Even when a boy he was forced to labor for his bread. In the first opening of manhood a terrible calamity fell upon him, in magnitude fit to form the mystery or centre of an antique drama. He had to dwell, all his days, with a person incurably mad. From poverty he passed at once to unpleasant toil and perpetual fear. These were the sole changes in his fortune. Yet he gained friends, respect, a position, and great sympathy from all; showing what one poor man of genius, under grievous misfortune, may do, if he be courageous and faithful to the end. (pp. 274–5)

Small wonder that one reviewer, working under this saintly atmosphere, concluded that Lamb "will never excite hostile criticism," that readers of Lamb will feel "a warmer, a more partial affection than Criticism knows how to express," and that criticism would gladly forgo judgment to "embrace the man as he is."[37]

A celebration of the joys of domesticity accompanied this fascination with what Pater later termed the "Greek tragedy" of Lamb's life.[38] De Quincey's 1848 review of *Final Memorials* for the *North British Review* delicately links the motifs of miniaturism, "compacted genius," family tragedy, and domestic comfort:

> They [the Elia essays] traverse a peculiar field of observation, sequestered from general interest; and they are composed in a spirit too delicate and unobtrusive to catch the ear of the noisy crowd, clamouring for strong sensations. But this retiring delicacy itself, the pensiveness chequered by gleams of the fanciful, and the humour that is touched with cross-lights of pathos, together with the picturesque quaintness of the objects casually described, whether men, or things, or usages, and, in the rear of all this, the constant recurrence to ancient recollections and to decaying forms of household life, as things retiring before the tumult of new and revolutionary generations; – these traits in combination communicate to these papers a grace and strength of originality which nothing in any literature approaches.[39]

Such complex nostalgia, which hints that the domesticity it celebrates has already slipped away in the face of modernity, gives way to more dramatic and aestheticized accounts later in the century. R. M. Milnes's review of Proctor's biography for *Blackwood's* notes, somewhat uncomprehendingly, the contemporary cult for "those modest, almost austere habits of his [Lamb's] daily life,"[40] and W. C. Hazlitt calls for yet another biography: "There is want of a volume yet, which should describe that for us, which should paint the Lambs' fireside, and present to us a view, or even glimpses, of those two, as they were and moved, even at the hazard of a little pre-Raphaelitish detail."[41] Earlier in the century critics had praised Lamb's expressive capacities as a master of the personal essay; now, Lamb's biography, hammered into a particularly Victorian moral emblem, had taken precedence.

Such a position is bound to engender extreme reactions. Walter Pater's discussion of Lamb in *Appreciations* and Augustine Birrell's essay in *Obiter Dicta* are each, in their own way, signs of decadence – in the positive and the negative sense.[42] Pater's insistence on the "fateful domestic horror" (*Appreciations*, p. 109) as precondition to – and not subject of – the Elia essays frees his discussion from the more crippling effects of the critical tradition. As reaction to the cult of "St. Charles," Pater's unlikely championship of Lamb's disinterestedness is refreshing:

In the making of prose he realizes the principle of art for its own sake, as completely as Keats in the making of verse. And, working ever close to the concrete, to the details, and with no part of them blurred to his vision by the intervention of mere abstract theories, he has reached an enduring moral effect also, in a sort of boundless sympathy.[43]

This move has the added attraction of making Pater attentive to aspects of the Elia essays unacknowledged since John Scott – Elia's ability to form, in his first editor's words, "so clear and fair an impression from facts" (*London Magazine* 2 [1820], 317) and to widen these perceptions into a larger social vision. Far from seeing Lamb as a "contracted genius," Pater finds power, surprisingly, in Lamb's penchant for reminiscence: "Seeing things always by the light of an understanding more entire than is possible for ordinary minds, of the whole mechanism of humanity, and seeing also the manner, the outward mode or fashion, always in strict connexion with the spiritual condition which determined it, a humourist such as Charles Lamb anticipates the enchantment of distance" (*Appreciations*, p. 117). Pater is very close to John Scott's sense of nostalgia as reflex of and possible cure for social and political discontent. The political and social charge may be different, as for Scott the "outward mode" of displacement was determined by the "spiritual condition" of a dispiriting political arena, but the mechanism is the same.

Birrell's bluff portrait directly contrasts Pater's wire-drawn account of Lamb. The hollowness and predictability of his remarks show the exhaustion of the tradition of criticism:

It should never be forgotten that Lamb's vocation was his life. Literature was his by-play, his avocation in the true sense of that much-abused word. He was not a fisherman but an angler in the lake of letters; an author by chance and on the sly. He had a right to disport himself on paper, to play the frolic with his own fancies, to give the decalogue the slip, whose life was made up of the sternest stuff, of self- sacrifice, devotion, honesty, and good sense. ("Charles Lamb," pp. 227–8)

The implicit dismissal of any artistic intent in the Elia essays is made possible by the steady dissolution of Lamb's work into Lamb himself. Birrell exults in the moral uplift of Lamb's works, although he fumbles to locate it exactly, remarking that "they do good by stealth" (p. 235). Like W. C. Hazlitt earlier, he ends his review with a hearty call for more of the same: "Let us have them [more letters] speedily, so that honest men may have in their houses a complete edition of at least one author of whom they can truthfully say, that they never know whether they most admire the writer or love the man" (p. 235). Reading the *bonhomie* of Birrell's last sentiment, one can understand the vehemence with which a new generation of critics attacked Lamb.

The centennial of Lamb's death revealed the exhaustion of the "St. Charles" tradition. E. V. Lucas, who had edited the letters and written the standard biography, cranked out a thin volume of musings and small discoveries about Lamb, aptly titled *At the Shrine of St. Charles*. A. C. Ward justifies his publication of a short biography, *The Frolic and the Gentle*, with the blunt assertion that "Charles Lamb is not, I think, a suitable subject for psychological investigation, philosophical disquisition, or critical ingenuity."[44] Ward's opening chapter, "The Genius of the Hearth," bristles with such defensive statements as "Charles Lamb's cleverness was a superfluity" and "most of his readers do not value him so much for what he wrote as for what he was" (*The Frolic*, p. 1). The question of "what Lamb was," of course, is never really broached by Ward, who takes the essays as pure autobiography.

When a writer is beyond criticism, a reversal is surely at hand. *Scrutiny* provided the stage for the attack on Lamb. Denys Thompson's scathing "Our Debt to Lamb" excoriates Elia as a pernicious stylistic and moral influence. Likening Lamb's craft to advertising, Thompson sees him as pander to the most banal of bourgeois tastes and illusions – providing comfort and uplift – and contrasts him with eighteenth-century essayists, who challenged their audience's prejudices and addressed their ignorances. Worst of all, the essays reveal a "recessive mind, shrinking from full consciousness."[45] This lack of engagement with life makes Lamb unfit for any audience. Graham Greene, in a review of centennial books by Blunden and Lucas, echoes Thompson's strictures. Conceding Lamb's "supreme literary skill,"[46] he laments its perversion in the sentimental inanities of the Elia essays. Greene rejects the tradition of Lamb as domestic hero, insisting that he only did what anyone would do in such a situation. Like Thompson, Greene dislikes Lamb's recessive nature: he is a "a man who sublimated, but not very effectively, his weakness of character into gentleness, his inability to face contemporary life with courage into an antique literary manner" ("Lamb's Testimonials," p. 512).

The ironies of such a situation are acute. Thompson and Greene denigrate Lamb for just what John Scott valued in the Elia essays. The difference lies in the more complicated interpretive stance taken by Scott. Where Thompson and Greene take Elia's "recessive mind" literally, Scott saw such a move as an informed political gesture – a displacement that fitted a particular historical circumstance. Modern critics, working in a tradition that had forgotten the specificities of Elia's moment, could only respond to Lamb as the Victorians' "St. Charles." Small wonder that the academic studies of Lamb that follow the collapse of his reputation tend to argue for an appreciations of Lamb as a Romantic poet in prose, as a stylist who constructs a persona to explore a "neutral ground" free of the burdens of will and decision, as a writer whose whole body of work merits attention from a phenomenological perspective: the reception history of the Elia essays, cluttered with a century's worth of loose ideological constructions, needed the cleaning that formalism could provide.

We will see Lamb and Elia more clearly if we accept what the publishing history of the essays bluntly suggests: that the essays come to us in two ways – as an intertextually oriented part of a magazine, and as the self-contained prose poems admired by readers of his two collections. Certainly such a complex orientation fits the ambiguity of Lamb's – and Elia's – authorial stance. The irony that the "Friend of the Late Elia" attributes to Elia's "doubtful speeches" aptly figures the political dimension of the essays: "He would interrupt the gravest discussion with some light jest; and yet, perhaps, not quite irrelevant in the ears that could understand it."[47] In Scott's ears, the essays had a political relevance, and his determined use of them in the *London Magazine* asks that we rethink the critical tradition of the Elia essays. And in doing so, we may develop the ears not only for the inflections given to Romantic texts by contemporary editors and readers, but for those given by the ideological and editorial practices of subsequent critics.

CHAPTER TWO

A conversation between friends: Hazlitt and the London Magazine

> There is no conversation worth any thing but between friends, or those who agree in the same leading views of a subject. Nothing was ever learnt by either side in a dispute.
>
> "On the Conversation of Authors"[1]

William Hazlitt's days as regular contributor to the *London Magazine* were few, but they mark a turning point in his career. His most lasting work, the essays written under the pseudonym "Table-Talk," were begun under Scott's tenure as editor. As in the case of Lamb's essays, Hazlitt's contributions stand in an active relation to the *London*, but the rhetoricity of the Table-Talk essays differs from that of the Elia essays. Despite their archaic style, Lamb's essays are much more the up-to-date commodity text than Hazlitt's. The diction may be quaint, but the Elia essays accord with the division of labor that marks the production of nineteenth-century periodicals. For all their jaunty modernity, Hazlitt's essays recall an older mode of production: the conversational relation between periodical and contributor established in the eighteenth century. To follow Hazlitt's career in the *London* under Scott, in the interregnum between Scott's death and the sale of the magazine to the firm of Taylor & Hessey, and under Taylor, is to examine the complex workings of a shifting array of factors – different conceptions of the magazine, different ideological tendencies, and different political commitments – in the production of meaning for Hazlitt's contributions. Moreover, just as the relation between a given contributor and the magazine can vary over time, the relations of contributors to the magazine can differ from each other in the same number or over a given run. If the literary magazine can be said to provide an informing context for the individual contribution, this context shifts according to time and to contributor.

Hazlitt had worked with John Scott in 1815 on the weekly *Champion*, but it was with some reticence that the editor of the *London* hired him as drama critic in 1820. A letter of January 18 to Baldwin spells out Scott's concerns:

At the same time I will engage for the gentleman, from what I know of his character, that he would be most ready to listen to suggestions and to strain every nerve for us, in return for a service. He is naturally grateful, and though an original, is an honest one. I have not spoken to him for several years until Sunday last, but I see that in a very short time I shall be able to influence him to proper subjects and to a proper manner of handling them. – I mean *proper* in regard to the Magazine: – generally speaking I should have little claim to be his judge or guide.[2]

The genteel, hierarchical world evoked by Scott's use of "gentleman" and "service" seems an incongruous place for an unyielding radical like Hazlitt, but it is just such a relation that Scott forges between himself and his contributor in the pages of the *London*.

This situation as drama critic was a timely one for Hazlitt. He had collected his journalistic pieces in *The Round Table* (1817), in *A View of the English Stage* (1818), and in *Political Essays* (1819); and he was completing his lectures on Elizabethan literature when he was hired by Scott. Hazlitt was again in need of money, and Scott in his letter to Baldwin makes much of his consequent serviceability. Much can be gleaned from the preface to his *Political Essays* concerning Hazlitt's general state of mind as he began his career with the *London*. His disaffection with the present parallels that of John Scott. As would his editor in the pages of the *London*, Hazlitt expresses alienation from each of the existing parties – Tory, "governed by sense and habit alone,"[3] bowing to might and to established authority at every instance; Whig, "but the fag-end of a Tory" (*Complete Works*, vol. VII, p. 19), or at best the unwitting partner of Tory programs; and Reform, "necessarily and naturally a Marplot" (vol. VII, p. 14), offering only a spectacle of frivolous and ultimately egotistical speculation. Throughout the preface Hazlitt presents each faction not so much in itself as in relation to the other two, each morbidly dependent upon its antagonists. Hazlitt sees the current political impasse as the result of the combined efforts of these three groups. Moreover, even when Hazlitt's assessments run counter to the more conservative strain of Scott's ideas, they demonstrate a debt to Burke similar to that of his future editor. Hazlitt's invective against Legitimacy, while itemizing the evils of Burkean presumption and prescription, nevertheless pays indirect tribute to Burke's analysis of the persistence of tradition:

But there are persons of that low and inordinate appetite for servility, that they cannot be satisfied with any thing short of that sort of tyranny that has lasted for ever, and is likely to last for ever; that is strengthened and made desperate by the superstitions and prejudices of ages; that is enshrined in traditions, in laws, in usages, in the outward symbols of power, in the very idioms of language; that has struck its roots into the human heart, and clung round the human understanding like a nightshade; that overawes the imagination, and disarms the will to resist it, by the very enormity of the evil; that is cemented with gold and blood; guarded by reverence, guarded by power, linked in endless succession to the principle by which life is transmitted to the generations of tyrants and slaves, and destroying liberty with the first breath of life; that is absolute, unceasing, unerring, fatal, unutterable, abominable, monstrous. (vol. VII, p. 12)

Hazlitt's disgust is Jacobin, but his analysis of the persistence of old evil is Burkean.[4] Though the sentiment may be that of Paine, it lacks his insouciant revolutionary dismissal of old corruption. There is no conversion trope, no light of reason to eradicate the darkness of oppression. The rhetorical reversal of such phrases as Paine's "He pities the plumage, and forgets the dying bird" has become, in the climate of the late Regency, ineffectual. The brisk critical mode of the Enlightenment has given way to consideration of the transmission, circulation, and reproduction of ideology.

Put another way, the question prompted by Hazlitt's situation is whether the critical energy of the Enlightenment, put in popular journalistic form by Paine, can be appropriated by more literary and belletristic writers. This powerful rhetoric, which works to a large extent by subtraction or reduction, conflicts with the growing awareness of the thickness of culture, the complex network of relations that constitutes society. That the clarification offered by the force of Reason is not eligible – that no one really seeks to counter an impressionistic and often contradictory view of society – is evident in Hazlitt's later essay on Godwin in *The Spirit of the Age*. There Hazlitt can only wonder at the revolution of Godwin's reputation between the "burning heat" of 1793 and the "below zero" of 1814 (*Complete Works*, vol. XI, p. 17). Godwin's fault, to Hazlitt's mind, is "ambition": he "conceived too nobly of his fellows," taking "abstract reason for the rule of conduct, and abstract good for its end" (vol. XI, p. 18). In his brisk summary of Godwin's philosophy, which "absolves man from the gross and narrow ties of sense, custom, authority, private and local attachment, in order that he may devote himself to the boundless pursuit of universal benevolence" (vol. XI, pp. 18–19), Hazlitt invokes a Burkean set of coordinates. He concludes with a flight of Burkean rhetoric:

We may not be able to launch the bark of our affections on the oceantide of humanity, we may be forced to paddle along its shores, or shelter in its creeks and rivulets: but we have no right to reproach the bold and adventurous pilot, who dared us to tempt the uncertain abyss, with our own want of courage or of skill, or with the jealousies and impatience, which deter us from undertaking, or might prevent us from accomplishing the voyage! (vol. xi, p. 19)

Hazlitt's extended figure elegantly charts his shift from insurgent criticism to intellectual critique: from Godwin's generalities to Burke's specifics, from consideration of principles to concern for the force of circumstance, from the sublime of abstract speculation to the more picturesque work of mapping the affections.

Hence Hazlitt is not pliable simply because of his finances and "naturally grateful" character; he is compatible with Scott's program for the *London* because he shares – at least for a time – many of the same principles espoused by Scott. Jacobin in sentiment, Hazlitt is Burkean in execution. His virtual farewell to politics in the preface to *Political Essays*, his sense of the futility of political discourse, and his status as Jacobin pariah condition the inward turn of his career during the early 1820s. This compatibility should not be confused with complicity or capitulation: Hazlitt and Scott, as we shall see, will disagree on a number of issues in the pages of the *London*. But the relation that emerges is more one of dialogue or conversation than confrontation.

This conversational setting was not achieved at once. Scott forced a kind of re-apprenticeship on Hazlitt in the first few numbers of the magazine. In a review of Hazlitt's recent lectures in the second number of the *London*, Scott expands on the misgivings about Hazlitt's politics that he expressed in his letter to Baldwin. Although Hazlitt's observations are always original, Scott argues, his argument is often left off "for the sake of a vehement sally." This "caprice" makes Hazlitt's work "vastly liable to terminate in unconscious habits of sophistication," gives openings to his enemies, and "impedes the good offices of friends" (*London Magazine* 1 [1820], 187). Whether or not this criticism affected Hazlitt's work, it aptly sums up one difference between his earlier essays, such as those collected in *The Round Table*, and those done for the *London* under Scott. It is only after Scott's death in February 1821 that Hazlitt resumes some of his former vehemence.

Scott must have been pleasantly surprised by the coherence of his contributor's monthly drama reviews. Unlike the desultory and circumstantial efforts of other drama critics, Hazlitt's first four reviews are noteworthy for their attention to the principles of drama criticism and to the dynamics of the theater. Discussion of contemporary performances either introduces general considerations or exemplifies them. "Drama. No. 1" opens with a series of epigrammatic comparisons between the traditions of drama and of literature: drama escapes invidious comparison between current and historical productions, and stage tradition, as it effectively covers only a generation, is less an encumbrance to actors than literary tradition to writers. Hazlitt then describes the dynamics of a stage performance. Audiences like to see the "study of humanity . . . brought home from the universality of precepts and general terms, to the reality of persons, of tones, and actions; and to have it raised from the grossness and familiarity of sense, to the lofty but striking platform of the imagination" (*London Magazine* 1 [1820], 65). This double action, which embodies abstractions as it refines experience, is the essence of Hazlitt's dramatic criticism. Like Lamb's analysis of acting in "On the Tragedies of Shakespeare," Hazlitt's dramatic criticisms tend to view acting as a series of signs – essentially as a semiotic system. Acting, Lamb argued, is like a language: gesture and voice are the means of translating the text. Like any system of signs, it is better suited for some tasks than others. Often the limits of acting as a language make it a poor match for some texts, as in the case of Shakespeare's tragedies. Hazlitt's general agreement with this view of acting is evident in his second column on the drama, in which he criticizes Mrs. O'Neill's "natural" style of acting. At times she is too lifelike, and her renderings of bodily suffering "are no longer proper for dramatic exhibition when they become objects of painful attention in themselves, and are not really indications of what passes in the mind – comments and interpreters of the moral sense within" (*London Magazine* 1, 165). "Drama. No. 3" begins with a survey of the minor theaters, but again the essay shifts to more general considerations. Small houses lend a kind of familiarity to the actors that ends in a kind of contempt: "By too narrow an inspection, you take away that fine, hazy medium of abstraction, by which (in moderation) a play is best set off" (*London Magazine* 1, 301).

But these efforts, while impressive, can be seen as prefatory to Hazlitt's fourth contribution on the drama, in which he addresses the relative lack of good contemporary work. He proposes that a bias toward abstraction has made recent productions tedious, that the French Revolution and subsequent upheaval have provided a much more gripping spectacle, and that the public realm has gained so much on that of the private that much drama seems petty. In fact, the decline is not so much the fault of writers as a failure of the audience:

But surely it is hardly to be thought that the poet should feel for others in this way, when they have ceased almost to feel for themselves; when the mind is turned habitually out of itself to general, speculative truth, and the possibilities of good, and when, in fact, the processes of the understanding, analytical distinctions, and verbal disputes, have superseded all personal and local attachments and antipathies, and have, in a manner, put a stop to the pulsation of the heart. (*London Magazine* 1, 434)

This sense of the loss of the personal and local echoes John Scott's "On Human Perfectibility," which appeared in the previous number of *London*. Scott argues that contemporary society has become degenerate through the "tyranny of the understanding." Feelings and sentiments have been separated from perception, and the result is that

people have no longer, either within them, or about them, anything but certain circumscribed and determined figures, which they call realities, because they are the objects of their commonest senses. All that is now known, is to combine and analyze ideas: there is a desire to understand, to define, and to demonstrate every thing, – and by means of so much demonstration the truth is missed. (*London Magazine* 1 [1820], 270)

This dissociation of sensibility that both Scott and Hazlitt perceive in contemporary life recalls Burke's oft-cited praise of the local in *Reflections*.[5] The avowed politics of each writer is, to some extent, less important than the commitment to the "truth" of "personal and local attachments and antipathies." Scott's distrust of Enlightenment modes of thought is more clearly stated – as in the above passage, where the by now formulaic "combine and analyze ideas" and "demonstrate" indicate his feelings exactly – but Hazlitt's arguments register the force of the "pulsation of the heart" as well.

Scott's "On Human Perfectibility" serves as a compact commentary on the Table-Talk essays to follow in the *London*. Scott dismisses the Whig idea of a progressive history as the product of the Enlightenment's mania for "distinct ideas" and "a falsification, alteration, and truncation of history." A proper history would start from below, not with abstractions, but with "particular examples; – that is, the various people which compose it; and, to know these last, it is necessary to examine each in what is proper and peculiar to itself. This is to be found in its language, usages, and history." In fact, if a general history is to be written, it ought to begin with a collection of local histories: "If we had a full collection, we should see that each presented a distinct view of human nature: the things possessed in common would reduce themselves to very few, and the differences would strike much more than the resemblances" (p. 271).

Scott's recognition of the thickness of culture makes current attempts at general history "contemptible and unsatisfactory" and leads him to an admirably compact conclusion, in which he strikes at the Enlightenment even more directly: "Were the above plan followed, it might be found perhaps, that general history, like general grammar, reduces itself to a small matter" (p. 271). Scott's apprehension of the striking differences within human nature leads him to a profound distrust of abstraction, even as he recognizes that the process of abstraction is essential to thought. While Hazlitt rarely goes as far as Scott in advocating so nominalist a view of history, he displays similar intellectual affinities. As the political content of his essays ebbs, these other tendencies become prominent, and his work accords surprisingly well with Scott's views.

Hazlitt apparently proved himself to Scott in his first four drama contributions. He writes seven more, but they are offhand at best, restating the ideas in the first four numbers, applying their insights to particular performances, and offering desultory remarks on other productions.[6] Hazlitt seems here to be turning his attention to the Table-Talk essays, the first of which appears in the June 1820 number. As in the case of Lamb's essays, these contributions are drawn into the network of Scott's *London*. But there is a salient difference in the use to which Scott puts Hazlitt's series: instead of emphasizing some elements of these essays with subtle editorial tactics, Scott encourages their conversational aspects. The essays themselves, which often include references to or echoes of arguments made by other contributors, simplify Scott's task. Ultimately the fact that Hazlitt, a middle-class radical, shares so many "leading views" with the far more conservative Scott, permits an unexpected exchange of ideas. What ensues is a conversation that charts the boundaries of discourse for the emerging middle class.

A recent critic has characterized the interplay between the articles in the *London* as dialogic in the Bahktinian sense, as if the magazine presented a medley of voices representing different social types or kinds of discourse.[7] While this assessment does the very real service of turning scholarly attention toward the magazine as a context for the essays of Hazlitt and Lamb, it overstates the diversity of speech types in this very middle-class journal. The dialogism of the *London*, especially in the case of Hazlitt and Scott, is more akin to that implicit in many eighteenth-century periodicals, in which the ubiquitous coffee-house analogy that defined the roles of contributors and readers was predicated on the acceptance of a particular discursive formation and the fulfillment of certain standards of property.[8] Though Scott and Hazlitt clearly do not display the fierce commitment to rationality or to the narrowly bourgeois concept of standing through property of their eighteenth-century forebears, their discursive commitments are equally exclusive and their allegiances to class are, if anything, more occluded than those of their periodical predecessors. The result is a kind of conversation which never rises to the level of a dispute over fundamental issues.

Critical treatments of Hazlitt's Table-Talk essays tend to address them as if they were written at Winterslow in a kind of vacuum.[9] Such discussions present Winterslow as a retreat, a respite in which Hazlitt was free to set loose his Montaignesque penchant for expansive treatment of subject and for introspection. The timeless quality that critics have seen in these essays is possibly more a product of the way these essays are now read – in collected editions – than of any intent on Hazlitt's part. For example, Hazlitt's first Table-Talk essay, June's "On the Qualifications Necessary to Success," is enmeshed in the time and place of the *London*. Hazlitt began the May drama column with a complaint about his exclusion from Drury Lane; in his June Table-Talk this incident exemplifies the way in which appearances and a failure to regard proprieties work against merit. Hazlitt adds to the simmering feud with *Blackwood's* with a jibe about their attention to class in their damnation of Keats and praise of Shelley. The relative weakness of Walter Scott's latest novel, *The Monastery* (reviewed by John Scott in the previous number), recurs as one of Hazlitt's examples of defensive vanity on the part of authors. Even the footnotes, in which Hazlitt peevishly notes his disaffection with writing ("I am somewhat sick of this trade of authorship, that I have a much greater ambition to be the best racket-player, than the best prose-writer of the age" [*London Magazine* 1 (1820), 653]) set up a sympathetic oscillation within a magazine so careful to cover fighting and other popular sports.

But the most prominent topic in this essay saturated with local detail and institutional reference is Benjamin Robert Haydon's exhibition of "Christ's Agony." Scott's May article had opened discussion of the picture in the *London*. There Scott had praised the picture, defended Haydon's practice of public exhibition against his detractors, and excused Haydon's self- promotion as the only avenue to success available in an era of limited patronage. Recalling George III's generous support of historical painting, he criticizes his son's niggardly attitude as Regent. Scott also defends Haydon's method in a more positive fashion: such promotions, by drawing attention to the fine arts, have resulted in more exhibitions and in the acquisition of the Elgin Marbles. Scott argues that any excesses on Haydon's part should be weighed against these achievements. Nevertheless Scott has some misgivings about the strategy of relying on the general public. Public exhibitions conducted by the artist himself are dangerous to his art because there is always "the temptation unduly to consider the popular taste in the selection of a subject, and to introduce accessaries calculated to gratify popular prejudice in the mode of treating it" (*London Magazine* 1 [1820], 584). Some of Haydon's hype – such as the sensational claim of "six years on the easel" – is less a cultivation of public taste than "something for those to repeat who could say nothing for themselves" (p. 586).

Hazlitt has none of Scott's cautious optimism about the entrepreneurial activities of Haydon. He lashes out at both Scott's model of highbrow reception as well as middlebrow consumption of art: "The majority go by personal appearances, not by proofs of intellectual power; and they are quite right in this, for they are better judges of the one than of the other" (pp. 652–3). He cites Wordsworth as an example of the grudging admiration given an artist by audiences both high and low: "Mr. Wordsworth has given us the essence of poetry in his works, without the machinery, the apparatus of poetical diction, the theatrical pomp, the conventional ornaments; and we see what he has made of it" (p. 646). More germane to success is a certain manner, a robust constitution, some personal quality not related to an artist's genius, or mere chance. Hazlitt and Scott are in essential agreement about aesthetic principles, but they differ widely in their expectations of these principles being applied. Scott hopes for a patchwork combination of revived patronage and improvements in public taste through increased exhibition; Hazlitt sees chicanery and fraud in the culture of consumption and malice and envy in the culture of reception.

The basis for this illuminating exchange lies in the intellectual common property that lies beneath it, the "leading views" that enable it. Here we have a conversation about aesthetics, reception, and the possibility of artistic success not from some outside, abstract position, but from within the circuit of artistic production and reception itself. Scott and Hazlitt, who have played a variety of roles in their literary lives – Scott as editor, critic, and author of travel books; Hazlitt as drama critic, literary critic, essayist, philosopher, and political journalist – bring a wide range of specific circumstances to bear on these issues. Their exchange, which suggests a harsh audience for the soaring aspirations of a Keats or Haydon, offers a more informed estimate of the conditions for artistic endeavor than we are likely to get in critiques of a more aesthetic turn.

If Hazlitt's first Table-Talk essay hints at the productive capabilities of the dialogic stance, the second in the series, "On the Difference Between Writing and Speaking," provides a more specific conversational opener. Hazlitt's thesis cuts against one of the eighteenth-century periodical pieties – that writing is a kind of speech, and that the periodical was a kind of coffee house in which free exchange and circulation of ideas could flourish. According to Hazlitt the chief difference between writing and speech is time, but more telling disparities arise as a consequence. Speech is fluency with commonplaces; it is bound by the apprehensions of the slowest auditors; it cannot deliver new ideas. It can only mobilize latent bias, and by doing so, can draw up a consensus: "Zeal will do more than knowledge" (*London Magazine* 2 [1820], 26). Writing, however, allows for original ideas, novel expression, and perhaps even truth. The written word "does not lie at the orifices of the mouth ready for delivery, but is wrapped in the folds of the heart and registered in the chambers of the brain" (p. 32). The speaker who wishes to load his remarks with ideas more fitted to written expression will meet, as did Burke, blank incomprehension. To speak in the House of Commons is to be in "a go-cart of prejudices, in a regularly constructed machine of pretexts and precedents" (p. 28). Hazlitt figures speech (or for that matter hearing) as mechanical or mechanistic throughout the essay, as a product always already in circulation. Such a position was uncongenial to Scott, who responds obliquely to Hazlitt's essay in the "Lion's Head" of the ensuing number. His reaction, a pointed inclusion of a letter praising debate clubs, is undeveloped, but characteristic of a man who valued, perhaps out of nostalgia, exchange within the public sphere.

If the August "Lion's Head" offers an implicit counterpoint to Hazlitt's attack on speaking in the July number, Hazlitt's September contribution, "On the Conversation of Authors," affords a synthesis of the two positions. Hazlitt begins by reasserting the superiority of writing, but he then praises various kinds of conversation. In doing so, he sets out a kind of theory of conversation: he carefully charts the differences in writing, speechmaking, and conversation; and he notes the limitations to each. The essay is remarkable in its attention to the rhetorical situation of writing and speaking – that is, how various situations condition the effect of each. As this contribution is the culmination of an engaging inquiry into the nature of various discourses, it is fitting that it concludes with a description of various talkers – both good and bad – among Hazlitt's friends and acquaintances.

Hazlitt's October contribution, "On the Present State of Parliamentary Eloquence," draws on ideas from earlier essays in the Table-Talk series. It begins by applying the principles outlined in "On the Difference Between Writing and Speaking" to the speeches of current Members of Parliament. While the greatest hits are made against the ministerial side, Hazlitt's survey of the political scene is contemptuous of the Whigs as well. His concern with the predominance of technique over matter, an exaggerated version of Scott's own alienation from all parties in politics, is entirely within the range of his editor's program for the *London*. The links between "On the Present State of Parliamentary Eloquence" and "On the Conversation of Authors" are even more prominent. If the essay is an application of the ideas in the writing and speaking essay, it is also an example of the conversational framework predicated by Hazlitt: in estimating the effectiveness of the various speakers in Parliament, Hazlitt comments implicitly on John Scott's characteristic position of alienation from all parties. His criticism of Scott grows out of an analysis of the style of Mackintosh and Brougham, a "didactic style of parliamentary oratory" that Hazlitt traces to "northern colleges and lecture rooms" (*London Magazine* 2 [1820], 373). (The reference here may be personal as well: Scott was from Aberdeen, and although he did not take a degree at Aberdeen's Marischal College he spent three years there.) Hazlitt's critique of Mackintosh and Brougham focuses on their failure to consider the rhetorical situation when they speak. By carefully sifting evidence, stating the question, considering fundamental principles, tracing down difficulties, setting oneself up as a judge rather than an advocate, these men ensure the defeat of their programs. Hazlitt insists on greater attention to the oratorical situation: "Others will find out the rotten parts of a question: do you stick to the sound – knowledge is said to be power: but knowledge, applied as we have seen it, neutralises itself." Against the "the resistance, the refrangibility of dense prejudice and crooked policy" (p. 374) of the audience, a speaker must appeal to the "soil of common feeling and experience" that constitutes the "springs of the human mind" (p. 375). Hazlitt measures the speaker according to his effect, and he has little patience with those who make a party to themselves: "In political controversy, as in a battle, there are but two sides to chuse between; and those who create a diversion in favour of established abuses by setting up a third, fanciful, impracticable standard of perfection of their own, in the most critical circumstances, betray the cause they pretend to espouse with such overweening delicacy" (p. 374). Hazlitt has again modified his earlier distinction between writing and speech: the literal distinction between the two in "Table-Talk. No. II" has now become a rhetorical figure for effectual and ineffectual persuasion. As Mackintosh, Brougham, and Scott become more writerly – that is, thorough – they lose the force made possible by appeals to their audience's "substratum of prejudice," and their discourse loses the "cement of interest" (p. 375).

Current events give piquancy to these remarks on political controversy. Scott had been commenting, somewhat reluctantly, on the Queen's trial for several months. What support he lent her – and the opposition – tended to be of the ineffectual variety criticized by Hazlitt. In the November "Historical and Critical Summary of Intelligence" Scott glumly surveys the humiliating spectacle of the trial by registering displeasure with all sides: the Queen is probably guilty, the ministerial party is unable to prove it, the proceedings were biased, and the newspapers have cynically taken up the Queen's cause. He insists on a standard of disinterested inquiry in this very political trial; while the actions of the ministerial party disgust him, Scott refuses to work his cause in Hazlitt's way. He concludes that the proceedings were so malignant and biased that this alone provides grounds for ruling in the Queen's favor. This consciously equivocal gesture is precisely what Hazlitt objects to.

Part of the interest of the "conversation" between Hazlitt and Scott lies in its capacity for increasing complexity – in the successive modifications of earlier formulations. The December Table-Talk offers not only a departure in tone and subject matter from the earlier four contributions but an implicit critique of one of the "leading views" that inform them. "On the Pleasure of Painting" is in part another careful consideration of writing – this time against painting rather than oratory or conversation. Hazlitt finds painting delightful because one need only look and follow nature in pursuing it. No angry passion intervenes, no audience need be considered, no adversary must be met. In this almost prelapsarian world the contraries of life are overcome: "The hours pass away untold, without chagrin, and without ennui; nor would you ever wish to pass them otherwise. Innocence is joined with industry, pleasure with business; and the mind is satisfied, though it is not engaged in thinking, or doing, any mischief" (*London Magazine* 2 [1820], 597). Writing essays is another matter. Hazlitt feels hurried, the work is unpleasant, and he hates to reread what he has written. The very means of expression is deficient: "words are necessary to explain the impression of certain things upon me to the reader, but they rather weaken, and draw a veil over, than strengthen it to myself" (p. 598). He speaks of his feelings being "melted down" into words which are subsequently forgotten. Painting is different: one does not discharge what one knows, one discovers new material. In painting, one is permitted to glimpse nature face to face.[10]

Hazlitt's analysis of writing in terms of painting leads him to conclusions that are consonant with two of Scott's more insistent aesthetic principles: fidelity to nature and the desire for displacement. Hazlitt attributes to painting what Scott attributes to good writing. His description of painting echoes Scott's assessment of Walter Scott: "He speaks just what is set down for him in the book of nature, and we know that its pages are always open before his eyes, and we feel assured that what we read in his, has been faithfully transcribed from them" (*London Magazine* 1 [1820], 12). But more welcome to Scott's political program would be the conscious displacement with which Hazlitt opens his essay on the pleasures of painting: "you have no absurd opinions to combat, no point to strain, no adversary to crush, no fool to annoy – you are actuated by fear or favour to no man. There is 'no juggling here,' no sophistry, no intrigue, no tampering with the evidence, no attempt to make black white, or white black" (*London Magazine* 2 [1820], 597). Read in the context of the 1821 *Table-Talk* or in a modern edition, this language loses much or all of its specificity. In the *London*, it is recognizable as a reference to the procedures of the ministerial party in the Queen's trial. Scott, in the previous number's "Historical and Critical Summary of Intelligence," had waxed indignant about ministerial manipulations of evidence and preparation of witnesses, and he had castigated supporters of the ministry and opponents of Radicals for calling it "our duty to call black white, and white black" (*London Magazine* 2 [1820], 570).[11] By recalling this language, "On the Pleasure of Painting" celebrates a Scott-like escape from the degradations of the public sphere.

As we have seen with the Elia essays, Scott knew well how such displacements might be deployed in the *London*. What is intriguing in the case of Hazlitt is the degree to which this hitherto unyielding radical complied with this program. Hazlitt has done more than mute his politics in the first five Table-Talk essays: he has at various times taken leave of politics, as when he asserts that he would rather be expert at fives than writing when the score is kept with "Whig and Tory notches"; he has analyzed parliamentary oratory in terms of form and style rather than with respect to cause; and in "On the Pleasure of Painting" he has presented a hierarchy of artistic endeavor which considers writing, which he describes in political terms, as an imperfect medium. Scott has little need to frame these essays in the way he did Elia's; Hazlitt's Table-Talk essays internalize the displacement the editor sought.

The last Table-Talk essay before Scott's death demonstrates Hazlitt's compliance with Scott's program of displacement. "On Reading Old Books" exhibits a Hazlitt tuned to an Elian key of wistful reverie.[12] "I hate to read new books," Hazlitt announces peremptorily: "I have more confidence in the dead than in the living. Contemporary writers may generally be divided into two classes – one's friends or one foes" (*London Magazine* 3 [1821], 128). This turn from the divisive politics of the contemporary scene frames a lush description of the pleasures of reading old books: they are "links in the chain of our conscious being. They bind together the different scattered divisions of our personal identity" (p. 129). Hazlitt revels in the affections conjured by the books of his youth, the alluring heroines who make up "the only true ideal – the heavenly tints of Fancy reflected in the bubbles that float upon the springtide of human life" (p.129). A very Wordsworthian lament over the waning of these pleasures follows. But perhaps key in his recollections are *Paradise Lost* and Burke's *Reflections*, a "double prize" bought together in 1798 and read with the fierceness that only youth can afford. In language that rivals the ecstatic account of his meeting with Coleridge in "My First Acquaintance with Poets," Hazlitt charts the effect of Burke on his own literary aspirations. Burke, who at first sight made all other prose writers seem "pedantic and impertinent," is yet the greatest of stylists for Hazlitt:

I did not care for his doctrines. I was then, and am still, proof against their contagion; but I admired the author and was considered as not a very staunch partisan of the opposite side, though I thought myself that an abstract proposition was one thing – a masterly transition, a brilliant metaphor, another. I conceived too that he might be wrong in his main argument, and yet deliver fifty truths in arriving at a false conclusion. (p. 133)

Here is the issue put baldly: the competing claims of, on the one hand, abstraction and, on the other, the rhetoric of the affections marshaled by "masterly transitions" and "brilliant metaphor." However much Hazlitt and Scott might disagree on the validity of Burke's "main argument," the "fifty truths" struck off along the way form the basis of a conversation that clarifies the persistence of Burke's ideas in Romantic thought. Ultimately Hazlitt's contributions are a monument to Scott's vision of literature generally as well as his reading of Romanticism, a line of transmission that became standard in the ensuing generation.

After John Scott's death in February 1821, the *London* became much less focused. Hazlitt's comments in an 1823 article for the *Edinburgh Review* entitled "The Periodical Press" provide an exaggerated but suggestive account of John Taylor's subsequent tenure as editor:

> The fault of the London Magazine is, that it wants a sufficient unity of direction and purpose. There is no particular bias or governing spirit, – which neutralizes the interest. The articles seem thrown into the letter-box, and to come up like blanks or prizes in the lottery – all is in a confused, unconcocted state, like the materials of a rich plum-pudding before it has been well boiled. (*Edinburgh Review* 16, 232)

Unlike Scott's *London*, which provides a kind of bibliographic code with which to read the essays in it, Taylor's "rich plum-pudding" proves more difficult to assess. Gone were such explicit statements of political purpose as Scott's "Signs of the Times" essay. Under Taylor, the "Monthly Register," in which Scott analyzed ministerial, parliamentary, and social activities, becomes almost entirely an entertainment section. The mysterious problem of moving bogs in Ireland receives more attention than the civil disturbances in Spain; stories of unhappy or unusual passion far outnumber calls for modest social or political reforms. For fourteen months John Scott had examined the relations among the political, the literary, and everyday experience, but such attempts at a totalizing cultural analysis – however reactionary, however mystified in themselves – are conspicuously lacking in the magazine under John Taylor and his assistant Thomas Hood.

Without a distinct editorial voice to provide a rationale for the magazine as an institution, the *London* appears more a combination of tendencies – some held over from Scott's editorial practices, some revived from eighteenth-century periodical traditions – than the focused intervention it had been. Scott made direct appeal to the utility, and even necessity, of the displacement from historical circumstances his magazine offered. He praised this tendency in reviews of other works, and he clearly valued it as a specific remedy to a specific historical situation. Taylor, by removing the conscious consideration of displacement, changes the dynamic. The political, under Taylor, becomes unconscious, or at least less conscious. Politics, instead of being particularly distasteful and vexing at this time, is simply distasteful and vexing. Escape is valued in itself, as a universal anodyne for the constrictions of bourgeois life. The *London* becomes more inward, more liable to focus on the personal experience of the middle classes, on connoisseurship, on improvement in social graces. The picture offered by the *London* is much the same, but it lacks the frame provided by Scott's distinct editorial voice.

By almost any standard, however, the *London* prospered under Taylor – at least until 1824.[13] It offered continuing series by Lamb, Hazlitt, Cunningham, and Wainewright; was bolstered by more frequent (and less derivative) contributions from Reynolds; and added De Quincey and H. F. Cary. Yet Hazlitt left at the end of 1821, and in an often-cited 1823 letter Lamb lamented the waning of the magazine.[14] Hence the *London* becomes interesting in an entirely different way, and it presents a different set of critical problems. It is possible to read Scott's *London* in terms of the timeworn model of text and context or, by considering Scott a kind of expert reader whose editorial activities codify his response, as a valuable and unusually clear record of the originary moment of reception. Taylor, less driven by ideology than by a combination of generally liberal tendencies and a sensitivity to market forces, presides over a far less static institution which serves less to stabilize the meaning of its essays than to unsettle them.

We can see indications of the change in the *London*'s tone in the number immediately after Scott's death. The March 1821 number – after a formal announcement of the death of Scott – begins with Horace Smith's "The Statue of Theseus, and the Sculpture Room of Phidias," an essay on the Elgin Marbles. It is a choice that points up several new tendencies in the *London*. Smith's article recounts a "reverie, or waking dream" in which the author is transported from the British Museum, where he has been admiring the Theseus of the Elgin Marbles, to Periclean Athens, where the same statues are being "exhibited to some of the most distinguished citizens, previously to the indiscriminate admission of the people" (*London Magazine* 3, 245).

Smith's reactions to the statues are not the analytical, wide-ranging forays into aesthetics that mark earlier essays in the *London*: he reports "indescribable awe," "silent reverence," "the thrilling delight with which minds of any susceptibility usually contemplate the beauty of exquisite proportion – of the vague apprehension inspired by gigantic bulk – and of that lingering homage still attaching itself to whatever has been once associated with the noblest and most solemn affections of the human heart, and contemplated as the figure of a divinity by the most civilized nations of the world" (p. 245). This drop in analytic and critical rigor is not incidental; Smith defines a very different reader than does Lamb or Hazlitt. Where the more famous essayists assume a familiarity with Greek and Latin culture, Smith unobtrusively yet carefully identifies each Greek character. The article does not elicit a response by naming certain classical figures; it provides the proper response. Smith is not so much calling upon a shared cultural background as he is catering to the desire for such a culture; the essay is a commodity to be consumed by an audience that desires the range of reference common to the public sphere evoked in eighteenth-century periodicals and coffee houses.[15]

Smith's flattery of the reader does not end here. The essay's prefabricated responses are accompanied by gestures that stress a continuity between Periclean Athens and the London of 1821. "I imagined myself to be sometimes at Athens, under the administration of the celebrated Pericles, and again at London, under the enlightened guidance of Lord Castlereagh" (p. 245), Smith begins. The comparison ultimately leads to a familiar thesis – that the great classical tradition has given way to a pathetic trickle of smaller, less vigorous works. Yet a nationalistic tenor creeps into the essay. When Zeuxis rebukes the painter Agatharchus, who has been boasting of his speed in painting, by saying he wishes to be remembered for the slowness of his production, Smith alludes to, without naming him, "the first of our modern artists," Benjamin Robert Haydon, "who, though he may be as deliberate as his Athenian predecessor, bids fair, at least, to rival him in celebrity" (p. 249). The essay ends with an ingenious comparison of audiences – of the readers of the *London*, spectators and connoisseurs by proxy, and the glorious list of Greek and Roman admirers of the statuary of the Parthenon: "Once more I surveyed the marble upon which the living eyes of all the illustrious persons I have mentioned had been formerly fixed – as well as those of Cicero, Pliny, Pausanias, and Plutarch, who have recorded their visits to the Parthenon" (p. 250). The figure here provides much more than flattery; Smith redefines the activity of appreciation. By a kind of parallax effect, the eyes of the reader and those of the famous dead are aligned, suggesting an equivalence based not on the quality or content of response but on the mere fact of a shared gaze. What one feels or thinks is of less importance than the fact that one looks on the same objects as did past worthies. The essay provides no real hint of what aesthetic appreciation or criticism might be; indeed, to reap the benefits of an entry into the exclusive sphere of the connoisseur, one need only assume the role of spectator. The transaction is one less based on some particular response to a work than a participation in the dynamics of cultural consumption. In fact, the essay itself demonstrates the irrelevance of the particular art work to this spectacular process. Nowhere does

Smith describe the Theseus in any detail. If the gaze is all that is necessary, then the gaze of the reader at the reproduction of the Theseus provided by the magazine is really all that is necessary for a complete experience. The essay is not only a commodity, but a time-saving commodity.

A quick recall of earlier essays on the fine arts in the *London* under Scott reveals quite a different critical tenor. Charles Eastlake's January 1820 article, "The Advantages and Disadvantages of Rome, As a School of Art" (*London Magazine* 1, 42 ff.), not only assumes a knowledge of Reynolds's *Discourses*, but also a considerable familiarity with many of the paintings of the Italian High Renaissance. Eastlake devotes much of the article to a close consideration of the facilities for study at Rome – studios, models, access to antiquities, and programs set up for study by various foreign governments. Equally technical is John Scott's May 1820 essay, "Mr. Haydon's Picture of Christ's Triumphal Entry into Jerusalem" (pp. 581 ff.), which examines closely the processes of production and exhibition adopted by Haydon for his historical paintings. Scott's remarks on the formal qualities of the picture presume a knowledge of technique and composition on the reader's part. Even the more perfunctory essays on the fine arts offer this easy range of shared reference: Scott's September 1820 introduction to a translation of a German essay on Hogarth assumes a more than passing familiarity of the part of the reader with Lamb's Hogarth essay (*London Magazine* 2, 277 ff.). Such articles aim at an audience of well-informed amateurs or professionals; Smith's essay serves the needs of an audience more interested in consumption than in reception.[16]

Other tendencies – also departures from Scott's institutional procedures – appear with the slackening of editorial control. One essay seems to look forward to the later periodical works of Arnold, Bagehot, Mill, and Carlyle. "On the Present State of Religious Parties in Germany" (possibly written by George Croly) combines a ready knowledge of German higher criticism (reference is made to Eichhorn and Paulus) with a shrewd capacity for hitting at the insularity and anti-intellectualism of the English clergy. Ostensibly a summary of an article in the German review *Hermes*, the article begins, however, with a few remarks on William Jacob's book on German society, a typical "view" of a foreign country. The writer ridicules Jacob's reactionary, sycophantic, and dogmatic principles, maintaining that his moralistic strictures on the speculative and philosophic turn of the German clergy betray a mind bent more on getting on within the English clerical establishment than one seeking religious truth. The essay makes a strong case for reasoned discussion and inquiry among the clergy as well as the flock, defending even that breeding ground of radicalism, the dissenting Scotch peasantry, as unruly not because of their disputatious training but because of their political situation.[17] All in all, the essay is Whiggish – celebrating reason almost to the point of fetishizing it, briskly attacking reactionary and dogmatic institutions, and applauding progressive educational ideas. Formally, it anticipates the "essay-like review" that Walter Houghton finds characteristic of later periodicals; rhetorically it approximates the conditions that Houghton sets out for the emergence of such a style of writing – a bifurcated audience made up of the more articulate classes as well as the common reader.[18]

Nevertheless, against the new tendencies of the articles by Smith and Croly, the March 1821 number offers articles that recall the tenor of the magazine under Scott. Lamb's essay, "A Chapter on Ears," bristles with recondite references. Even in this, perhaps the most slight of his essays, Lamb assumes a community of reference. One of the number's essays on the fine arts, the "Ambrosian Codex of Homer, with Ancient Paintings" (*London Magazine* 3, 273ff.) offers an extremely technical appraisal of a recent foreign publication of the illustrations to Homer in a codex held by the Biblioteca Ambrosiana. Reference is made to current German scholarship in the classics, and to forthcoming German collections of similar illustrations. Another essay, on Rossini's "Maometto Secondo," requires considerable knowledge of musical technique and operatic tradition. On the whole, the March number is uneven – unsure of its audience and perhaps its purpose.

Scott's death must have precipitated this transitional period, in which the *London* loses the tight focus provided by its first editor's Burkean–Coleridgean literary culture. What is less clear is Hazlitt's part in all this. If, as many scholars have maintained, Hazlitt were editor in the interim period between Scott's editorship and that of Taylor (aided by subeditors Hood and Reynolds), it seems odd that he would have placed such work as Smith's in so prominent a position.[19] Perhaps his capacity here was more limited, more piecework than a position of any real editorial control. The death of Scott, who was a substantial contributor in addition to the editor, may have left a gap in submissions that was difficult to fill in the short run. But given Hazlitt's facility as a writer and the fact that the *London* leads with these two articles, this seems doubtful. The magazine seems to be sliding toward a change in tone and emphasis that makes Hazlitt's departure inevitable.

Hazlitt's Table-Talk essay for March, "On Personal Character," seems intended for Scott's *London*. Hazlitt's epigraph from Montaigne, "Men palliate and conceal their original qualities, but do not extirpate them," suggests a balance and polish that would fit well with the consciously evasive politics of the late editor. The entire argument, in fact, fits the reactionary tenor of Scott's system: if character is fixed at birth, if the natural bias determines how experience is processed, then certainly the millennial hopes of reformers become tenuous. If man as he is will always preclude the production of man as he could be, then reform is largely specious. If "the mind contrives to lay hold of those circumstances and motives, which suit its own bias and confirm its natural disposition" and if "[t]he will is not blindly impelled by outward accidents, but selects the impressions by which it chuses to be governed, with great dexterity and perseverance" (*London Magazine* 3, 295), then little change can be brought about by reform. Hazlitt offers a Burkean view of habit and prejudice: "Do we not say, habit is second nature? And shall we not allow the force of nature itself?" (p. 297).

When politics does flash out in the essay, it shines in a form particularly congenial to Scott's procedures: "The Jacobin of 1794 was the Anti-Jacobin of 1814 . . . they drifted with the stream, they sailed before the breeze in either case" (p. 298). Such sentiments echo Scott's own excluded sensibilities. The moral drawn by Hazlitt would be even more welcome to the former editor: "we should mind our own business, cultivate our good qualities, if we have any, and irritate ourselves less about the absurdities of other people, which neither we nor they can help" (p. 298). This withdrawal, in which the thoughtful observer registers the pain of inaction, squares with the sense of political futility of Scott's *London* perfectly.

The persistence of Scott's editorial influence can be felt in the following number – one in which Hazlitt's editorial role is unclear – as well. Although "Table-Talk. No. ix. On People of Sense" begins as an attack on mystification by various professions, it moves toward an attack on the utilitarians. The essay, as Hazlitt's essays often do, enacts its own conclusions. Hazlitt's attack on the utilitarians' proclivity for a mathematical neatness in their reasoning and for dismissing the mixture of feeling, custom, and rhetoric involved in any practical question, is prefaced by a historical sketch of the excesses of people of "sense" that is itself marked by murky reversals and ambiguous turns. According to Hazlitt, the destruction of unwieldy and obfuscatory systems such as Aristotelean philosophy and Popery was once a heroic undertaking, yet the result has been a modern French philosophy equally abstruse. Only poets and painters have managed to avoid these excesses and deviations from common sense. Notably, their efficacy is denied by the utilitarians. Ultimately, poets and painters emerge in Hazlitt's essay as commonsensical, reasonable, and skeptical. Accustomed to flights of fancy and imagination by nature, they are proof against the wild absurdities of those who are new to such territory. Poets are now less prophets and harbingers, as they were formerly, than skeptics and conservatives.

Hazlitt carries out his attack on Bentham in "On People of Sense" under the aegis of Burke. For Hazlitt the hostility of the utilitarians to Burke's practice of reasoning through figures and rhetoric indicates their distance from common sense and feeling. By couching his attack on the Benthamites in a Burkean rhetoric, Hazlitt pays yet another tribute to the power of Burke's style. Further, his allegiance to Burke's style, especially within the skeptical, experience-rich genre of the familiar essay, almost inevitably leads him to arguments that could be effortlessly absorbed by Scott's institutional frame – even by Scott's conservative politics. Scott is dead, but Hazlitt's contributions carry on the conversation begun in the previous year.

Other contributions by Hazlitt in this editorial interregnum are more than simply liable to co-optation: they could be mistaken for collaborations between Hazlitt and John Scott. In the May 1821 number Hazlitt takes up the former editor's "Living Authors" series with an examination of George Crabbe. He begins with a brisk attack: "The object of Mr. Crabbe's writings seems to be, to show what an unpoetical world we live in" (*London Magazine* 3, 484). Hazlitt asserts that Crabbe misapprehends the generic requirements of poetry: he substitutes literal, painstaking, relentless fidelity for invention. He attends to nature, but only to the meanest, most unsettling parts of it. Hazlitt speculates on the causes of the vogue for Crabbe's work. Part of its success lay in timing: it emerged when weaknesses in other arts were beginning to be redressed. Painting was just emerging from a ruinous commitment to academic theory, which "had enfeebled and perverted our eye for nature," and the precision and intricacy of Crabbe's descriptions struck this sickly eye with the force of truth. Poets, even nature poets, up to that time had largely taken the response of the individual to nature as their subject, not nature itself. Crabbe goes to the thing itself – however wretched: "Pope describes what is striking, Crabbe would have described merely what was there" (p. 485). Unimpressed by arguments for Crabbe's healthy demystification of country life, Hazlitt wonders whether the pastoral mythology of other poets, always a construction, needed debunking. If one wishes to insist on "unwelcome reality," Hazlitt asks, why not simply turn to prose and statistics? If there were a moral here, one might understand Crabbe's obsession, but there is none. Perhaps most telling in Hazlitt's strictures is his attack on Crabbe's attitude toward the people whose lives he portrays: "He does not indulge his fancy or sympathise with us, or tell us how the poor feel; but how he should feel in their situation, which we do not want to know" (p. 486).

Hazlitt's objections partly stem from his own pragmatic attitude toward social activism. Crabbe's pictures of rural suffering and poverty are true, but they will not serve to move those in a position to help. Hazlitt would take the audience, as well as the subject, into account:

By associating pleasing ideas with the poor, we incline the rich to extend their good offices to them. The cottage twined round with real myrtles, or with the poet's wreath, will invite the hand of kindly assistance sooner than Mr. Crabbe's naked "ruin'd shed": for though unusual, unexpected distress excites compassion, that which is uniform and remediless produces nothing but disgust and indifference. (p. 486)

This sensitivity to the rhetorical situation of poetry, while not surprising in a writer so thoroughly versed in the journalistic and periodical trades, leads to an unexpected convergence with Scott's conscious program of displacement in literature. Hazlitt approvingly singles out two lines in a long quotation as "worth nearly all the rest of his verses put together." The couplet describes the feelings of children, following the bier of a superannuated man who died in the workhouse. They recall that he had made them toys and had participated in their games: "Him now they follow to his grave, and stand / Silent and sad, and gazing, hand in hand." In appreciating this moment, Hazlitt turns to a discussion of the aims of poetry:

It is images, such as these, that the polished mirror of the poet's mind ought chiefly to convey; that cast their soothing, startling reflection over the length of human life, and grace with their amiable innocence its closing scenes; while its less alluring and more sombre tints sink in, and are lost in an absorbent ground of unrelieved prose. Poetry should be the handmaid of the imagination, and the foster-nurse of pleasure and beauty: Mr. Crabbe's Muse is a determined enemy to the imagination, and a spy on nature. (pp. 488–9)

Such a poetics – succinctly evoked by the term "polished mirror," which recalls yet modifies other figures for the mimetic function of art – coincides perfectly with Scott's ideas about art and literature: that these activities are admittedly mildly escapist, willed displacements. Some truths are to be displaced, some transformed, and some revealed as they are – but each according to the rhetorical situation.

May's Table-Talk installment is similarly consistent with the Burkean bias of the magazine under Scott. "On Antiquity" begins with a consideration of the "strange, mysterious, visionary, awful" feelings attendant on our perception of the past. While registering the power of such feelings and associations, Hazlitt seeks their cause as well. He examines the process by which the past has "become ancient." Antiquity is a trick of perception, a term that suggests more about our relation to the past than the past itself. But the hold of such habitual perceptions is powerful: "It is only by an effort of reason, to which fancy is averse, that I bring myself to believe that the sun shone as bright, that the sky was as blue, and that the earth was as green, two thousand years ago as it is at present." Recognizing the trick fails to change one's perception: "How ridiculous this seems; yet so it is!" (*London Magazine* 3 [1821], 527). The stance here is complicated: Hazlitt reveals the mechanism by which antiquity is produced, yet he is still subject to it. In such an analysis two styles of thought – one more proper to an Enlightenment program of reason, the other suggestive of a Burkean (and to my mind, Romantic) procedure – persist in an uneasy solution. As in Hazlitt's later essay on Godwin in *The Spirit of the Age*, custom and tradition make up a kind of circumference to reason, a hedge on its activity. The past, no matter what analysis we apply to it, has a claim on us that reason cannot break. Hence Hazlitt's subsequent point, that after a certain time we simply repeat our old ideas "at stated intervals, like the tunes of a barrel-organ."[20]

In a sense the essay is a tribute to Burke. Hazlitt re-enacts, in perhaps his clearest statement among his *London* contributions, what was for him the ultimate failure of the Enlightenment: a persistent and intriguing shadow accompanies the "light" of reason. Hazlitt's position, while different from that of his former editor, remains well within the bounds of the "conversation" they pursued in the pages of the *London*. While Hazlitt, unlike Scott, clings to the ideals of the French Revolution – "hatred of tyranny" and contempt for "the fashionable doctrine of Divine Right" – he admits that Burke's *Reflections* still sparkle as well.[21]

In his only contribution to the June number of the *London*, Hazlitt applies these political sentiments to aesthetic considerations. "Pope, Lord Byron, and Mr. Bowles" reviews Byron's famous open letter to his publisher, John Murray, which answers Bowles's argument that Pope was not a poet. Always keen to unravel the rhetorical force of writing, Hazlitt opens by rather dismissively defining the circumstances surrounding the publication of the letter. He anatomizes the advantages to Murray and to Byron: "This is a very proper letter for a lord to write to his bookseller, and for Mr. Murray to show about among his friends, as it contains some dry rubs at Mr. Bowles, and some good hits at Mr. Southey and his 'invariable principles'" (*London Magazine* 3 [1821], 593). Hazlitt notes that the letter does not settle the critical issues it broaches: in it Byron strikes an attitude more akin to a lord ordering his servants about than a critic reasoning with his audience. Hazlitt further unwinds the rhetorical construct Byron employs against his audience: Byron whines (in a preface to one of his tragedies) about the poor reception given nobles like Walpole, when to Hazlitt's mind everything Byron writes or does is read in the favorable light of his peerage. After analyzing the role of class and privilege in the entire argument, he rates Byron's remarks as no better than desultory conversation on this topic: "It might be had anywhere. Then why this letter all the way from Ravenna full of our own commonplaces?" (p. 593).

Hazlitt quickly resets the rhetorical coordinates for his own audience. He includes a sly reference to Jem Belcher (one of the combatants in "The Fight"), who, when asked if he did not feel "awkward" at facing a tall opponent, replied "An please ye, sir, when I am stript to my shirt, I am afraid of no man" (p. 594). This nicely sounds the basis of the argument that follows: that literature should be a more egalitarian province, one not subject to the hierarchies and received distinctions of class. The exchange between Byron and Bowles concerns the definition of such terms as natural, artificial, and art. Hazlitt defines poetry this way: "real poetry, or poetry of the highest order, can only be produced by unraveling the real web of associations, which have been wound round any subject by nature, and the unavoidable conditions of humanity" (p. 602). Byron differs, finding the poetical not in the natural but in the artificial: in ruins, in ships that recall heroic naval battles. To return to the original example in the dispute, whether the sun shining on a ship at sea is poetic in itself or because it recalls associations attendant on the man-made ship, Hazlitt would say that the associations with the sun – the deep, quasi-universal appreciation we might have for it that has, over time, become a kind of natural association – are more poetic because they are available to a wider audience without the special pleading of the particular colors of the boat or particular recent naval battles. The question becomes not one of whether associations are central to poetry, but which class of association: those that have been forgotten, that lie deep beneath the visible social order, or those that still call to mind their construction. The question is, whether we have forgotten the forging of the association so as to make it natural, or if the impress of the event is still so fresh as to make us think of the production of meaning:

> where the hand has done every thing, nothing is left for the imagination to do or to attempt: where all is regulated by conventional indifference, the full workings, the involuntary, uncontrollable emotions of the heart cease: property is not poetical, but a practical prosaic idea, to those who possess and clutch it; and cuts off others from cordial sympathy; but nature is common property, the unenvied idol of all eyes, the fairy ground where fancy plays her tricks and feats. (pp. 600–1)

Noteworthy in this poetics is the use of property as an analogy.[22] Hazlitt was well aware of the "leveling" involved in his aesthetics: "A man can make any thing, but he cannot make a sentiment! It is a thing of inveterate prejudice, of old association, of common feelings, and so is poetry, as far as it is serious." (p. 602). Hence the material of the highest poetry is not property that is owned by some, but communal. One theory of poetry is inclusive, leveling; the other is, perhaps inevitably, exclusive.

This article, as "On Antiquity" before it, marks one of the high points of Hazlitt's contributions to the magazine. There are better essays in the Table-Talk series, but none so cogently analyzes the aesthetic questions involved in the choice of subject matter for poetry. Hazlitt's treatment of the exchange between Bowles and Byron, saturated with the conflicting epistemological concerns of "On Antiquity," is remarkable for the rigor with which Hazlitt employs an astringent Enlightenment mode of reason as well as a Burkean feel for sentiment. There is no synthesis here, but this is perhaps all the more reason for admiration. Hazlitt, without anxiety, without easy recourse to irony as a defensive principle, was fully prepared to assess the limits of his conceptual tools and to accept the inevitable ambiguities they produced.

As Hazlitt upbraids Byron for arguing against his own practice in his best poetry, he draws a kind of circle of kindred spirits: "His Lordship likes the poetry, the imaginative part of art, and so do we; and so we believe did the late Mr. John Scott" (pp. 599–600). Only when read through the constricted gaze afforded by the *Collected Works* does the appearance of John Scott in the essay seems somewhat unexpected. In the context of the magazine, the reference becomes a highly pointed and appropriate one that memorializes the editor and recalls the highly successful "conversation" that characterized their collaboration.

Hazlitt's June 1821 memorial to Scott marks the moment at which his own relation to the magazine shifts. By contributing five consecutive Table-Talks from January to May, he had shouldered much of Scott's burden in the editorial interregnum (no less than four articles in May), but only one article appeared in June, and none whatsoever in July. His subsequent contributions are greatly reduced: three more Table-Talk essays in August, November, and December. In January of 1822 he moves the series to Henry Colburn's *New Monthly*, and, with the exception of a January review of W. Scott's *Pirate*, and occasional essays on the fine arts, effectively leaves the *London*.[23]

The circumstances of this removal are various. Surely the *New Monthly* was a more convenient place for his Table-Talk series. After the failure of John Warren, Hazlitt's publisher for the first volume of *Table-Talk*, Colburn had undertaken to publish the second volume. This arrangement presumably allowed Hazlitt to display his wares: three essays from the second volume of *Table-Talk* appear in the first three numbers of the 1822 *New Monthly*.[24] Colburn had a reputation as a sharp trader and a vulgarian, but his business practices were highly successful.[25] Moreover, Colburn paid his contributors well. Such considerations must have been attractive to Hazlitt, coming off the failure of Warren's firm. Hazlitt began his stint with the *New Monthly* with panache: his first Table-Talk essay was the estimable "On Going a Journey," and he contributed "The Fight" in February. But behind this easy fit between writer, magazine, and publisher lies a difference of opinion between Hazlitt and the new owner/editors of the *London*. Hazlitt's July hiatus is sign of the transactions behind the pages of the magazine.

The occasion for the breach between Hazlitt and Taylor & Hessey was his submission for the July number of the *London*, "Guy Faux." Hessey's reaction to the essay can be seen in a letter of 5 October 1821 from Hessey to Taylor that describes a visit to Hazlitt:

On my asking him if we were to expect a No. of the Living Authors he observed that he felt no Interest in them or their works and that he considered such Papers as mere fat work which cost him no effort and brought him no fame. He then spoke of the Table Talks as being the papers on which he valued himself and which he wished to continue but said that he felt so annoyed and cramped in his mind by the fear of alteration or objection or perhaps rejection altogether that he could not write freely as he was accustomed to do. – He spoke of Guy Faux and its rejection, and very much pressed its admission saying at length that he must candidly confess that if Guy Faux were not inserted he should never write a line with pleasure for the Magazine. I told him we had decided objections to certain parts, but for those parts (as is always the case) he feels the greatest Affection and he proposed again the qualifying of them by a Note. He said he wished much to see the Magazine write down all its rivals by superiority of talent, and expressed a desire to assist in the good work by all the means in his Power. All he wished was to have his Liberty in the Table Talks and in everything else he was ready to do whatever we wished. But Guy Faux seemed to be the sine qua non. I told him I did not think we could with any regard to our own safety insert the Article, but I brought it away with me to look it over again and see what alterations might make it passable, for I did not wish to cut with him and in fact I scarcely knew what were the passages actually objected to. – It does however appear to me that we could not insert it as it is, and therefore I must either tell him so and say that when you return you and he can decide as to any alterations if you think that when altered it may be admitted – or else I will say we cannot receive it at all, and leave him and Mr. Baldwin to settle the matter themselves.[26]

Notice that Hazlitt will settle for a qualifying note, one of Scott's customary practices in disagreements with him. The essay was rejected, as Hessey feared it must be, and Hazlitt turned to the *Examiner*.[27]

It is not difficult to see why Hazlitt felt so strongly about the essay. What he finds in Guy Faux is an admirable fervor and devotion, as well as an "absolute disinterestedness" (*Complete Works*, vol. xx, p. 98). He did not act out of any consideration of self, but out of conviction and faith:

We have no Guy Fauxes now: – not that we have not numbers in whom "the spirit is willing, but the flesh is weak." We talk indeed of flinging the keys of the House of Commons into the Thames, by way of a little unmeaning splutter, and a little courting of popularity and persecution; but to fling ourselves into the gap, and blow up the system and our own bodies to atoms at once, upon an abstract principle of right, does not suit the radical scepticism of the age! (p. 99)

One might venture that Guy Faux, even though he labors under what Hazlitt terms a "strange infatuation" (p. 98) or a "mischievous fanaticism" (p. 99), is the kind of partisan that the last *London* Table-Talk in December 1821 applauds. Hazlitt heaps praise on Guy Faux for his devotion to abstract principle:

To have an object always in view dearer to one than one's self, to cling to a principle in contempt of danger, of interest, of the opinion of the world, – this is the true ideal, the high and heroic state of man. It is in fact to have a standard of absolute and implicit faith in the mind, that admits neither of compromise, degree, nor exception. (p. 99)

Behind this kind of assertion, as often in Hazlitt's political writing, lurks the counter-example of Burke, who had famously sketched the attachments of each man as radically local in *Reflections*. Here Hazlitt

has tipped the scales back to abstract reason. Hazlitt describes contemporary practice as contrasting starkly with Guy Faux's disinterested championship of abstract principle: "a safe, underhand
persecutor, an anonymous slanderer, a cringing sycophant, promoting
his own interest by taking the bread out of honest mouths, a mercen-
ary malignant coward, a Clerical Magistrate, a Quarterly Reviewer, a
Member of the Constitutional Association, the concealed Editor of
Blackwood's Magazine!" (p. 101). This is a wonderfully controlled bit of
invective on Hazlitt's part, moving from the general to the specific and
from the timeless to the topical. The essay then considers modern
advocacy. Guy Faux's fanatical devotion to cause is no longer possible;
the present allows no such focus, no such narrowness: "A devoted and
incorrigible attachment to individuals, as well as to doctrines, is weak-
ened by the progress of knowledge and civilization. A spirit of
Scepticism, of inquiry, of comparison, is introduced there too, by the
course of reading, observation, and reflection, which strikes at the root
of our disproportionate idolatry" (p. 103). Hazlitt then cites three
examples from the *Cid* (translated in 1808 by Southey)[28] that show the
focus on the ideal and the abstract necessary for true heroism. Since
modern times run against the exercise of such physical heroism,
Hazlitt aspires only to "mental courage" (p. 112): "In little else I have
the spirit of martyrdom: but I would give up any thing sooner than an
abstract principle" (p. 112).

As in other essays by Hazlitt, the argument runs on two levels. Hazlitt
laments the trimming and tergiversation that characterized the political
thought of many of his contemporaries. Again he figures himself as carrying the good fight alone to his reactionary and monarchal enemies.
But the essay also examines the springs of conviction, the ease and fervor
with which personal interests are pursued, and the difficulties of holding
an abstract principle. Hazlitt's paradox here, as in his May Table-Talk
essay for the *London*, "On Antiquity," is the seeming impossibility of
melding the abstract and the social with the personal and local. Hazlitt
provides a very precise description of the causes of this difficulty: "the
course of reading, observation, and reflection" made possible – and
inevitable – by the "progress of knowledge and civilization." While fully
aware of the constitutive powers of these inevitable commitments,
Hazlitt also ponders their inescapable limits. "To walk," as Coleridge
would have it, "in the light of one's own knowledge" is to leave behind
the vital heat that brings about change.

It is not difficult to see why this essay aroused Hessey's fear of prosecution, especially given the shadowy threat of the newly organized Constitutional Association.[29] Hazlitt's celebration of Guy Faux, who tried to destroy Parliament, and Margaret Lebrun, a would-be assassin of the Queen, could hardly have been welcome. But behind this particular breach lies a more general editorial decision. The political reservations of Taylor and Hood so apparent in Hessey's letter inform the shape taken by the *London* over the next few numbers. The new owners take full control in the July 1821 number, in which Hood officially takes over the "Lion's Head." That number's lead article, John Hamilton Reynolds's "Warwick Castle," is a reliable indication of things to come in the magazine. Close attention to "Warwick Castle" reveals that, despite a superficial congruence with Scott's program of conscious displacement, the new *London* has adopted a much more evasive political stance. If such essays as that of Reynolds are the new standard, the magazine affords little room for work like Hazlitt's.

In early 1821 Reynolds was a coveted periodical writer. In addition to his legal duties and his tireless boosting of his friend Keats in the periodical press, he had worked with John Scott on the weekly *Champion*; he had published in the *Edinburgh* (through Hazlitt's helpful intervention); he was a regular contributor to Constable's *Scot's Magazine*; and his book of poems, *The Garden of Florence*, had been well received by all but the most partisan critics. Scott had almost employed him as drama critic for the *London* in 1820, but the post eventually went to Hazlitt. In 1820, he had published a witty mock biography of a boxer, *The Fancy*, which garnered much praise.

Reynolds's politics were generally liberal, as his long association with the *Champion*, the *Yellow Dwarf*, and the *Edinburgh* suggests.[30] But unlike Hazlitt's "Love me, love my dog" views, Reynolds's were more pliable. At least he seemed so to his contemporaries: in 1819 the *Blackwood's* camp made a concerted effort to hire him. A letter from P. G. Patmore to William Blackwood of 7 April suggests that Reynolds thought more of his personal friendships, especially those with Hazlitt and Hunt, than of the political considerations in refusing Blackwood's lucrative offer.[31] In many ways, Reynolds's attachments were all personal; even in his *Champion* days, when his editor John Scott's politics were much more to the left than they were in the *London*, one would be hard pressed to find a statement that has the overt political tendencies of those of Hazlitt or John Hunt. Reynolds's relations with Leigh Hunt and Keats in 1820 show his ability to negotiate a comfortable passage though a contradictory situation: he allowed Hunt to reprint his defense of *Endymion* in the

Examiner while dissuading Keats from dedicating his "Hyperion" frag-
ment to Hunt out of concern for the young poet's public reputation.[32]
Reynolds is no tergiversant – a 20 October 1816 review of Wordsworth's
"Thanksgiving Ode" praises the imaginative and poetic aspects of the
poem while lamenting the Tory line it presents – but he does not let his
politics block his prospects as a periodical writer.[33]

"Warwick Castle" counters Hazlitt's "Guy Faux" in both form and
content. It counsels a static, legitimizing political posture through a consistent application of the picturesque as the dominant mode of presentation. The disengaged narrator of the essay seeks – and assumes his
readers seek – escape from contemporary events in picturesque encounters. Nothing like Hazlitt's fierce analysis of "antiquity" as a puzzling
mode of perception is in evidence here: Reynolds's antiquity is a little
Eden where "the world is shut out" and "Adam's banishment seems
reversed." Reynolds's descriptions of the grounds and servants inevitably evoke political expression. The beautiful park has particularly agreeable groupings of trees: "not of those slim, young things, – saplings, I
would call them, – which usurp the name of trees in these impoverished
times, – but of old solid family trees, trees of character, and long standing" (*London Magazine* 4 [1821], 6). The play between the recent saplings,
which undercut the picturesque effects, and the established and distinguished "family trees," turns in part upon the force of "usurp."
Reynolds's concern with the apparent degeneracy of the aristocracy in
modern times chimes in with Scott's earlier calls for a counter-revolutionary resurgence of the "natural political guardians" of the people.

The gardener, irritating at first encounter, becomes acceptable as he
is read through the dictates of the picturesque. Reynolds's description
quickly moves into the figural world of associations; the gardener might
be "a quaker of the forests – a romantic sectarian . . . let loose by the
Earl to ornament the grounds more by his presence, than by his labour"
(p. 7). More observation begets more poetic reverie: the gardener quickly
becomes "an ideal gardener only," who simply suggests the function of
gardener by occasionally pretending to prune and arrange, and who
does not carry tools. His plants have a "superior odour, foliage, and
shape" that Reynolds attributes to the occupants of the castle: "The
nobility of the family seemed to have passed into leaf and blossom, –
and the myrtles and geraniums grew as of stately birth. They were lux-
uriant, without a sign of decay" (p. 8). This political commentary continues as Reynolds describes the housekeeper. On the eve of the troubled
coronation of George IV, in the wake of the tenuous monarchial

restorations on the Continent, at a moment when some of the more arbitrarily (re-)established claims of legitimacy have begun to respond to various local rebellions in Naples and in Spain, Reynolds carefully inscribes the housekeeper within the aristocratic tradition:

The keen sensible expression of her countenance, the easy, yet respectful familiarity of her address, and the pointed and pretty neatness of her laced cap and silken garments, quite recommended her to my favour. She made no formal and marked curtsey; her whole manner was subdued, quiet, and extremely polite, being quite of the *old school*. Her body seemed to have settled into a perpetual curtsey; and time had crystallized her politeness. (p. 11)

Here we have another "ideal" character, whose body is bent by her office in the hierarchy to the perfect expression of her function. As the gardener is the ultimate semiotic expression of gardener, so is the housekeeper a social sign of deference, a "perpetual curtsey."

As the housekeeper takes the group into the galleries, Reynolds's persona imagines her as "a happy work of the old masters, and partook of the kindness of Time!" (p. 11). The metamorphosis of the housekeeper into a painting is itself expressive of the workings of Reynolds's picturesque, but also suggestive is the vagueness of the transfiguration. There are Rubens, Raphaels, Guidos, and Vandykes to be seen, but Reynolds does not describe them. Nor does he offer, as Hazlitt often does in similar situations, personal recollections. The paintings serve less an aesthetic than a social and a semiotic role in the essay. They are utterly subordinate to their social setting: The housekeeper "prizes the glowing canvas, more on account of its station in Warwick castle than for its bearing the magic hues of a Rembrandt or a Titian" (p. 11). Their "magic hues" again provide an instance for a ready-made picturesque sentiment, not a particular aesthetic experience. Reynolds's delight in the housekeeper's picturesque qualities again turns political: "The lofty rooms, the cedar-lined walls, the glossy wainscots, all speak to her of patient and never-dying grandeur. What to Mrs. Hume is the meanness, the modern noise, the foppery of this working-day world? – she knows it not!" (p. 11). Mrs. Hume, who knows her place and the timeless feelings she should have in it, stands in stark opposition to the atmosphere of crisis in the fallen present. Reynolds hears "the voice of antiquity" in nearly everything about him at "Warwick Castle," but unlike Hazlitt he does not care to hear the particular words.

Lamb's Elia essay in the July 1821 number, "Mackery End," explores a rather different kind of antiquity than that of Reynolds.[34] An account of a visit to a farmhouse in Hertfordshire – an old place that has become familiar through reminiscence by Bridget Elia – the view of "antiquity" in "Mackery End" recalls that of Hazlitt. Where people are picturesque in Reynolds's essay, they are presented without reference to such a conceptual scheme in Elia's. Though they make an affecting picture, it is not at all a ready-made one. Unlike the Countess Reynolds imagines to complete the ideal garden of Warwick Castle, Bridget is not drawn from an Italian print; she is rendered up with her edges and crotchets. The cousin who welcomes Elia and Bridget does not so much fit a preconceived notion of welcome as stand for a pattern of it: she "might have sat to a sculptor for the image of Welcome" (*London Magazine* 4, 30).

The difference between these two essays can be put another way. Hazlitt's essay on Byron and Bowles proposed a distinction between the natural and artificial in poetry. Reynolds's essay, which simply taps the pre-existing sentiment of the picturesque, contains no discussion of common natural affections, nor the oblique meditation on the nature of cousinship that dominates Lamb's essay. Reynolds presents a castle, a hierarchy, and royal personages that have passed into literature and ballad; Lamb presents an old farmhouse filled with Brutons and Gladmans. Reynolds, despite his frequent self-referential gestures, has no particular character within the essay: he may be irritated or delighted by what he sees, but he responds only in terms of the picturesque aesthetic the essay employs and celebrates. Lamb's essay begins with a long and highly specific autobiographical passage. He is so unlike his reader – even so little like his cousin Bridget – that his discovery of cousinage at Mackery End, his easy subsumption into the give and take of common recollection and generosity, is given great force: even the singular, quaint Elia can discover these common feelings residing in his breast. Elia truly has Hazlitt's leveling muse here. The sentiments expressed are common, neither the exclusive property of some readers nor ready-made responses dictated by the picturesque. Reynolds's essay, try as it might to present its sentiments as universal and timeless, cannot escape the charge of artifice. Read together, the essays embody a live debate: will the traditions so important to the restoration of legitimacy become "natural" through a forgetting of their rhetorical status, or will this term be used for moments like those described – even celebrated – by Elia?

Reynolds's new prominence in the *London*, taken with Hazlitt's virtual withdrawal, suggests that the legitimate and the picturesque mark out the magazine's future tendency. John Scott's program of nostalgia, evasion, and displacement ostensibly worked toward such a tendency, but it was a conscious, and more importantly, a historically informed choice. Superficially, the *London* under Scott and the *London* under Taylor seem to provide the same tonic for the political and social anxieties of their middle-class readership, but Scott carefully brackets his suggestions with a knowledge of the historical contingencies that produce the situation. Scott's program, while often marked by inaction and political alienation, presumes a critical stance toward the present. Displacement, for Scott, was itself a criticism.

The tension between Elia's recollections and Reynolds's pursuit of the picturesque in the July 1821 number illustrates the magazine's radical swerve from Scott's program. In this new context, Lamb's essay could easily be read as taking issue with the apolitical – that is, legitimizing – stance of the *London*. "Mackery End" might well have been incorporated into Scott's program of conscious displacement (in its move from urban to rural, its establishment of near-Burkean local and specific familial bonds, its fall into history, its celebration of these contingent ties); in Taylor's *London* it runs weakly against the current, countering the line articulated by Reynolds. Ultimately the Elia incorporated here is the Elia that endures: reading the Elia essays in Taylor's *London* is much closer to the experience of reading them in the 1823 *Elia* or the 1833 *Last Essays of Elia*.

Hazlitt's return to print in the magazine, August 1821's "On the Landscape of Nicolas Poussin," is marked by indirection as well – albeit an indirection that lacks the consistency of "Mackery End." The general remarks on painting are familiar: he has presented them in other Table-Talk essays (most notably in "On the Pleasure of Painting"), and here Hazlitt need only modify them for the particular situation of the historic painter: "The historic painter does not neglect or contravene nature, but follows her more closely up into her fantastic heights, or hidden recesses. He demonstrates what she would be in conceivable circumstances, and under implied conditions . . . His art is a second nature, not a different one" (*London Magazine* 4, 177). Hazlitt follows this with a discussion of the failures of second-rate historical painters. As in the earlier Table-Talk on painting, Hazlitt revels in the pleasure of the aesthetic experience: "A life passed among pictures, in the study and love of art, is a happy, noiseless dream: or rather, it is to dream and to be awake at the same time; for it has all 'the sober certainty of waking bliss,' with the romantic voluptuousness of a visionary and abstracted being." Hazlitt further explores an escapist response to art in a footnote, in which he defends Poussin's repetition of subjects: "It is hard that we should not be allowed to dwell as often as we please on what delights us, when things that are disagreeable recur so often against our will" (p. 177).[35]

This praise of displacement in the aesthetic experience culminates in the essay's unexpected turn to Napoleon in the final paragraph. Noting the fine collections of paintings in England – "a privileged sanctuary . . . where the eye may doat, and the heart take its fill" – he meditates on the return of the Louvre's "triumphant spoils" after Napoleon's defeat, and finally eulogizes Napoleon: "he, who collected it, and wore it as a rich jewel in his Iron Crown, the hunter of greatness and of glory, is himself a shade! – " (p. 179). This provides a fine, albeit oblique tribute to Napoleon. Hazlitt beautifully recalls the reader to the essay's opening analysis of Poussin's "Orion," a hunter himself. This spectacular bit of eulogy conflates Poussin's painting of Orion – blind, setting out on a journey to recover his sight, the obscure mists of morning rising around him, who "reels and falters in his gait, as if just awakened out of sleep, or uncertain of his way" (p. 176) – with Hazlitt's fallen hero.

This tribute to Napoleon has generally gone unnoticed in critical analyses of the essay, which critics tend to discuss only in terms of Poussin and aesthetics.[36] But when read against Hood's remarks in "The Lion's Head" on Napoleon's death, the essay offers other readings: "Napoleon Buonaparte's death will surely be the cause of ours. Will the reader believe that we are up to our middles in mourning verses? . . . We have elegies enough to paper all the tenements in St. Helena, and should be very glad to contract for furnishing linings to any respectable builder of bonnet boxes" (*London Magazine* 4 [1821], 119– 20). Even if Hood's dismissive tone were less obvious, his editorial moves would speak eloquently about his feelings toward Napoleon: no "mourning verses" appear in the *London*. Given this situation, Hazlitt's essay becomes a clever way of slipping an indirect eulogy for his dead hero past an unsympathetic editor.

While the Poussin essay is no "Guy Faux," its sympathies with Napoleon sharply contrast with the rest of the number. Reynolds's effusions on the splendor and magnificence of the aristocracy in "The Coronation," some five pages after Hazlitt's tribute to Napoleon, make this emphatic. Reynolds frames his report as a "Letter from a Gentleman in Town, to a Lady in the Country," and his preparatory description of the gentleman as a fop, dwelling on his clothes and his splendor as he prepares for the day of the coronation, is a superb bit of satire. Reynolds' correspondent takes particular notice of familial warmth among the peerage, which is apparent in the welcome of new arrivals to their seats: "the young daughter of the Duchess was kissed as frankly and tenderly, as though she had had no diamond in her hair, and her eyes had been her only jewels" (*London Magazine* 4 [1821], 187). Given the spectacular lack of domestic order in the Regent's own household, this seems to be a kind of compensation.

Reynolds's account of Caroline's attempt to enter Westminster and claim her right clarifies the politics of the essay. Reynolds reports slight confusion, "but the gates were presently reopened, and all proceeded as gaily as ever" (p. 186). Such a representation aligns Reynolds with the ministerial papers, which dutifully reported a "few cries" of "The Queen! The Queen!" which either "shortly subsided" or "were speedily suppressed."[37] Reynolds's description of the King's entrance could well have been written by a Tory hack:

You would have thought that such magnificence was not of the earth, but of the fancy; – not made by mortal hands, but wrought by fairy spell out of wonders of the sea and air. It seemed that being once in existence, it could never pass away; but would glow for ever so brightly, so beautifully, so full of matchless romance. The King looked down his hall of state with a proud expression of delight; and the eyes of the attendant ladies seemed to sparkle thrice vividly with the consciousness of their being the living lights and jewels of the scene. (p. 187)

This reads more like the *Quarterly* than the *London* under Scott. This is hardly what the *London*'s former editor meant when he suggested a "credible, uplifting ceremony" that would stir the respect latent in the breasts of the people.[38]

The articles by Reynolds in the July and August numbers signal a change in editorial policy. The fact that the latter number contains some criticism of the ministerial party is essentially irrelevant, since the criticisms focus on particular corrupt members or practices. Unlike Scott, who saw support of the monarchy in Burkean terms, that is, mindful and accepting of the radical contingency of the situation, the new editors celebrate legitimacy as a good thing in and of itself. Reynolds's part in this new institutional formation, his serviceability and pliability, might be considered unprincipled, given his dissenting background, his generally liberal tendencies, and the many anecdotes of his truculent radicalism in his old age.[39] But Reynolds had always been interested in getting on, in enhancing his reputation as well as, to his great credit, those of others. If Hazlitt, as we have seen, could be curbed by the demands of the magazines for which he wrote, a lesser talent like Reynolds was even more vulnerable. Reynolds's pliability testifies eloquently to the state of affairs among middle-class periodical writers and intellectuals in the late Regency and the early 1820s: real radicalism, that is, one not characterized by reaction and defensive maneuverings, had all but vanished.

The November 1821 number codifies the changes signaled in the July and August numbers of the *London*. This new formation has three main components: one essentially epistemological, one literary, and the last political. Together, they form a powerful reading of contemporary culture and shrewdly presage the literary climate of the rest of the decade.

The epistemological strand may be seen in Hood's "A Sentimental Journey, From Islington To Waterloo Bridge, in March, 1821." The journey is framed by an exchange between a cockney, who would like to travel out of London, and a philosopher, who attempts to persuade him that a walk through London would give him all the benefits of foreign travel.[40] The author overhears this argument and decides to test it – by walking to Waterloo Bridge:

A traveller, said I, should have all his wits about him, and so will I. He should let nothing escape him, no more will I – he should extract reflections out of a cabbage stump, like sun-beams squeezed out of cucumbers; so will I, if I can – and he should converse with every and any one, even a fish-woman. Perhaps I will, and perhaps I will not, said I. Who knows but I may make a sentimental journey, as good as Sterne's; but, at any rate, I can write it, and send it to the LONDON MAGAZINE. (*London Magazine* 4 [1821], 509)

This walk becomes an exercise in interpretation, in which the city and its inhabitants serve as a text to be read by the sophisticates who write for or read the magazine.[41] Ultimately, the article seeks to construct a particular kind of urban observer, a bourgeois *flâneur* whose researches into the varieties of life on the street aim less at comprehensive understanding than heightened self-consciousness.

The narrator's first encounters show this clearly. An unfortunate female, very near his doorstep, makes him think of Sterne's Maria. The narrator prepares to act out the sentimental role set by the text, but the scene is interrupted when he realizes that she is drunk, not needy – "rather bewitched than bewitching" (p. 509). He pushes on, his eyes charged with tears, but with no object to lavish them on. An encounter with a street-sweeper reinforces this demystification. After giving him a half-penny, the narrator watches him quickly pocket two more from other walkers. The sweep has garnered one half-penny out of inconvenience, one out of convenience, and one out of charity. The narrator concludes that humans, whether giving or receiving charity, act according to self-interest. He then enters into a quarrel between a man and his wife that blossoms into a debate over the "rights of women" and the "freewill of man" (p. 511). Assuming the role of arbitrator in the dispute, he suggests a compromise, to raucous applause, but his reforms, which pointedly recall basic tenets of French and domestic radicalism, are at once overturned. The tendency of these encounters is unmistakable: as responses to modern urban life, sentiment, charity, and political reform are signal failures.

Nevertheless such equivocal and gently self-mocking experiences prepare for the staging of other ideological commitments. The narrator, nonplussed, stares idly at the shop-windows on the Strand. Admiring the workmanship and craft of the products displayed, he meditates on the constantly improving industry of his countrymen: "May they still travel onwards in the path of improvement, and, surmounting all obstacles which a meaner ambition would plant in their way, reach that point of excellence and perfection, to which man in this world may be destined to attain!" (p. 514). This hymn to the enterprising spirit of the emerging merchant and industrial class briskly encapsulates the bourgeois ideology that informs the speaker's observations and interpretive procedures. The neatly ordered shop-windows become an island of order and excellence amid the vivid but incomprehensible variety of social types described earlier. Merchandizing and manufacture are themselves a mode of travel – indeed a quest – which organizes the discontinuous experience of city life.

Hood's article then returns to the overtly literary world in which it commenced. The narrator winds up his tour in a bookseller's shop, where he ponders the relation of happiness and ignorance. Convinced that learning is a help to happiness, he picks up *The Prayse of Ignorance*; reading it, he summarily decides that ignorance truly is bliss. Such a view is far from that of the *London*'s first editor. If literature had "much to do with" English manners, politics, and social life generally according to Scott, here literature is more a talisman whose exact relation to society is elusive. Scott, always averse to reductive views of the relation of literature to culture, had a deep appreciation of the subtle work it was capable of doing. Hood's essay essentially removes literature from the workings of the culture that he observes.

"A Sentimental Journey" concludes with the narrator's return to Islington by coach. As he rides, he arranges his travel adventures for publication. He begs indulgence of the editor if his style is "rugged and uneven" and if his matter is "abrupt and unconnected" – asking that this be attributed to the "unpleasant jolting of the stage, and the frequent interruptions and stoppages that it met with" (p. 515). The representation of London in the magazine has changed radically: Scott's mimetic

program of rendering of the "form and pressure" of London has given
way to a reductive and mechanical registering of urban life – one in
which the discontinuities of the city are less events to be considered
deeply by an author than events which register themselves on an author.
Hood's more semiotic approach, in which inexplicable social types and
practices are decoded, has replaced Scott's organic view of society, in
which classes were bound together by reciprocal duties.

Such a program has literary ramifications, and two other contributions to the November number – one by Charles Phillips[42] and one by
Reynolds – sketch these conveniently. Phillips's "Life of Hölty" sets out
a crude but lamentably durable paradigm for poetic achievement – a
dead Romantic poets' society. The essay expounds upon the "romantic"
character of Hölty: his love as a boy for the "terrific," which led him to
visit churchyards "and other appalling places" (p. 518); his longing for
sentimental rural scenes; his unspoken love for his Laura; his wide
reading in languages; his love of old ballads; his fervent nationalism; his
fascination with dreams; and, perhaps most typical, his death from consumption while young. His poetic thoughts are often simply the assertion
that he has had them. What they might be is, as in the earlier case of
Horace Smith's appreciation of the Elgin marbles, irrelevant. A quotation from one of Hölty's letters, presented as typical by Phillips, suggests
that the poetic experience is either ineffable or merely empty: "I often
lie at dusk on a hay-stack, and indulge my fancies, until the silver moon
comes forth upon the sky, and agreeably surprises me" (p. 525).[43]

That Hölty's life fits a pattern familiar to the readers of the *London* is
indicated by what follows Phillips's tribute: John Keats's "Sonnet, – A
Dream." The link is clear: here is another dead young promising poet.
The Hölty account stresses Hölty's deep reverence for love; Keats's
sonnet, in which the speaker descends into Dante's *Inferno* to give a kiss
to one of the fair forms enduring "that melancholy storm" (p. 545),
expresses a similar sense of poignant feeling and profound exclusion.[44]
Whatever the merits of Keats's sonnet in other contexts, in the *London* it
fulfills familiar expectations.

Unsurprisingly, John Hamilton Reynolds wrote the second of the
essays that trace the literary aims of the *London*'s new institutional commitments. Reynolds's contribution extends the tendencies seen in the
essay by Phillips as it recalls the attitude of Hood's "Sentimental
Journey." An exemplary commodity text, it diverts, flatters, and reas-
sures the reader it seeks. Consciously self-referential, jauntily urban, and
obsessed with deciphering the world it represents, it trades upon a

common knowledge of stereotypes and conventions that define both the reader of and the writer in the *London*. "Edward Herbert's Letters to the Family of the Powells, No. II: Greenwich Hospital" continues the series begun earlier with "The Coronation." This installment, again cast as a letter to a friend, clearly specifies its audience:

You know that my knowledge of London had previously arisen principally from the books which I had read, and that my actual experience of life had been gained chiefly from the small life of market towns and country revels. How often, Russell, have we ejaculated wishes to each other, when standing at a wrestling match, or looking upon the lads of single stick, or, when walking over the most celebrated houses "for miles round," – that we could see and admire those higher and more exciting struggles and combats of the great city, – those theaters, temples, and palaces, of which we had so often read, even to dreaming – that we could watch and wonder at the workings of that tremendous hive, into which – rash drone as I am! – I have at length ventured to creep. (*London Magazine* 4 [1821], 527)

Note the circularity of the pattern of perception here. Herbert read of London, then came to describe it to others who will in turn read of it.[45] Reynolds then mentions his recent adventures, essentially coming attractions in the *London*.

As in his earlier Coronation article, Reynolds shrewdly exploits the potential female audience, at once invoking them as readers ("The buildings, the theaters, the court, will have gaiety and beauty enough to interest the ladies' minds"), promising to cater to their particular sensibilities ("what female heart is proof against pointed lace, or can contemplate ruffles without emotion?" [p. 527]), and simultaneously winking to his male readers at the charming superficiality of the weaker sex. Reynolds effectually recreates the parlor here, constructing a kind of conversational sphere that will include polite society, the emergent middle class, and those aspiring to the middle class.

Then follows a description of the family into which he has been introduced, the Mortons. Reynolds's portrait of Mr. Morton manages to incorporate most of the features of the High Victorian paterfamilias: silent but central, powerful, acute, enforcing an absolute separation of activity between home and an office "somewhere in the city." While celebrating the comforts of the cozy domestic fireside, the passage mystifies, and simultaneously disparages, the economic basis of these comforts.[46] Mrs. Morton at once supports and subtly deconstructs Morton's centrality and authority. Her role is at once supplementary ("The silence and worldly inaptitude of her life-partner have called forth the powers of her

mind, and given a constant exercise to her fine judgement") and ena-
bling ("It is her chief desire to make Mr. Morton appear superior to
herself, and to that end, her voice and manners are gentle and subdued
in his presence, as though she took all her feelings, thoughts, and wishes,
from his heart and mind: – though to those whose observation is acute,
it is evident that her knowledge is far more profound than she chuses to
lay open"). A wide and knowledgeable reader, and a good critic of painting, Mrs. Morton "enlightens common walks, the idlest evening rambles,
with talk, all breathing information, and pleasure, and truth. The distant
gloomy landscape reminds her of this or that picture; and she points out
the disposition of the lights and shades which frames the resemblance"
(p. 529). She is a "queen" into whose court Reynolds's narrator is proud
to be admitted.

The Morton nieces and nephews are types as well. The eldest,
Prudence, is a blue-stocking, whose incessant literary chatter never devi-
ates from received parlor opinion. The youngest, Agnes, is the angel of
the house: "one of those sweet little fairy creatures which we seem to recognize as the realization of some dim poetic dream, or favorite beauty
of the fancy" (p. 530). She embodies many of the qualities celebrated in
the Keats sonnet that directly precedes the essay. She forms an implicit
comment on her sister: "Her elf-like shape, melodious tones, and retired
looks, seem contrived by nature as contrasts to the gigantic figure, vehement voice, and vampire gaze of Miss Prudence" (pp. 530–1). Her
brother, Tom, completes this brace of conventional figures. A middle-
class version of the Regency buck (minus the immorality), he spends his
time in pursuit of sport and spectacle: fighting dogs, cockfights, and the
"green rooms" of various theaters.

Reynolds then remarks on the efficacy of his portraits. Throughout
he has insisted that the reader fill in the gaps, which suggests that the
types he conveys are well known to the audience. In a telling phrase,
Reynolds asserts that the picture "is not 'done in little, ' I think, but man-
ufactured after the style of poor Dr. Primrose's family group – huge,
awkward, and unsatisfactory" (p. 532). The manufacture of the predictable is the core of the commodity essay. Beneath the seeming variety of
incident in Reynolds's "Edward Herbert" essays lies a grid of invariable
truth – a bourgeois ideology that sets out the new formation of the
London.

The actual visit to Greenwich Hospital – a rest home for sailors – is
uneventful. Old sailors are contemplated, met, and spoken to, but no
real conversation is recorded. Reynolds notes the strolling sailors:

But the walk below . . . at the edge of the water, narrow, inconvenient, and thronging with watermen, sailors, and other bronzed men, – was a delight to walk. There do the maimed and weather-tried tenants of the place saunter out their indolent and late holiday of existence. There do they sit for hours, like Crabbe's Peter Grimes, but without his crimes, looking upon the flood. There do they lean, – there stand, – there recline, – there sidle about. The passing of a packet, – the heavy slumber of a Dutch vessel, – the arrowy course of a wherry, – are all beheld and thought over with an unchangeable profundity and a deathless silence. (p. 535)

Again we see experience offered up as fragmentary, though picturesque impressions. The reader is in the presence of "profundity," although he may not know what exactly that means. It is enough, for the purposes of the magazine, that the sailors seem to be in some transcendent state, which can be commodified. That it is empty makes the transaction no less valid.

Such articles seem almost prescient. Their satiric eye, their urban bias, their smug complacency make them a piece with much of the periodical literature of the next few decades. There is little content to the easy kitsch of such articles; clearly we are far from the aspirations of John Scott, however modest they might have been. But perhaps most revealing of the shift from Scott's literary program is the evasive politics at work in the November number. This, the last of the three strands of the *London*'s institutional formation under Taylor, can be seen in Hartley Coleridge's essay, "On Parties in Poetry." Coleridge offers a political classification of "our most considerable writers": "Constitutionalists, Legitimates, and Revolutionists" (*London Magazine* 4 [1821], 476).

The great excellence to which our political constitution approximates, is the fair and balanced representation of all the great interests of society, and, as resulting from thence, the due subordination of every part of the body politic to the whole. An analogous excellence is discoverable in the writings of our great dramatists, and dramatic poets (under which title Chaucer may be fairly included,) up to the age of Milton. These, therefore, we call the upholders of our poetical Constitution. They were the elect of nature, and uttered, as it were, the common voice of mankind. They preserve the balance between the various elements of humanity; between those simple energies and primary impressions, which it has been the fashion of late to call exclusively natural, and the complex regards that arise from artificial society. The grave and the gay, the rustic and the refined, the town and the country, are adequately represented in their writings. They never introduce characters, as corrupt ministers are said to have sometimes appointed members of parliament, merely in order to utter their own opinions, their likes and dislikes, through many mouths; nor do they dispose incidents so as to maintain their peculiar theories. There is no self, no idiosyncrasy in their writings. They speak, in short, for the whole estate of human nature, not for that particular plot of it which themselves inherit. This praise belongs to Shakespeare pre-eminently, yet in large measure it is due to his predecessors, contemporaries, and immediate successors. (p. 476)

Coleridge employs the analogy not so much to tie the poetic and the political realms together as to separate them more completely. For all the prominence of politics in the essay, its function is purely metaphoric. The essay has much more to do with other schema of general decline, such as Peacock's "Four Ages," than with the historically conscious criticism of John Scott. Where Scott examined the contingencies of history, Coleridge opts for a master narrative so abstract that it ceases to be history.

The essay details the breakup of the organic constitutional formation. The metaphysicals are corrupted constitutionalists: they upset a "balanced representation" by "giving undue preponderance to the speculative intellect" (p. 476). The "Legitimates" Dryden and Pope countered the overabundant representation of the "head," but their critical principles "tended to prohibit all poetry that was not like theirs" (p. 480). Such views were "as detestable in taste as the political tenets of certain persons, who, because monarchy is good while it co-exists with freedom, wish to establish it upon the ruins of all social privileges, however hallowed by antiquity, or imperiously demanded for the welfare of mankind" (p. 478). The constitutionalist impulse returned in Gray, Mason, and the Whartons, who "assisted to break the legitimate spell, by reconciling the public to bolder metaphors, stronger images, and more varied cadence." Their attempts, however, were too faint, as they lacked "that universality, that deep and germinative knowledge, which distinguishes the earlier Constitutionalists" (p. 479).

Given the currency of such analyses in periodical literature, Coleridge's argument seems derivative, although perhaps more detailed in its depiction of the decline from gold to silver ages in poetry. Coleridge is more original in his treatment of the revolutionary school: "Dogmas, which had been held indisputable, were weighed in the balance, and found wanting; and the portentous creations of German fancy affected poetry much as the American revolution influenced politics." The name "revolutionary" owes not just to their contempt for "legitimate" prescriptions, but to a "deeper propriety": "Both politicians and the poets of the school referred every thing to nature, to pure unmodified nature, as they imagined her to exist before the growth of social institutions." This departure from the standard of an organic society constitutes a fall:

But licence sprang up with liberty; the strong used their strength tyrannously, and the feeble, casting away the restraints which had served to conceal and bolster up their feebleness, exposed themselves pitiably. All mankind became statesmen, and a very large part of them, to say nothing of womankind, became poets; and the Revolutionists of both classes had a strong tendency to form associations, as witness the "Florence Miscellany," and the "Corresponding Society." Happily, the poetical anarchy has not been succeeded by despotism; but, on the other hand, many approaches have been made to the restoration of the true old Constitution. (p. 480)

Notwithstanding his earlier insistence upon the necessity of both Freedom and Monarchy, Coleridge rehearses the familiar reactionary assessment of the French Revolution – licence followed by anarchy and Napoleonic despotism. The linkage of the *Florence Miscellany* and the London Corresponding Society is a cleverly Anti-Jacobin touch – mutual guilt by association. Coleridge's final remarks figure the "Constitutionalist" phase as an Eden from which his contemporaries are exiled. While not going as far as Peacock's dismissal of poetry as a "mental rattle," Coleridge paints a bleak picture:

It is too often forgotten, moreover, that neither states nor men can return to infancy. They may, indeed, sink back to its ignorance and impotence; but its beauty, its innocence, and docility, once past, are flown for ever. It is a paradise from which we are quickly sent forth, and a flaming sword prohibits our regress thither. Those who cry up the simplicity of old times ought to consider this. Human nature, and entire human nature, is the poet's proper study. With external nature he has nothing to do, any farther than as it influences the passions, the affections, or the imaginations of his fellow-men. Besides, Nature, as presented to the senses, is mere chaos. It is the mind that gives form, and grace, and beauty, and sublimity; and from that same mind the institutions and the prejudices of social life derive their being. Poetry, in short, has become too romantic, and the world is too little so. (pp. 480–1)

This line of analysis effectively closes the period which has come to be called Romantic, and, in its determined shift from nature to the activities of society, ushers in a Victorian sensibility. (Clearly his father's hopes for Hartley, that he would "see and hear / The lovely shapes and sounds intelligible / Of that eternal language, which thy God utters" and that "all seasons be sweet" to him, were not fulfilled.) The pseudonym chosen by Coleridge – Thersites – reaffirms his detachment and pessimism. The comfort of wit, however, remains to the writer amid the keen sense of the inadequacy of the contemporary literature: "It is a little remarkable, that the most strenuous supporter of poetical Legitimacy in the present day should be the encomiast of Napoleon, and the derider of all social institutions; while the most loyal of laurelled Bards continues a decided Revolutionist in the state of the Muses" (pp. 480–1). The paradoxes described in the final paragraph, sly hits at Byron and Wordsworth, are typical. The politics that back this stance are reactionary less through conscious commitment than disappointment, passivity, and spleen.

A *London* of this stamp was no place for Hazlitt. As the magazine became less overtly political and more attuned to the needs of a middle-class reader, Hazlitt's long quiet political bias was growing restive. While unable to place the incendiary "Guy Faux" in the magazine, he lit the path of his exit with a pair of Table-Talk essays that trace his turn from conversationalist to partisan. November's "On Consistency of Opinion" reveals Hazlitt in a jousting mood. He slashes away at some of his old friends – notably S. T. Coleridge – and baldly states: "I would quarrel with the best friend I have sooner than acknowledge the right of the Bourbons" (*London Magazine* 4 [1821], 485). The essay moves to a discussion of modern polemics. After outlining his own method of thinking about an issue – to draw as many opposite arguments as possible in order to be forearmed and in order to get at the truth – he sketches the character of those who have "sudden and violent changes of principle." Their reversals are a product of their intellect:

All their notions have been exclusive, bigoted, and intolerant. Their want of consistency and moderation has been in exact proportion to their want of candour and comprehensiveness of mind. Instead of being creatures of sympathy, open to conviction, unwilling to give offence by the smallest difference of sentiment, they have (for the most part) been made up of mere antipathies – a very repulsive sort of personages – at odds with themselves, and with everybody else. (p. 486)

Gone is the withdrawal prominent in Hazlitt's writing for the *London* under Scott; Hazlitt chooses sides and proceeds accordingly. In emphasizing zeal rather than knowledge, Hazlitt reasserts himself as the old partisan radical, not the conversationalist elicited by Scott.

Yet the way in which Hazlitt's radicalism re-enters the *London* is noteworthy: it is through the lingua franca of personal attack, as the following remarks on Wordsworth's tergiversation show clearly:

Mr. Wordsworth has hardly, I should think, so much as a single particle of feeling left in his whole composition, the same that he had twenty years ago; not "so small a drop of pity," for what he then was, "as a wren's eye," – except that I do not hear that he has given up his theory that poetry should be written in the language of prose, or applied for an injunction against the Lyrical Ballads. I will wager a trifle, that our ingenious poet will not concede to any patron (how noble or munificent soever) that the Leech Gatherer is not a fit subject of the Muse, and would sooner resign the stamp-distributorship of two counties, than burn that portion of the Recluse, a Poem, which has been given to the world under the title of the Excursion. The tone, however, of Mr. Wordsworth's poetical effusions requires a little revision to adapt it to the progressive improvement in his political sentiments: for, as far as I understand the Poems themselves or the Preface, his whole system turns upon this, that the thoughts, the feelings, the expressions of the common people in country places are the most refined of all others; at once the most pure, the most simple, and the most sublime: yet, with one stroke of his prose-pen, he disfranchises the whole rustic population of Westmoreland and Cumberland from voting at elections, and says there is not a man among them that is not a knave in grain. In return, he lets them still retain the privilege of expressing their sentiments in select and natural language in the Lyrical Ballads. So much for poetical justice and political severity! An author's political theories sit loose upon him, and may be changed like his clothes. His literary vanity, alas! sticks to him like his skin, and survives in its first gloss and sleekness, amidst "the wreck of matter, and the crush of worlds." (p. 487)

Just as Hazlitt wound his August tribute to his hero Napoleon into what was ostensibly a discussion of Poussin's painting, here he subordinates politics to a story of personal failure. The focus is less on radicalism than on inconsistency. Nevertheless, as the *London* submerges politics, Hazlitt's radicalism resurfaces.

Hazlitt's last Table-Talk for the *London*, December's "On the Spirit of Partisanship," leads one back to the principles of politics offered earlier in 1821 by John Scott in his "Signs of the Times." Where the partisan was a sign of corruption and degradation to Scott, it becomes an essential way of operating for the more politically engaged Hazlitt. The "strict dependance" of politics "on local and temporary circumstances" (*London Magazine* 4 [1821], 154) deplored by Scott is simply accepted by Hazlitt as the price of the ticket: "You cannot support measures unless you support men; – you cannot carry any point or maintain any system, without acting in concert with others" (*London Magazine* 4 [1821], 620). Much of what Hazlitt and Scott have to say in their conversation depends not so much on different views of the social and political condition of England but on different assessments of these situations. Hazlitt is less offended by the chicanery, bad faith, and outright fraudulence he sees in current politics; in fact, he expects it. He unabashedly shows his partisan bias in the account he provides of the victory of reactionary forces – an account which is less measured analysis than hustings bravado. He traces the flagging hopes of the liberal cause to its content:

the liberals espouse a "speculative proposition"; their opponents "practical interests" (p. 623). "They beat us in courage and in intellect, because we have nothing but the common good to sharpen our faculties or goad our will; they have no less an alternative in view than to be uncontrolled masters of mankind, or to be hurled from high" (pp. 622–3).

But if Hazlitt emerges from the uneasy apprenticeship forced on him by Scott, he does so in terms that would be amenable to Scott's principles. Hazlitt ends with a discussion of another "use" of partisanship: as a way of ensuring that "antipathies and ill-blood" are discharged in a harmless way. A partisan is, in Hazlitt's scheme, a "good-hater," but he holds a noble view of humankind. He believes that error and evil are the results of "sects and parties, classes and creeds," not inherent to humanity:

There is nothing that is a greater damper to party spirit than to suggest that the errors and enormities of both sides arise from certain inherent dispositions, common to the species. It shocks the liberal and enlightened among us, to suppose that under any circumstances they could become bigots, tools, persecutors . . . The spirit of partizanship is not a spirit of our misanthropy. (pp. 625–6)

Such a conclusion bears the impress of Hazlitt's time with the *London*. Hazlitt has redefined partisanship here – forging a kind of synthesis out of the thesis of his own radicalism and the antithesis of Scott's conversational, Burkean mode of thought. In Hazlitt's last *London* Table-Talk, to be a partisan is to have a sense of historicity, to begin to see the constructed nature of the self and one's opinions, to see the local and specific as well as the timeless and universal, to be a Romantic rather than an Enlightenment thinker.

Ironically, Hazlitt's thoughtful reconsideration of one strain of Romanticism emerges just as the *London* has taken a form that precludes its further development. John Scott's *London* sought to explain its representation of society in terms of deeper continuities and relations; the new *London* blithely accepts the discontinuities of urban social life and offers a selective reading of its signs. The satisfactions of Scott's Burkean–Coleridgean literary culture – "the collation of present with the past" and the habit of tracing feeling and opinion to idea and principle – have given way to the more fleeting gratifications of recognition. Taylor and Hood clearly thought that such a configuration would find the audience that Scott's more thoughtful approach had not. The relentless pressure to find readers, and the concomitant pressure to distinguish one's product from that of competitors, led the magazine to an inconclusive reorganization and an eventual collapse in 1825.

Nevertheless, the first two years of the *London* demonstrate several aspects of literary magazines. The meaning of a particular contribution takes shape amid the relations between that contribution and others that surround it, both immediately in the number and over time in the run. The *London* creates meaning in two ways: by providing a context that stabilizes or emphasizes a certain interpretation, as in the case of Scott's handling of Lamb's Elia essays, or by a less deliberate, open-ended, and dialogic process, as in the conversation pursued by Scott and Hazlitt. Because meaning is a function of the magazine, not simply the contribution, meaning tends to go beyond the intentions of the contributor, and, as we shall see in the next chapter, the editor. In reading literary magazines such as the *London* or *Blackwood's*, one can trace the elusive relationship between what writers consciously command in their writing and what they do not, between their intentions and the intentions that inform the medium in which their writing emerges. The rhetorical situation of the poet described by Wordsworth – "a man speaking to men" – simply does not obtain in such a system: a literary magazine ensures that meaning be perceived as inescapably corporate.

CHAPTER THREE

The burial of Romanticism: the first twenty installments of "Noctes Ambrosianae"

There are many extraordinary achievements in literary magazines between 1820 and 1825: Lamb's Elia essays, Hazlitt's Table-Talk, De Quincey's "Confessions of an English Opium Eater," and Landor's "Imaginary Conversations." But while one might argue that the magazine provides the space and opportunity for the talents of each writer, and that specific features of literary magazines (personality, periodicity, commodification) inform each of these conspicuous successes, it is only in the "Noctes Ambrosianae" of *Blackwood's Magazine* that writers begin fully and consciously to exploit the particular resources of the literary magazine. "Noctes Ambrosianae," at least in its first twenty installments, internalizes the dialogism implicit in the form of the literary magazine in order to carry out a searching analysis of its effects. It persistently blurs the line between literature and criticism, and in doing so it calls into question the very critical authority it asserts. Finally, by inviting the reader to consider the complications attendant upon figural uses of language, it encourages a particularly knowing kind of reader, one sensitive to the fictionality as well as the fiction of the literary magazine.

To explore these aspects of "Noctes Ambrosianae" it is necessary to shift our interpretive procedures from the abstractions of the class-based reading of *Blackwood's* employed earlier to an account of the collaborative efforts of a small group of highly individual writers. If the cultural work of *Blackwood's*, considered broadly, concerns the pursuit of gentility (for contributors and readers alike), the description of the place of culture in this magazine requires the kind of attention that Hazlitt brought to bear on periodical literature.

The origins of *Blackwood's Edinburgh Magazine* are familiar. In 1817 William Blackwood, having gained at forty a foothold as bookseller, sought to leave the shop for the more gentlemanly pursuit of publisher. As his occasional London partner John Murray put it, "you may improve to a most valuable extent the foundations already laid of a solid retail business, which in a few years may be consigned to the care of attentive clerks, while you will be gradually from this time rising into the higher duties of cultivating the young men of Genius of the day."[1] The attractions of Murray's description of the activities of publisher – one that blurs bourgeois "foundations" in a mist of patrician "higher duties" – for Blackwood, himself formerly one of those "attentive clerks," are obvious.[2] Blackwood had little relish for a gradual rise, however; he impatiently sought the means of putting himself on a competitive footing with his Edinburgh rival Archibald Constable.

Three lucrative ventures evince the prowess of Constable's firm: his continuing relation with Walter Scott, his assumption in 1812 of the copyrights for the *Encyclopedia Britannica*, and his publication of the *Edinburgh Review*. Blackwood had tried to pry Scott loose, but Constable had managed to keep him and the lucrative *Tales of My Landlord*. Blackwood then shifted his attentions to a more difficult, but ultimately more telling means of competition: periodical publication. He hired two experienced, if not inspired, hands, Thomas Pringle and James Cleghorn, and commenced publication of the *Edinburgh Monthly Magazine* in April 1817. The venture was not a success: by the second number the editors complained of the publisher's interference, and Blackwood was unhappy with the magazine's fusty tone, antiquated format, and surprising support of the *Edinburgh Review*'s writers and Whig politics. Blackwood recast the magazine, ousting his editors and promoting two "young men of Genius" that the magazine had managed to "cultivate": John Gibson Lockhart and John Wilson. In them, Blackwood found the blend of ideological fervor (both were staunch Tories), literary talent, ambition, and recklessness necessary to launch a successful challenge to the *Edinburgh Review*.[3]

The new formation, retitled *Blackwood's Edinburgh Magazine*, appeared in October 1817 with tremendous éclat. The opening number contained the infamous and libelous "Chaldee Manuscript" as well as the first installment of Lockhart's venomous series, "On the Cockney School of Poetry." Critical accounts of *Blackwood's* typically stress the scurrility and outrageous personality of the "Chaldee," but equally presumptuous is the self-aggrandizement of this satiric vision, which recounts the magazine's false start and predicts Blackwood's eventual triumph over his rivals. Blackwood appears as a reverential "man clothed in plain apparel"; Pringle and Cleghorn as two "beasts" whose loyalties to the "Book," that is, the magazine, are alienated by Constable, styled here "the Crafty"; Lockhart, Wilson, and James Hogg figure as a scorpion, a leopard, and a wild boar who replace the "beasts" and bring about "a great rushing, and the sound as of a mighty wind," which terrifies "the Crafty." The future of Constable is set out at the end of the manuscript: "Verily, the man which is crafty shall be defeated, and there shall not escape one to tell of his overthrow." Readers of the first number of *Blackwood's* may have snickered over the wit and personality of the "Chaldee," but the durability of Blackwood and Son's and the 1825 collapse of Constable give prominence to the raw commercial ambition shrouded in this Biblical parody.

If the "Chaldee" created the buzz necessary to make the magazine in 1817, "On the Cockney School" has transfixed the gaze of scholars and critics of Romantic literature ever since. "Z," the anonymous author of the series, has found few apologists. Even institutional accounts of *Blackwood's*, such as Margaret Oliphant's, register shock and dismay over the virulence and recklessness of this attack and the ones that follow.[4] But while in no way extenuating, the circumstances of this near universal critical reaction to the articles by "Z" merit close attention. One need only think of the relentless personality of Hunt's "Fat Adonis" caricature of the Prince Regent in the *Examiner*, Coleridge's vituperative attack on Maturin's *Bertram* in his *Biographia Literaria*, Byron's description of Castlereagh as an "intellectual eunuch" (and references to him as "it" in succeeding lines), or John Wilson Croker's ready expansion of the *Blackwood's* attacks on Keats in the *Quarterly* to see that Lockhart was traveling a well-worn path of scurrility. Moreover, we should pay particular attention to the way in which literary history itself has shaped our response to "On the Cockney School." Our response to Lockhart's attacks on Hunt and Keats has more to do with the change in poetic sensibility that made the marginal and "vulgar" John Keats emblematic of Romantic aspiration and tragedy than with any intrinsic difference between the venom of "Z" and that of contemporary periodical writers.

At issue here is one of the effects of this critical tradition. The reevaluation of Keats that occurred in the ten years after his death has systematically distorted our view of the early history of *Blackwood's*, narrowing it to the magazine's first three or four years, those of the "Z" attacks. If we can avoid – without ignoring – this critical basilisk, we might profit from the remarkably canny and dense account of Romantic literature provided later in the first twenty installments of the "Noctes Ambrosianae." Here, in this apparently desultory production, we find so powerful an intensification of the tendencies inherent to the magazine as a form that a new kind of critical writing emerges, at least momentarily. The "Noctes," in their early incarnation, are the pure product of the magazine, an experiment in writing that creates effects that go far beyond any conceivable intent. An inquiry into this particular achievement of the early "Noctes" will require a careful reconstruction of the literary scene in which the series participated, a recollection of the history of *Blackwood's*, a description of the "Noctes," and an analysis of its relation to the magazine.

The literary scene between the appearance of the first "Noctes," in March 1822, and the twentieth installment of June 1825, is difficult to capture for several reasons – chief among them the politically charged atmosphere of magazines and reviews. No review of literature in the *Edinburgh*, *Blackwood's*, or the *Quarterly* would avoid politics, even if reviewers occasionally praise across party lines. To use terms offered by *Blackwood's* in a January 1823 critique of the first number of *The Liberal*, "a common word, when applied to party purposes, or adopted by a party as a name or watch-word, at once acquires a new signification; and although it does not lose the old one, the *party* and the *ordinary* significations are sometimes the reverse of each other"(*Blackwood's* 13, 109). Here the writer apparently attempts to demystify partisan discourse, but in doing so he is caught up in the same cycle of "party" and "ordinary" meaning. Moreover, as *Blackwood's* is full of knowing references to this process of signification, we can assume that the move is deliberate. Hence the blistering attack on *The Liberal* supports two exclusive readings: one that naively accepts the overt point that *The Liberal* is less liberal than Jacobin, and another that would trace, perhaps approvingly, the production of "party" signification – here Tory – for literary works. The subversion of "ordinary" signification, insofar as it is knowing, is, of course, endless.

Yet it is useful to recall generally the shape of the literary scene, at least as it is registered in the great periodicals and borne out by some of the facts of circulation. We should begin with the list of deaths: Keats in 1821, Shelley in 1822, and Byron in 1824. The sales of poetry had fallen sharply; in the words of one *Blackwood's* reviewer, it was a "drug" on the market.[5] Reviewers noted declining vigor in former greats, notably in the case of Thomas Campbell, whose long-awaited *Theodoric* and *Loves of the Angels* were failures. Southey largely confined himself to prose. Byron's greatest sales – at least in a form that would make money for his publisher Murray – were behind him as well. Wordsworth's reputation grew steadily through this period, but his output was represented by the modestly successful *Ecclesiastical Sonnets*. By 1824, the audience for poetry was largely sought through the poetic annual or keepsake, a commercial innovation lauded by reviewers for its astute mingling of verse and elegant entertainment.[6] Walter Scott's novels sold briskly during this period, but reviewers noted a sameness to the characters and a lack of the innovation in form or in subject matter so prominent in *Waverley* and *Ivanhoe*. There were no sensations like the previous decade's *Lalla Rookh*, *Childe Harold*, or *Corsair*.

On the other hand, the great quarterlies and a few magazines enjoyed considerable success, especially if one takes into account the size of the market and their price. The *Quarterly*, however stolid, had circulations of around 12,000 at this time. Those of *Blackwood's* ranged between 7,000 and 10,000, and those of the *Edinburgh*, while dropping somewhat from the last decade's 12,000, remained high.[7] In a sense, the widening market for periodicals represents a shrewd choice by the audience: increasingly, periodicals themselves were literature. The combination of original essays, such as those of Elia, the Opium-Eater, and the author of Table-Talk, with the extensive quotation of poetry in reviews provided great value for a literary audience at a time when books were expensive. Periodicals achieved greater circulations later in the century, but they never dominated the literary market as they did in the 1820s.

When the "Noctes" began their long run, the contributors to *Blackwood's* were no longer the incendiary crew that had launched the "Chaldee" and the stinging criticisms of Coleridge and Hunt in the first number. 1821 was a particularly sobering year. The Scott–Christie duel had damped the spirits of Lockhart, and his father-in-law, Walter Scott, had urged him to distance himself from *Blackwood's*, "that mother of mischief." The magazine had faced libel action by John Leslie, a Professor at Edinburgh University whom the magazine had accused of various lapses from religious orthodoxy. Blackwood, who had made his way into the first rank of publishers, was clearly ready for a more uneventful tenure. A letter of June 18 to James Hogg, rejecting his submission of a piece in the spirit of the "Chaldee," shows Blackwood's desire for more respectability: "the Magazine is now too serious a concern to be trifled with. It has got quite above attacks and malignities, and I shall take good care never again to give them any handle for saying that they were entitled to speak of it as they once did."[8] The shift in tone implied by the letter is matched by a change in the circumstances of Lockhart and Wilson, who had more respectable ambitions of their own to pursue.

Between 1821 and 1825 the two produced seven works of fiction (which Francis Jeffrey, in a snippish review article for the *Edinburgh*, placed among the "Secondary Scottish Novels."[9]) Hence Lockhart and Wilson, while writing the "Noctes," draw on an unusual blend of experience and facility: as periodical writers (Lockhart himself was able to write thirty-two columns in a day without strain[10]), as intermittent editors, and as novelists. The comprehensive view of the literary scene afforded these writer-critics is the basis for one of the most powerful assessments of literature since the French Revolution.

The origins of the "Noctes Ambrosianae" are somewhat nebulous. As often is the case with matters in the early days of *Blackwood's*, the principals enjoy mystifying their activity. Whether or not the series was the idea of William Maginn or of Lockhart, it is clear that the majority of the first twenty installments were a collaboration among Lockhart, Maginn, and Wilson, and William Blackwood occasionally fitted parts by various contributors together.[11] The cast of the "Noctes" included North, the fictional editor of *Blackwood's*;[12] Timothy Tickler, a waspish reviewer for the magazine; Sir Morgan Odoherty, Maginn's alter ego, a stereotypically irascible Irishman; and the Ettrick Shepherd, loosely based on James Hogg. The "Noctes" were presented as a transcript of an evening's talk and song – as well as a record of some truly epic drinking and eating – at a local Edinburgh tavern, Ambrose's. Occasional visitors, drawn from a variety of real and literary venues appear as well (among them Byron; Vivian Joyeuse, fictional editor of *Knight's Quarterly Magazine*; the Opium-Eater; Pen Owen and Sir Andrew Wylie, eponymous heroes of 1822 novels; and "the seven young men," mentioned in the "Chaldee" but who take on further existence in the subsequent pages of *Blackwood's*).

Such a scheme is a suggestive one. The setting, recalling the license and freedom of Falstaff's Boar's Head Tavern, and the slippery ontologies of the dramatis personae give the "Noctes" an unusual sophistication and volatility.[13] Yet what becomes most prominent in reading the series is the intensification of the tendencies of the magazine. Features of *Blackwood's*, and of magazines more generally, are distilled into the "Noctes," but in the process they often become something quite different.

A description of the relation between the "Noctes" and *Blackwood's* might begin with their dialogic qualities. As noted in the discussion of Elia and the *London* in chapter 1 and Hazlitt and John Scott in chapter 2, the tendency of the magazine-miscellany is toward a kind of conversation. Editors such as John Scott made obvious attempts to give their

magazines coherence by organizing material in ways that produce complicated resonances among articles by different hands. *Blackwood's* not
only aims for such effects, but, as is often the case in the magazine, displays a kind of self-consciousness about the practice. For Tickler, attention to echoes among individual contributions is one of the protocols in
reading periodicals. In his reviews of rival periodicals, he proceeds
through a given number article by article and comments upon inconsis-
tencies and contradictions. The "Noctes," however, carry this process to
an extreme, as the case of the May 1823 installment shows. "Noctes" 8,
largely written by Lockhart, features Tickler and Odoherty, two prominent contributors to the magazine, as well as the less regular
Kempferhausen and Hogg. As the discussion begins, the German is hor-
rified by the Shepherd's zest for public executions, one of which he has
come to town on purpose to see. Odoherty, who coolly claims to have
seen one hundred and fifty, takes up the question of the actual means of
death in hangings with a less eager but well-informed Mullion. After a
comparison of the aesthetics of hangings and beheadings, the conversation shifts to ease of departure, the execution of one Lucky M'Kinnon
being mentioned as the most pacific hanging in recollection. The
Phrenological Society's interest in M'Kinnon's skull occasions an anecdote from Mullion about a hoax played upon the phrenologists in which
the cast of an enormous turnip was presented to them for professional
scrutiny. The conversation, by means of an intricate series of rapid associations, turns to Scott's latest novel, *Quentin Durward*, which even the
egotist Hogg confesses to be his best in a long time. Tickler's comments
on *Quentin* clinch this sequence: "It has all the novelty of another
Ivanhoe – and yet all the ease and lightness of another Guy Mannering
– and by the way, Hogg, the author seems to be as fond of hanging-
matches as yourself – what capital characters those two ladder boys are
– and their never stirring without rope and pulley, any more than a
parson without a corkscrew!" (*Blackwood's* 13, 594). Each topic in this allusive conversation has palpable connections with the articles that surround the "Noctes" in *Blackwood's*. Appreciations of popular spectacles,
reports of advances in medical – or more particularly, coroner's –
science, attacks on the inanities of phrenologists, and epigrammatic literary evaluation recall typical fare delivered elsewhere under the signa-
tures of Tickler, Odoherty, and the Ettrick Shepherd. This exchange in
the "Noctes" serves to put these articles into an intensely dialogic relation – one far more open-ended and speculative than any produced by
Scott in the *London*, and one that might well go beyond the intentions of

the *Blackwood's* contributors. From the heterogeneity of the exchange, one might simply conclude, in familiar New-Historical fashion, that "literary and non-literary 'texts' circulate inseparably"[14] and rather freely in the 1820s. But the "Noctes" make a much more extravagant claim about the possible relation of the literary and the non-literary. Here high and low cultures are not simply mingled suggestively but ordered. The shock registered by Kempferhausen at the depravity of Hogg and Odoherty results from a series of misapprehensions; not only are such spectacles proper for discussion among literary men at Ambrose's, they are intrinsic to part of the pleasure readers take in Walter Scott's novels. The "Noctes" do not simply blur the boundaries between popular and elite cultures, they locate one culture within the other.

In a sense, such exchanges rely on what might be called performative strategies at the expense of constantive ones. The speed of development, the reliance on association,[15] the slant recollection of signed articles by Ambrose regulars in the magazine but outside the "Noctes" proper, do not so much constitute an argument as provide the spectacle of a argument. Such exchanges organize impressions and information, but they do not attempt to justify or even examine the reasoning behind the development of such a view. At times, it seems that the rest of the magazine, or at least the parts that attempt systematic exposition and reasoned argument, exists simply to provide a reference for the ideologically charged moments of the "Noctes."

Wilson shares Lockhart's penchant for staged spectacle. In "Noctes" 5, he marshalls the political dogma of *Blackwood's* into parade order to celebrate George IV's royal visit to Edinburgh. The installment is divided into three acts, the first two of which follow the allusive and rollicking pattern of other stretches of the "Noctes." Wilson mines the third act, set in the kitchen and spence of a "Farmhouse in Girnaway," with his heavy ideological charges. The Gudeman and Gudewife who host the festivities, patterns of the yeoman class lauded throughout the magazine, voice the conclusions made by the magazine's more discursive articles. Gudeman repeats the economic analyses of *Blackwood's* regulars "Y. Y. Y." and "Bandana," that landlords must take lower rents and return to less inflated pre-war pricing; he insists that the king is not, as the Whigs put it earlier in the sketch, "just like other men" or the "chief magistrate"; and he provides comfort to *Blackwood's* nervous middle-class reading audience by reporting that, although seditious books circulate freely, they are largely spurned by a contented rural population. The Gudewife, breathless between country dances, nevertheless finds time to remark, again in ways that would relieve an anxious, post-revolutionary middle class, on the ideological efficacy of *Blackwood's*: "Siccan a bulk I never read afore. It gars ane laugh, they canna tell how; and a' the time ye ken what ye're reading is serious, too – Naething ill in't, but a' gude – supporting the kintra, and the King, and the kirk" (*Blackwood's* 12 [1822], 387). Wilson closes his performance with a speech by North. After settling a dispute between the local miller and smith by reminding them of their value to the community, North toasts the King. The sentiments are predictable; the miller's response provides the real focus: "A' the time you were speaking, I felt as if I could hae made a speech myself" (p. 391). The truths of this celebration of a Tory organic society are not argued, but staged, in a sophisticated performance that emphasizes emotion and sentiment but relies on the recollection of the more reasoned arguments in the articles that surround the "Noctes." Gudeman and Gudewife may not, as Coleridge puts it, "walk in the light of their own knowledge,"[16] but the articles and arguments that surround their remarks bathe them in a bright light of highly self-conscious Tory doctrine. At moments such as this, the "Noctes" convert the rest of *Blackwood's* into an authority that gives resonance to what are offered as natural, spontaneous statements of truth.

The "Noctes" transform others features of *Blackwood's* as well. Lockhart and Maginn regularly produce articles under the pseudonym "Tickler" that review recent issues of other periodicals. These contributions vary widely in terms of the writer's engagement with the material: at times "Tickler" will reproduce elaborate arguments very precisely, at others he dismisses them summarily and disparagingly. Yet the focus throughout the series remains steadily on the content of other publications. In the "Noctes," magazines and the literary world are a staple of conversation, but the emphasis is less on content than on the market for periodicals. The "Noctes" are punctuated with succinct and knowledgeable assessments of circulation, government regulation of the press, and the nature of audiences. When content is mentioned, it is usually in the context of differentiating *Blackwood's* from its rivals in terms of possible market share. The effect of this emphasis upon the material circumstances of publication is partly to debunk the idealistic claims of the rest of the magazine, as in "Noctes" 19, when North lists the familiar principles of the magazine "The religion of our fathers – the institutions of our fathers – the edification of the public," but adds "and our own emolument" (*Blackwood's* 17 [1825], 380). Yet at other moments this immersion in the dynamics of the publishing world gives the "Noctes" a powerful analytic capacity. Such conversations provide succinct explanations of the effect of market forces upon circulation, as when North explains the effects of a repeal of the taxes on newspapers and advertisements in "Noctes" 16. Tickler's spirited defense of the tax provides unusual clarity to the exposition: North's somewhat progressive analysis proceeds according to the "common-sense" objections of his interlocutor. The sensitivity of *Blackwood's* to the literary and periodical world is unusual among magazines, but in the "Noctes" this sensitivity takes on a particularly capacious form. The assessments of the literary and periodical world in the "Noctes" are short, but their attention to the material basis of publication makes them unusually trenchant. The contributors to *Blackwood's*, especially when writing in the "Noctes," are well aware that, as New Historicists often remind us, "every expressive act is embedded in a network of material practices."[17]

Finally, the dialogic form of the "Noctes" offers singular possibilities for critical discourse. *Blackwood's* had, from its inauguration, published contradictory articles on various literary figures. The turnabout on Coleridge, whom the first article of the first number directed by Lockhart and Wilson abused and whom later numbers handle reverentially, is memorable, but hardly singular. *Blackwood's* often presented competing views only to settle them with a culminating article, and some political issues were debated through letters to North and largely left open. But the "Noctes" carry this tendency further, and, in doing so, give it a new efficacy. In the hands of the writers of the "Noctes," this adversarial tendency becomes a complex and highly self-conscious way of exploring a literary work. Positions taken in articles can be loosened or unsettled by exchanges in the "Noctes," and much more tentative modes of critical assertion can be employed. This can be seen in the reception of L. E. L.'s first book of poetry, *The Improvisatrice*. Maginn reviewed the work formally and enthusiastically in the August 1824 number (albeit with a condescending gallantry that renders his remarks grating). After regretting that the papers had "pawed" the book, thus making quotation difficult, he provides extracts and assures his audience that there are "many other as swelling and Coleridge-like passages through the poem" (*Blackwood's* 16, 191). She is, according to Maginn, "the cleverest girl in print," and he concludes that it "will be in her own power to arrive at more positive distinction" (p. 193). The "Noctes" that culminates the August number takes up L. E. L.'s reputation as well, recalling the earlier review, but putting its assertions into play:

ODOHERTY. Literary Gazettes! – What a rumpus all that fry have been keeping
up about Miss Landon's poetry – the Improvisatrice, I mean.

NORTH. Why, I thought you had been one of her greatest admirers, Odoherty.
Was it not you that told me she was so very handsome? – A perfect beauty,
I think you said.

ODOHERTY. And I said truly. She is one of the sweetest little girls in the world,
and her book is one of the sweetest little books in the world; but Jerdan's
extravagant trumpeting has quite sickened every body; and our friend
Alaric has been doing rather too much in the same fashion. This sort of
stuff plays the devil with any book. Sappho! and Corinna, forsooth! Proper
humbug!

NORTH. I confess you are speaking pretty nearly my own sentiments. I ran over
the book – and I really could see nothing of the originality, vigor, and so
forth, they all chatter about. Very elegant, flowing verses they are – but all
made up of Moore and Byron.

ODOHERTY. Nay, nay, when you look over the Improvisatrice again, I am sure
you will retract this. You know very well that I am no great believer in
female genius; but nevertheless, there is a certain feminine elegance about
the voluptuousness of this book which, to a certain extent, marks it with
an individual character of its own. (*Blackwood's* 16, 237–8)

Beneath the condescension lies a real consideration: how to place a
pleasant, worthwhile, but essentially derivative book. The dialogue does
not permit, but more importantly it does not require the development of
this point, a delicate one which might in itself be harmful to a young
poet's reputation. Instead of a judgment, the reader feels the pull of
competing views. The elasticity of the dialogic form of the "Noctes"
allows its writers to say and not say what they are not yet sure they mean:
their remarks can reflect the uncertain apprehension that is more
common in the reception of new work than the history of reviewing
would suggest.

Moreover, in addition to this more objective consideration, the
exchange in the "Noctes" concerning L. E. L. draws attention to an
aspect of the critical act that reviews typically obscure: the part played
by subjectivity in critical response. North's remarks blur the term
"admirers," as well as the distinction between Landon and her work.
Odoherty's defense continues this double reference, as when he insists
upon the "certain feminine elegance" and "voluptuousness" of the
book. This studied imprecision cleverly reflects the force of personality
in literature: Odoherty, who reads *The Improvisatrice* with an eye to the
Improvisatrice herself, basks in the imaginary glow of her sweet verse
and "perfect beauty"; North, reading strictly in terms of the book itself,
finds much less pleasure. Odoherty, less judicious and more enthusiastic,

reads in terms of the age, in terms of Byron's self-stagings and market-wise autobiographical titillations. Finally, in doing so, Odoherty cleverly extends the remarks laid down in "Noctes" 1 concerning personality: "In reviewing, in particular, what can be done without personality? Nothing, nothing. What are books that don't express the personal characters of their authors; and who can review books, without reviewing those that wrote them?" (p. 362). And what, Odoherty's remarks suggest, are reviews that do not express the personal characters of the reviewers?

Hence the first twenty numbers of the "Noctes," by virtue of their contributors' immersion in the worlds of literature and of periodicals, by their fortunate circumstance of covering the waning days of a conspicuous literary movement, because of the unusually wide range of reference available in *Blackwood's* generally, because of the power and flexibility of the dialogic form, and because of their intensely self-conscious critical practice, provide an unusually fine lens through which to view what we subsequently have called Romantic literature. From the beginning of the "Noctes," the remarks of Lockhart, Wilson, and Maginn on this literature are nostalgic – meditations on what has been done, not what is left to do. At the center of these critical pronouncements, predictably, is Byron, whose difficulties in the general collapse of the market for poetry, flagging poetic powers, and untimely death provide the occasions for evaluations of the spirit of the age. The remarks, taken together, form something of a burial service for Romanticism – part nostalgia, part judicious analysis, part ritual marking of the passing of this literature.

The first "Noctes" begins much in the same key as Byron's *Don Juan*, with a smart, impatient, and worldly survey of the literary scene and its competitors. Odoherty, in an exchange with North concerning payment for articles, stands in the role of a literary hack who provides all manner of material, writes for everyone, and cannot remember half of what he has done. Byron's complaints about the debased heroism produced by newspaper puffery and his dismissive remarks on his rival poets are echoed by lamentation over periodicals, particularly the expansion of advertising. Chit-chat about the London periodical scene leads to a generalization about the changing taste of the early 1820s. Odoherty insists on the delicacy of the age; North, while agreeing, notes that "any production of genius" can be shown to "contain that which they pretend to abhor" (*Blackwood's* 11 [1822], 374). The test case for this change in sensibility is Byron, whom North celebrates for having "a little of *what's wrong* in his works" (p. 374). North notes the poet's difficulties with the Chancellor: "if Cain be prosecuted, it will be a great shame. The humbug of the age will have achieved its most visible triumph" (p. 375). The exchange culminates with Odoherty delivering what he claims to be the original version of Bryon's open letter to his publisher Murray concerning charges of blasphemy against *Cain* – suitably in *ottava rima*.

Byron's outsize presence in discussions of literary matters can also be seen in North's sonorous assessment of the age later in "Noctes" 1:

Why, we live in an age that will be much discussed when 'tis over – a very stirring, productive, active age – a generation of commentators will probably succeed – and I, for one, look to furnish them with some tough work. There is a great deal of genius astir, but, after all, not many first-rate works produced. If I were asked to say how many will survive, I could answer in a few syllables. Wordsworth's Ballads will be much talked of a hundred years hence; so will the Waverley Novels; so will Don Juan, I think, and Manfred; so will Thalaba, and Childe Harold's Pilgrimage, and the Pilgrimage to the Kirk of Shotts, and Christabel. (*p. 361)[18]

This list, if we except the jocular reference to the latter "Pilgrimage," is a fairly accurate one, especially in the case of Byron. It does not take into account the change of taste in the late 1820s that raised the reputations of Shelley and Keats, but it serves as a valuable reminder of the contours of the literary scene in 1822. North does not give reasons for naming these particular works; Tickler interrupts him and the conversation shifts to good-natured raillery. But, as often in the "Noctes," the rationale for a particular statement can be drawn from other articles in the magazine. Reviews of Scott's novels in *Blackwood's* put much emphasis on original subject matter, such as in *Waverley* or in *Ivanhoe*, and "Christabel" is often cited as the formally innovative work that inspired much of the poetry in the first decade of the century. (Ever market-wise, contributors also cite it as an example of Coleridge's bad timing; when Coleridge finally published "Christabel" in the 1817 *Sybilline Leaves* the familiarity of derivative works made it, paradoxically, seem derivative.) Hence the three works of Byron mentioned, all striking innovations and conspicuous successes, fit perfectly into North's list of "first-rate works."

North's comments on the state of literature, delivered in a brisk and seemingly offhand conversation about literary reputations, mark the beginning of a consideration of Romanticism that culminates in "Noctes" 15 and 19. In the intervening two years, this rough pecking order of Wordsworth, Scott, and Byron will become a descriptive typology in which each writer represents one of "three different great veins of thought and sentiment which are prevalent in this age of the world" (*Blackwood's* 15 [1824], 714). The reputations of Wordsworth and Scott are, as North's remarks suggest, largely settled – by the apparently obvious achievements of the *Lyrical Ballads* and the Waverley novels. That of Byron, however, is in play, and nowhere more brilliantly than in the pages of *Blackwood's* from March 1822 to May 1825. Almost all of the *Blackwood's* regulars follow and comment upon Byron's vicissitudes, both personal and professional, and their accounts differ sharply. The "Noctes" echo this variety of opinion and then incorporate it into a description of Romantic literature. The resulting consensus is itself subject to examination, in a self-conscious turn that exposes the pragmatic basis of such literary assessments.

The April 1822 number's "Letter From Paddy" sets out the main lines of attack on Byron. The "Letter" follows directly the "Critique on Lord Byron," a bland survey of Byron's works, in heroic couplets, which serves to recall his career generally. The topic started, Paddy insists that Byron's work is derivative (naming the source in each case), dismisses his blasphemy as unoriginal, and laments that the poet has lost his sense of Englishness among foreigners. Although the article, as an unsigned letter to North, lacks the status of other contributions to *Blackwood's*, it nonetheless summarizes what a reader might have been expected to bring to the debate in the spring of 1822.

The July number not only counters these attacks but suggests a radically oppositional approach to reading periodical criticism. The number concludes with "Noctes" 4, in which Odoherty is "Transferred (by poetic license) to Pisa" and speaks to Byron himself. The installment reads like a typical "Noctes," which on one level slyly incorporates Byron into *Blackwood's*, with drinking, song, and some racy personality. Then Odoherty takes up one of the popular criticisms of Byron's work: "Consider, my Lord – consider, I say, what a very immoral work Don Juan is – how you therein sport with the holiest ties – the most sacred feelings – the purest sentiments. In a word, with every thing – the bottle is with you – that raises man above a mere sensual being" (*Blackwood's* 12 [1822], 103). Part of the subtlety of this dialogue lies in the dramatic aspects of this moment. Odoherty's situation humorously undermines his point: as he passes the bottle – and very emphatically not for the first time – the Ensign speaks of spirit and the sacred. Byron's rejoinder, in addition to meeting his detractors, articulates what the contradiction between Odoherty's speech and action implies: "I meant to call people's attention to the realities of things. I could make nothing of

England or France. There every thing is convention – surface – cant. I
had recourse to the regions where Nature acts more vividly, more in the
open light of day"[19] (p. 103). Odoherty's further strictures allow Byron
further opportunity to defend his work, most notably "Cain," against
charges of blasphemy. The "Noctes," with considerable humor and
cleverness, have allowed *Blackwood's* to stage objections to the line of
criticism which it, like the *Edinburgh* and even lately the *Quarterly*, had
taken.

But these reversals are in themselves preludes to a more profound critique launched by Odoherty against periodical criticism generally:

BYRON: As for all your humbug of Reviews, Magazines, &c. why, you are, at
least, as much as any man alive, up to their nothingness.

ODOHERTY. 'Tis the proudest of my reflections, that I have somewhat
contributed to make people see what complete stuff all that affair is.

BYRON: I admire your genius, Mr. Odoherty: but why do you claim this
particular merit?

ODOHERTY: Merely as a great contributor to Blackwood. That work has done
the business.

BYRON: As how, friend Morgan?

ODOHERTY: Call another flask, and I'll tell you – Ay, now fill a bumper to old
Christopher.

BYRON: With three times three, with all my heart. The immortal Kit North!!!
!!! !!! [*Bibunt ambo*]

ODOHERTY: Why, you see what with utterly squabashing Jeffrey, and what with
giving Malagrowther an odd squeeze or so, – but most of all, by doing all
that ever these folks could do in one Number, and then undoing it in the
next, – puffing, deriding, sneering, jeering, prosing, piping, and so forth, he
has really taken the thing into his own hands, and convinced the Brutum
Pecus that 'tis all quackery and humbug.

BYRON: Himself included?

ODOHERTY: No – not quite that neither. As to two or three principles – I mean
religion, loyalty, and the like, he is always stiff as a poker; and although he
now and then puts in puffs of mediocre fellows, every body sees they're put
in merely to fill the pages; and the moment he or any of his true men set
pen to paper, the effect is instantaneous. His book is just like the best book
in the world – it contains a certain portion of *Balaam*.

BYRON: And this sort of course, you think, has enlightened the public?

ODOHERTY: Certain and sure it has. People have learnt the great lesson, that
Reviews, and indeed all periodicals, merely qua such, are nothing. They
take in his book not as a Review, to pick up opinions of new books from it,
nor as a periodical, to read themselves asleep upon, but as a classical work,
which happens to be continued from month to month; – a real Magazine
of mirth, misanthropy, wit, wisdom, folly, fiction, fun, festivity, theology,

bruising, and thingumbob. He unites all the best materials of the Edinburgh, the Quarterly, and the Sporting Magazine – the literature and good writing of the first – the information and orthodoxy of the second, and the flash and trap of the third. (pp. 105–6)

This exchange brilliantly undercuts, as it provides a forum for, Byron's complaints. Odoherty postulates a discerning reader, one who would be able to participate in the joke of *Blackwood's* discourse, while not excluding more naive readers. Although Odoherty insists on an authoritative discourse at work in the book – Blackwood's "two or three principles" – the admission that part of every number is "Balaam" puts every statement in play. As we have seen earlier, the performative aspects of the magazine are emphasized at the expense of informative or constantive aspects.

A quick comparison with John Scott's "Prospectus" to the *London* clarifies the unusual stance Odoherty assigns to *Blackwood's*. Scott had elegantly announced his magazine's mimetic program by recalling Hamlet's advice to the players: "to convey the very 'image, form, and pressure' of that 'mighty heart' whose vast pulsations circulate life, strength, and spirits, throughout this great Empire" (*London Magazine* 1 [1820], iv). By recourse to this familiar passage from Shakespeare, Scott signals that sophisticated kinds of representation are allowable, such as the figural representations of city life offered later by Elia, the author of Table-Talk, and the Opium-Eater, but the goal of the magazine remains mimetic – as he puts it, "to catch, condense, and delineate" (p. v). Odoherty's description of *Blackwood's* largely dismisses this function for the more playful and various role of "classical work." Scott's program – direct, sober, respectful of boundaries between the facetious and the serious – is directed to an audience that reads with the expectation that what is said is said straightforwardly and unironically. Odoherty's entertainment requires a very active, if not altogether suspicious reader on the lookout for "Balaam." Where Scott emphasizes content and intelligibility, *Blackwood's* foregrounds form and the medium itself.

Of course, such a mode of presentation is unstable. Although Odoherty posits a clear distinction between "Balaam" and moments when "true men set pen to paper," the terms he has introduced make judgments treacherous, if not impossible. Odoherty, like recent New Historicist critics, is well aware "that every act of unmasking, critique, and opposition uses the tools it condemns and risks falling prey to the practice it exposes."[20] In fact, his own unmasking performs just such a reversal. As Odoherty claims that *Blackwood's* enlightens its audience, his

use of the term "Brutum Pecus" slyly puts this enlightenment into question. The strategic use of a Latin phrase which recalls Edmund Burke's
infamous "swinish multitude" dissolves any positive statement in a wash
of ironies. At best the enlightenment bruited by Odoherty functions as
a paternalistic manipulation of part, if not all, of his audience.

Ultimately "Noctes" 4 celebrates the sheer joy of articulation. When
Byron mentions the Italian *improvisatori*, Odoherty at once boasts of his
own skill. The challenge is taken up, and he produces a neat Latin
version of the raucous drinking song "Back and Side go Bare." Later
Byron turns his lyric "There's not a joy that life can give" into "There's
not a joy that wine can give like that it takes away," which surveys the
damage of a descent into a drunken stupor. Odoherty, half boastful and
half exhilarated, celebrates the triumph of parody and counterfeit:
"Style – as to style, that is all fudge. I myself have written in all kind of
styles, from Burke to Jeremy Bentham" (*Blackwood's* 12 [1822], 109). The
final directions for the dialogue could not be more appropriate to the
writerly and speakerly pleasure celebrated within: Byron and Odoherty
are "Left Speaking" (p. 114).

The numbers of *Blackwood's* that follow do not keep up this chummy
attitude toward Byron. As is often the case in periodical literature, some
of the most telling moments of literary criticism come in unexpected
places – sandwiched into political discussions, as digressions in accounts
of travel, as sidelights to arguments about other literary works. August
1822's "Wordsworth's Sonnets and Memorials" repeats the earlier criticism that Byron's work is derivative, and it expands the charge that he
has lost his Englishness. Byron "has often forgotten, and often misre-
membered, his native country," whereas "The soil of his [Wordsworth's]
mind is English" (*Blackwood's* 12, 187). October's "Letter from Italy"
remarks on Byron's extensive debt to Italian poets. The indirect and
occasional nature of these criticisms of Byron adds to their force: they
have the status of accepted fact, not that of claims to be argued. A discussion of *The Liberal* in the December 1822 "Noctes" inaugurates a new
line of criticism: that Byron, now middle-aged, should "cut the
Cockney" and consider "taking up" lest he be dismissed as "incurable."
Odoherty puts this program of reformation most clearly: "The odd fish
is only just trying how far he may go: give him line, he'll soon come in"
(*Blackwood's* 12, 700). In this context, such words as "in" and "taking up"
have a political resonance, not, as would be somewhat irreconcilable to
the drinking party atmosphere of the "Noctes," a moral one. The regulars hope that Byron, now fat, nearing forty, [21] and experienced, will turn

Tory at last. The year's work on Byron in *Blackwood's* ends with a disman-
tling of *Werner* by Odoherty, which duly notes the poet's decline in ability,
prestige, and circulation. Much of the review is taken up with a discussion of the merits of the novel (by Harriet Lee) which Byron supposedly
"translated" for his *Werner*.

The sharks begin to circle in earnest with the new year. George Croly, in
registering his dismay at the abundance of cheap editions of seditious and
salacious works, notes that if Voltaire, writing in exile, was the motive force
behind the French Revolution, then Byron, operating from Pisa, might be
the unintentional cause of an English rebellion.[22] Croly dismisses Byron's
"Heaven and Earth" as implausible, though not, like previous efforts, libelous.[23] In April, the reviewer of "The Age of Bronze" insists that the work
is counterfeit and happily attacks it as an instance of Cockney presumption.[24] The publication of *Don Juan* 6–8 in July receives instant notice in
Tickler's letter for the same month. Lockhart and Maginn, writing together
under the name of Tickler, bring the criticisms of Byron to a point: so
"shockingly bad" are these cantos that Leigh Hunt, the King of the
Cockneys, could have written them. Maginn further remarks on Byron's
poetic decline in the "Noctes" that concludes the number.

The publication of Cantos 9–11 of *Don Juan* in September, however,
breaks the unanimity in the year-long assault on Byron. Lockhart,
writing under the signature of Odoherty, specifically responds to
Tickler's remarks in July. The latest cantos, like earlier ones, may well be
"wicked, base, vile, obscene, blasphemous," but they show abundant
intellect. Odoherty appeals to North to recognize the difference: "It was
in your pages that justice was first done to Lamb and to Coleridge –
greatest of all, it was through and by you that the public opinion was first
turned in regard to the poetry of Wordsworth himself . . . 'Stick to your
own good old rule – abuse Wickedness, but acknowledge Wit'"
(*Blackwood's* 14 [1823], 282). Odoherty admits many of Tickler's strictures
and shares his disgust with Byron's disparaging remarks on Castlereagh
and others in *Don Juan*, but he insists, whatever the moral failings of the
poem, that the function of the critic is to recognize genius: "[Byron]
ought to be told plainly, distinctly, solemnly, and with a total negation of
all humbug, that he is a writer of extraordinary talents – that Don Juan
contains the outline of an extraordinary poem – and that he is voluntar-
ily ruining both himself and his production" (p. 283). It is important to
note the veiled agency of much of this critical exchange. Both Lockhart
and Maginn, through pseudonyms, have taken both sides of the issue.
Lockhart helped to write the July attack by Tickler, and, as Odoherty,

Lockhart repeats many of the arguments he used in the anonymous "John Bull's Letter to Lord Byron," an 1821 pamphlet that defended, while at the same time, selectively censured Byron in what at best might be termed an insolent tone.[25] Maginn, as Odoherty in July, censures, but Maginn, in "Noctes" 4, gives powerful articulation to a defence of Byron. One cannot simply see the dispute as a disagreement between critics, a conversation between static entities in the magazine. The conflict lies not only between, but within critics. From one perspective, this is another example of *Blackwood's* notorious inconsistency, which aggravated John Scott to the point of a duel; from another, it demonstrates the flexibility and critical freedom that this most conservative, yet paradoxically innovative, magazine offered.

With their July and September 1823 articles, Odoherty and Tickler have set the terms of the disagreement over Byron, and *Blackwood's* seems content to let the issue lie for almost a year. Byron's death in April 1824 provides occasion for a more searching examination of his legacy in the June number. Even in May a kind of sea-change is perceptible in the *Blackwood's* line on current literature. Tickler's letter for the number, written by Maginn and Lockhart, cites a recent remark by Francis Jeffrey in the *Edinburgh* approvingly: "all is vanity and vexation of spirit, except the charming flow of the benevolent affections – the delights of friendship – the luxuries of HOME" (*Blackwood's* 15 [1824], 565).[26] This surprising bit of coincidence among rival critics receives expansion later in the May number in Maginn's "Maxims of Mr. Odoherty," a series which customarily offers a collection of rebarbative apothegms – mostly advice on drinking, eating, smoking, women, and books. Maxim Thirteenth concerns the present state of literature:

Poetry does not sell again in England for thirty years to come. Mark my words. No poetry sells at present, except Scott's and Byron's, and these not much. None of even their later poems have sold. Halidon Hill, Don Juan, &c. &c. are examples of what I mean. Wordsworth's poetry never sold: ditto Southey's: ditto even Coleridge's, which is worth both of them put together: ditto John Wilson's: ditto Lamb's: ditto Lloyd's: ditto Miss Baillie's: ditto Rogers': ditto Cottle's . . . There was a pause in poetry-reading from the time of Pope till the time of Goldsmith. Again, there was a dead stop between Goldy and the appearance of the Scots Minstrelsy. We have now got enough to keep our fancy from starvation for thirty or forty years to come. I hate repletion. (p. 602)

Maginn strikes this note again in the next number, in a review of Robert Sulivan's dramatic poetry. Poetry, Odoherty writes, is a "drug" on the market. The Byronic episode – dark-eyed cutthroats with gloomy dispositions – has passed into caricature, that is, *Don Juan*. Scott has retreated to prose; others – Moore, Southey, and Campbell – to prosiness. Coleridge is silent, Rogers punning, and Crabbe parsoning. Nobody, save Wordsworth, really writes poetry anymore. Odoherty's rhetoric is broadly comic, but beneath the humor lies the recognition of a lull in literary production, a real sense of an end to an era. Odoherty is not enthusiastic about Sulivan's work, but he does see possibility in Sulivan's homely subject matter. Byron's "Ruffian Amiables" (p. 676) are out of fashion, as are Wordsworth's peddlers and idiots; perhaps a return to the human affairs of those not *in extremis* is in order.

While one might dwell on the prescience of this assessment of the new direction for literature (especially as Maginn's comments sketch a climate most favorable to a poet like Felicia Hemans), what concerns me here is the emphatic finality of Maginn's dismissal of the Romantic poets still alive. What in "Noctes" 1 was a suspicion has now become fact. Appropriately, the death of Byron becomes the moment for a summative statement about the nature of Romanticism, and the least reckless of the *Blackwood's* critical triumvirate – Lockhart – rises to the task. "Noctes" 15 mourns Byron as the problematic third term in the familiar typology set out in "Noctes" 1.[27] Here the familiar triad of Wordsworth, Scott, and Byron become the basis for a critical description of Romanticism.

Many "Noctes" open casually or with fragmentary remarks, but "Noctes" 15 makes unusual demands on the reader. It opens with Odoherty's concession to Tickler in an argument, the gist of which the reader must infer. While the discussion refers to the future prospects of a drunken young guest, Jonathan Spiers, who has written "a romantic tale . . . interspersed with verses" (*Blackwood's* 15 [1824], 706), it is some time later that Hogg clarifies the situation by returning to what must have been Tickler's contention: "That there *is* no opening in the literary world" (p. 708). Despite Hogg's characteristically rosy view – half ignorance, half egotism – Odoherty's reaction and his earlier admission that he opposed Tickler "merely for the sake of conversation" (p. 706) show clearly how closed a question he deems it. The decline of poetry and literature is, at this point, axiomatic.

The conversation winds through various editorial or periodical projects young Spiers might take up, but it opens on, almost inevitably, the memoirs of Byron and his autobiography.[28] (The multiple levels of play characteristic of the "Noctes" can be seen in Tickler's suggestion that

Odoherty take up the task of a memoir; Maginn had in fact been charged with the task by Murray.[29]) Tickler, at the thought of Byron and his death, thinks of his own end, and with a sonorous quotation from Homer, looks forward to "enjoying the conversation of Byron himself" (p. 710) in the afterlife. Odoherty hopes he would keep better company in Hell. With this medley of argument, raillery, and sentiment setting the tone, the consideration of Byron begins in earnest. The end, to some extent, is predetermined; one hardly expects even the reckless crew of *Blackwood's* to speak poorly of the recently dead (and a lord at that). The real interest of this exchange lies in the intricate and suggestive development of associated literary and critical issues – chief among them the formation of reputation and the development of a literary tradition.

The first dispute concerns how modern writers are known. According to Odoherty, the abundance of books in modern times dampens (presumably, as Maginn puts it earlier, by "repletion") reputation. However estimable Byron's "fine bits," the existence of the "mass of lumber" he also produced obscures their virtues. In a moment typical of the complex nostalgia of *Blackwood's*, Odoherty attacks the "infernal engine of the press" (p. 711) for limiting the flight of readerly imagination; as ever in the "Noctes," litigants are painstakingly mindful of material considerations specific to modernity. Tickler counters this by arguing that a concomitant shift in the attitude of the audience has occurred: that readers attend not to the body of work but to individual works. In short, he argues for the continuing commodification of literature. The exchange does not seek to resolve the changes in literary sensibility effected by material and technological development, but the articulation of these changes, as often in the "Noctes," is precise and authoritative.

Tickler's estimation of Byron begins with a simple classification: that he is the "third name in one great era of the imaginative literature of England" (p. 712), trailing only the author of the *Bride of Lammermoor* and that of "Ruth." He expands upon this seemingly idiosyncratic evocation of Scott and Wordsworth at once, noting their "original invention," which he opposes to Byron's "original energy" (p. 712). Odoherty, still unconvinced of this high valuation, responds by listing the derivative aspects of Byron's work. However, as at other points in this exchange, this oft-cited criticism ramifies into an astute evaluation of Byron. After dismissing Byron's poetry completely, Odoherty then proposes that his real medium was prose. Verse is, after all, a "drug," and the English language is not "over-melodious." Odoherty cites selected letters – among them, mischievously, an attack on Blackwood – in insisting, over

Tickler's protests that "quizzing" is out of bounds in Ambrose Tavern, that "Byron's prose works, when they are printed, will decidedly fling his verse into total oblivion" (p. 713).

Tickler, for the moment, is reduced to quoting Byron's verse in response, much to Odoherty's disgust and Hogg's delight. But Odoherty's attack on Byron spurs Tickler to an unusually systematic development of his point:

there are three different great veins of thought and sentiment prevalent in this age of the world; and I hold it to be equally clear, that England has furnished at least one great poetical expositor and interpreter for each of the three. This, sir, is the Age of Revolution. It is an age in which earth rocks to and fro upon its foundations – in which recourse is had to the elements of all things – in which thrones, and dominations, and principles, and powers, and opinions, and creeds, are all alike subjected to the sifting of the winds of Intellect, and the tossing and lashing of the waves of Passion. – Now, there are three ways in which the mind of poetic power *may* look at all this – there are three parts among which it may choose. First, there is the spirit of scorn of that which is old – of universal distrust and derision, mingled up with a certain phrenzy of indignation and innovating fury – Here is Byron – Then there is the high heroic spirit of veneration for that which has been – that still deeper, that infinitely more philosophical distrust, which has for its object this very rage and storm of coxcombical innovation which I have been describing – This is Scott – the noble bard of the noble – the prop of venerable towers and temples, beneath which our fathers worshipped and did homage in the days of a higher, a purer, a more chivalric race. – This is the voice that cries – *In defence* – ! . . .

> "Faster come, faster come,
> Faster and faster, –
> Page, vassal, squire, and groom,
> Tenant and master:
> Come as the winds come,
> When forests are rending;
> Come as the waves come,
> When navies are stranding!"

And there is yet a third spirit – the spirit of lonely, meditative, high-souled, and yet calm-souled men – of him who takes no part in sounding or obeying the war-pipe of either array – the far-off, philosophic contemplator, who, turning from the turmoil, out of which he sees no escape, and penetrated with a profound loathing of all this mighty clamour, about things, at the best, but fleeting and terrestrial, plunges, as it were, into the quiet, serene ocean depths of solitary wisdom, there to forget the waves that boil upon the surface – there to brood over the images of eternal and undisturbed truth and beauty. – This is Wordsworth. (p. 714)

Such passages as this separate *Blackwood's* from its rivals. Francis Jeffrey's literary criticism in the *Edinburgh* is largely negative. His greatest heat is reserved for acts of exclusion, for the suppression of any work he considers innovative. For Jeffrey, to review is to judge work against an unchanging standard; ambitious attempts at a description of contemporary literature, such as Tickler's above, simply do not figure in the tight, bounded world of the *Edinburgh*.[30] Similarly, the largely political campaign of *Quarterly* insured that its criticism, while pungent and occasionally amusing, would take the most limited views of the literary scene.

Tickler's description of Romanticism is characteristically biased toward Tory politics, but, if we read with this bias in mind, he makes a plausible case. He begins, as do a number of his contemporaries, with the French Revolution as both historical event and symbol to which writers react. He takes care to register its effects both politically and intellectually: with the tottering of "thrones, and dominations" comes the more troubling loosening of "opinions, and creeds." Tickler's typology also retains a fidelity to the literary scene as it was visible to what, for all intents and purposes, would have been the audience in June 1824 – the readers of major periodicals. If Scott, Wordsworth, and Byron receive outsize attention, that is just the attention given them in the *Edinburgh*, the *Quarterly*, and *Blackwoods* – as well as the *London* and the *New Monthly*. Moreover, in comparison with many modern descriptions or theories of Romanticism, the Lockhart/Tickler typology is far more inclusive. Jane Austen's careful critique of aristocratic dereliction, her Johnsonian insistence on good sense and the moral tradition, and her profound distrust of innovation certainly have a place within the Scott vein of literary Romanticism. Shelley's Jacobin poetics finds place within the Byron vein, and "to brood over the images of eternal and undisturbed truth and beauty" fits much work by Keats as well as Wordsworth. Finally, the Tickler/Lockhart account is surprisingly self-conscious. Each account of the "great poetical expositor and interpreter" is, above all, critical: neither Wordsworth or Byron expressed their purposes in such terms, and I doubt that Scott would have been entirely comfortable with the largely reactionary description Tickler offers of his work. Moreover, because of the irreducible heterogeneity of its "three different great veins," the Lockhart/Tickler account avoids the most typical (and problematic) move in the history of Romantic criticism – the assertion that literature "gives access to unchanging truths" or "expresses inalterable human nature."[31] There is a thoroughgoing historicism to the typology.

Such an elastic description of Romanticism has much to recommend it. But perhaps even more suggestive is the occasion of this relatively disinterested criticism. In burying Byron, Tickler has effectively buried Romanticism: what ensues will be something different, something that approximates Jeffrey's exasperated turn to the "luxuries of HOME" – a tendency that emerges among the coordinates of poetic "repletion," of an increasingly moralistic middle-class audience eager to see themselves in what they read, and of the market-wise introduction of poetic annuals and albums. The timing of this assessment is exquisite.

Whatever the critical merits of Lockhart's typology, it is at once swept up into the continual play and dialogism of the series, a critical arena in which performance rules. Hogg, affected by Tickler's quotation of Wordsworth's description of the "poet's tomb" in "Glen-Almain," expresses the desire to be buried "beside Yarrow" as well. This characteristic bit of hubris allows Odoherty, seemingly halted by Tickler's grand demonstration, to shift ground by attacking the Shepherd. If Hogg will be buried, he will be "dug up, no doubt, quite fresh and lovely, like this new hero of yours, one hundred summers hence" (*Blackwood's* 15 [1824], 715). With this quip, Odoherty, in suitable "Noctes" fashion, both insults Hogg's intelligence and puffs his recent book, *The Confessions of a Justified Sinner*.[32] This brief comic relief, however, intensifies the pathos of Byron's death and refocuses the discussion of Romanticism. Tickler, having delivered his burial service, muses on the fitness of Byron's final resting place: "his suspiration was originally from thence" (p. 715). But Odoherty turns the conversation back to Byron's reputation, and in doing so he unsettles Tickler's carefully wrought typology. Byron, according to Odoherty, was no "Jacobin Bard" (p. 715); he always felt the weight of his coronet in every line that he wrote. Tickler concedes the point:

Byron took the walk that I mentioned, but he did not take it in that singleness of heart and soul with which the two other gentlemen took theirs. No, sir, he was too good by nature for what he wished to be – he could not drain the blood of the cavaliers out of his veins – he could not cover the coronet all over with the red night-cap – he could not forget that he was born a lord, a gentleman, an English gentleman, and an English lord; – and hence the contradictoriness which has done so much to weaken the effect of his strains – hence that self-reproaching melancholy which was eternally crossing and unnerving him . . . (p. 715)

This modification of his earlier description, a politically happy one for the Tory ideologists of *Blackwood's*, collapses the typology: the revolutionary vein is essentially an empty category, and its primary exponent a crypto-Tory. Tickler quotes a long passage from Canto 13 of *Don Juan* – the description of Newstead Abbey, the poet's "lost, forfeited, ancestral seat" (p. 715) – in defense of his claim about Byron, which sets up the ultimate turn in the consideration of Byron. Hogg, whose remarks have largely been dismissed throughout this exchange, gets the last word. Moved by the quotation and brushing aside the "grand divisions and sub-divisions" made in the foregoing typology, the Shepherd makes his own tribute:

I shall never see a grand blue sky fu' a stars, nor look out upon the Forest, when all the winds of winter are howling over the wilderness of dry crashing branches, nor stand beside the sea to hear the waves roaring upon the rocks, without thinking that the spirit of Byron is near me. In the hour of awe – in the hour of gloom – in the hour of sorrow, and in the hour of death, I shall remember Byron! (p. 717)

Hogg's personal and very readerly take on the Byronic episode – along with usual toast and song – punctuates the discussion. The critical efforts of Tickler – both his relatively disinterested typology and his politically driven modification of it – collapse into expressions of purely personal feeling.

This elaborate spectacle, in which two critics argue closely the legacy of Byron and offer a suggestive description of Romanticism only to swing back to a radically affective approach to literature, demonstrates the strength of the *Blackwood's* style of criticism as it is distilled in the "Noctes." The critical tenor prominent at the beginning of the exchange is set in stark contrast with the political mystifications of the subsequent revaluation of Byron and with Hogg's straightforward emotional response. Somewhere between these extremes lies the politically motivated modification of the typology. There is an end to the exchange, but there is no real sense of resolution; no approach to literature – be it critical, political, or radically affective – is given precedence. The personalities of the exchange – Tickler, Odoherty, and Hogg – allow for the development of a variety of approaches and allow each its swing. This style of critical inquiry allows the writer to put the critical voices he creates in a discourse that is open-ended – one that allows, and perhaps even cultivates, a divided and ambivalent response to literature. There is no authoritative center in the foregoing exchange among Tickler, Odoherty, and Hogg. The response of each figure to Byron is a function of the particular persona developed for each over time in the specific circumstances of the "Noctes." Odoherty's hotheaded patriotism bristles at what, in his final tribute to Byron in song, he terms the poet's "hot censure / Or rash laughter" for "that church, and that state, and / That monarch I loved" (p. 718). Hogg, whose poetic effusions are constantly regarded as unthinking, responds in an eloquent gush of feeling. In a sense, the "Noctes" perform a flexible and suggestive act of particularly Romantic criticism.

A review of Landor's *Imaginary Conversations* in April 1824 reveals the self-consciousness with which writers in the "Noctes" employed the dialogue form. While praising Landor's breadth of knowledge and genius, the reviewer notes his shortcomings:

No man can know better the prodigious and numerous difficulties of the Dialogue; and he seems in a great measure to have shunned them, contenting himself with giving a general impression of the characters and opinions of the different interlocutors, without striving to throw over them any of those varied and changeful lights, which, intermingling with each other, and fluctuating over all the composition, would have given both truth and beauty to each separate picture. (*Blackwood's* 15, 457–8)

It is just this fluctuation and intermingling, this sense of ebb and flow in conversation, this insistence on the position of the subject, that the "Noctes," at their best critical moments, embody. Landor's marmorial creations lack the dramatic snap of the shifting scene at Ambrose Tavern, and his critical opinions lack the performative values of the "Noctes." Insofar as Landor's work avoids the dialogic tradition, it fails. The review of *Imaginary Conversations* sketches an *ars dialogica* for the early "Noctes."[33]

A comparison of the treatment of Byron in "Noctes" 15 to that in February 1825's "Lord Byron" makes the superiority of this critical style clear. "Lord Byron," also by Lockhart, announces itself as the authoritative statement of the magazine. Lockhart admits that *Blackwood's* has been inconsistent on the topic, but defends that stance with the usual disdain for explanation:

because the notion of unity of mind, in a Journal like this, is quite a thing below our contempt, and because it was wished to make our pages reflect, as to this subject, the feelings and opinions floating about in society in regard to it – with this one *proviso* only, that we should have nothing to do with the opinions of dulness, or the feelings of envy. (*Blackwood's* 17, 132)

Now, according to Lockhart, is the time to speak out clearly on the subject of Byron. His magisterial tone might lead a reader to expect great things from what is to follow, but the article founders almost at once. In seeking to defend Byron's reputation as a man, Lockhart manages to obscure his poetic reputation in a a cloud of detail and petty circumstance. This positive case fails, notably, whereas the defense in the "Noctes," which "nothing affirmeth," triumphs. The monologic style of criticism taken up by Lockhart, with its impatience of hesitancy, ambiguity, and ultimately complexity, simply cannot do justice to a mercurial figure such as Byron, or to the variety of response his work elicits. Lockhart was much more effective when his work reflected "the feelings and opinions floating about" than when he sought an *Edinburgh*-style fixity.

The value of Lockhart's account of Romanticism in "Noctes" 15 becomes even more apparent when we examine it through our present critical concerns. Virtually no critical method could be more sensitive to specific historical circumstances: the personae in the "Noctes," with the exception of the pastoral Hogg, have a remarkable sense of their historical moment. We may not share their interpretation of recent historical events, such as the Revolution, or their distrust of democratic ideas, but they are fully conscious of their moment – often surprisingly so. These are writers whose immersion in politics and polemic leaves them ready to articulate their beliefs, often, in comparison with their waffling opponents, the Whigs, in telling ways. There is no "political unconscious" at work here, which gives their commentary an unusual salience.

Once developed, this particular dialogic critical style did not persist in the "Noctes." In 1825 Lockhart left *Blackwood's* for the more respectable post of editor of the *Quarterly*. Maginn had been for some time in London, and he was increasingly occupied with other projects.[34] Wilson took up the "Noctes" thereafter, with only occasional returns of his original crew, and he gave the serial a more stately aspect: at times, unfortunately, edging toward the static effects of Landor's work. The series, at least at first, does remain remarkably self-aware. In "Noctes" 19, Wilson seems to take stock of what the series has been and look toward what he will make it in the years to come. North, who will become more and more Wilson's alter ego, discusses the political situation. Given that the war is over, industry and agriculture thriving, taxation down, and the Whigs routed, the ministers are free to discuss systemic changes in government. Rather than talking for victory, they can turn their talents toward substantial issues. When asked by Hogg whether the division of the ministerial cabinet disturbs him, North praises this very quality, considering it important to the judicious settlement of fractious and difficult issues. Because a variety of entrenched interests are involved in each case, the divided Cabinet represents the country in an important way. There will be sacrifices when these issues are settled, and those who will sacrifice need to know that their interests have been vigorously considered. Hence the value of a divided Cabinet, in which, as Tickler puts it, "you would rather have what Eldon, Canning, Wellington, Liverpool, Peel, Robinson, and Huskisson, agree in considering the most practically prudent thing, than what any one of them thinks the thing most in unison with the dictates of absolute or abstract wisdom" (*Blackwood's* 17 [1825], 381). When Hogg insists that North apply this rule to the magazine, North replies that such is the case already. North's idea of consensus, the affirmation of "the most practically prudent thing" above more "absolute or abstract" claims, aptly describes a part of the dialogic approach of the previous "Noctes," but Wilson does not develop his idea dialogically. He speaks *ex cathedra*, using Hogg and Tickler, as he will in his later "Noctes," largely as a means of unpacking his opinions or as foils for North. "Noctes" 19 says one thing, but it does another, and this disparity characterizes the series under Wilson.

Hence, as is so often the case in literary periodicals of this period, the experiment of the first twenty "Noctes" is not continued. Moreover, it is not clear that the qualities I have discussed in this chapter would have found lasting acceptance among *Blackwood's* readers. When Ferrier brought out what must be considered the first authorized edition of the "Noctes" for the firm of Blackwood in 1855, he printed only those contributions that were demonstrably Wilson's.[35] In defending his editorial procedures Ferrier tells us much about the difficulties a series presented along dialogic principles might have encountered:

whatever the merit of the omitted colloquies may be – and it is sometimes considerable – they are so totally different in tone, spirit, style, topics, sentiment, and character – in short, in their whole treatment of men and things – from the Noctes Ambrosianae of Professor Wilson, that they could not have been introduced into the collection without destroying entirely that unity of design and dramatic consistency of execution for which the series, in so far as it proceeded from his hand, is in the highest degree remarkable. (*Noctes Ambrosianae*, ed. Ferrier, vol. 1, p. vii)

Ferrier's preference for the more cohesive and less ironic work of Wilson suggests little tolerance for the inconclusive exchanges of earlier "Noctes." Writing in the great age of the novel, Ferrier prefers exposition of character to the characteristically Romantic considerations of the position of the knower, and a grand harmony to the more centrifugal and ironic force of dialogism. In a sense, he has come not to praise

Romanticism, but to bury it, and his edition of the "Noctes," like most criticism of the period, obscures this most impressive of Romantic literary achievements.

Less thought than thinking, less product than process, the early papers of the "Noctes Ambrosianae" are one of the high points of the literary magazine as well as the era. Although the "Noctes," and *Blackwood's* more generally, appear to be a freewheeling exchange in self-expression, they are instead a method of production that could assimilate work of different hands yet find a disciplined coherence. Rarely has a literary production contained such energy, range, and order. As Byron said of his own masterpiece, *Don Juan*, "it may be profligate – but is it not *life*, is it not *the thing*?"[36]

CHAPTER FOUR

Magazine Romanticism: The New Monthly
1821–1825

Before examining the third great literary magazine of the 1820s, the "New Series" of Henry Colburn's *New Monthly*, a brief recapitulation of the aims and formal features of its rivals, *Blackwood's* and the *London*, is in order. Literary magazines, as we have seen, provide distinct versions of the world and embody distinct kinds of Romanticism. John Scott, the editor of the *London*, sought to go beyond mere "intelligence" and to "catch, condense, and delineate" what he termed "the spirit of things generally" (*London Magazine* 1 [1820], v). He sets out his intentions with his usual candor in a "Prospectus," which he follows closely until his death fourteen numbers later. *Blackwood's*, characteristically, has no prospectus, and its self-descriptions appear after-the-fact, if not simply tactical or occasional. Nevertheless, Odoherty's designation of the magazine in the fourth installment of "Noctes Ambrosianae" as a "classical work" (*Blackwood's* 12 [1822], 106) marks out the essential difference between these two magazines: the bias of Scott's *London* is toward representation; that of *Blackwood's* is toward performance.

Hence the spirit of the early numbers of the *London* is, above all, critical and objective. In it, John Scott seeks to balance an Enlightenment sense of order, one that emphasizes reason, clarity, analysis, objectivity, and balance, with a characteristically Romantic emphasis on sensibility, resulting in what I have termed a Burkean–Coleridgean literary culture. Scott's commitment to representation leads him to cast a wide net, as his remarks to Baldwin concerning the inextricability of politics and literature, as well as the connections among politics and "English trade, English amusements, Manners, thought, and happiness," demonstrate.[1] Such a posture requires a strong, active editor, one willing to sustain and defend his claims, to avoid slippery, manipulative arguments, and to hold his contributors to similar standards. Given this editorial vision, it is no wonder that Scott took it upon himself to police such practices as those employed by *Blackwood's*, which included the use of pseudonyms for mystification as well as anonymity, the staging of arguments for effect and interest, the recourse to personalities, and politically motivated reviewing.

We can trace the tenor of *Blackwood's* from its ideological commitments as well. To say it is ultra Tory and counter-revolutionary is true, but insufficient to account for its form. As deep as its political credo runs, it would not, without its contempt for the qualified Enlightenment principles held by Scott, be *Blackwood's*. Where Scott pursued something like Hazlitt's "conversation between friends," contributors such as Lockhart, Wilson, and Maginn show a deep distrust of discussion, of analysis, and of the possibility of any eventual enlightenment. This skepticism has a linguistic aspect as well: they are, paradoxically, rhetorically sophisticated in part because of their distrust of language and discourse. Masters of affect, innuendo, manipulative presentation, circumlocution, nicknaming, circular argument, begging the question, satire, and *ad hominem* attack, they seek to move, not inform and convince their audience. Their commitment to rhetoric and persuasion, which they openly defend as expedient in what they repeatedly term a good cause, makes the pages of *Blackwood's* a continual linguistic experiment, in which literal meanings are dissolved in a wash of rhetoric. Hence the magazine's parodies, ventriloquism, reversals of "ordinary" signification, confessions of "Balaam," mystifications of signature, hoaxing, and deceptively referential discourse. Even the editor was a kind of fiction: a variety of contributors, as well as the owner, shouldered the editorial duties. Their piecemeal efforts created the spurious textual emanation "Christopher North," who, with fatal irony, was "real" enough to cause two men to "walk out" with each other.

Each magazine projects a version of Romanticism as well. In the first few pages of the *London* Scott begins to develop his ideal of a Burkean–Coleridgean literary culture with an analysis of Walter Scott's novels in the "Living Authors" series. In subsequent treatments of Wordsworth, Godwin, and Byron, Scott carefully measures each writer against "The Great Unknown," and he returns to this surprisingly flexible account of contemporary literature throughout his tenure as editor. The *Blackwood's* account of contemporary literature is, as one might expect, far less official – it emerges during one of the exchanges in "Noctes Ambrosianae" – but this informality and tentativeness should not blind us to its merits as a particularly well-informed and broadly applicable theory. In tying contemporary production to the French Revolution, Tickler offers a typology of response: Walter Scott, Wordsworth, and Byron each exemplify one of the strains of Romanticism.

For the most part, the *London* and *Blackwood's* contrast neatly. Where Scott's magazine is urban, analytical, rational (but not Benthamite), and consistent, its northern rival is rural, rhetorical, distrustful of reason, and, outside its "two or three" Tory principles, proudly inconsistent. John Scott, with his heightened sense of order, place, and boundaries, keeps his reader clearly informed as to which parts of the magazine, such as Vinckboom's disquisitions on art, are humorously sportive, and which parts are serious. *Blackwood's* deliberately blurs such distinctions. Nevertheless, these two magazines share one premise: that politics and literature cannot be separated. Whatever one might think of their politics, there is no "political unconscious" in either of these two magazines.[2]

Like its two great rivals, Henry Colburn's *New Monthly* offers a distinct version of the world. Less self-conscious than *Blackwood's*, and less critical than the *London*, the *New Monthly* is neither a representation in the large sense that John Scott intends, nor a "classical work." Colburn and his editor Thomas Campbell position the magazine securely within the emerging middle-class social order, an order more economic than political, and one comfortable with a separation of politics and literature. As such, the *New Monthly* departs from the formal and informal considerations of Romanticism undertaken in either the *London* or *Blackwood's* and embodies a kind of Romanticism that these two magazines fail to account for.

One might be tempted to describe the *New Monthly* in terms of Mario Praz's "Biedermeier" Romanticism, as a timid, socially ambiguous exploration of domestic comfort and private feeling, as a lamentable attenuation of the energies of an earlier phase of Romanticism. But a more precise model exists: Carl Schmitt's analysis of the movement in *Political Romanticism*.[3] While Schmitt's "definition"[4] has serious limitations when applied to the range of English writers normally considered Romantic, it provides a useful account of the kind of Romanticism that the *New Monthly* inaugurates.

Schmitt's criticism of Romanticism begins with a recognition of its relentless aestheticization of the world:

Romanticism transposed intellectual productivity into the domain of the aesthetic, into art and art criticism; and then, on the basis of the aesthetic, it comprehended all other domains. At first glance, the expansion of the aesthetic leads to a tremendous intensification of artistic self-consciousness . . . Straightaway, however, a thoroughly typical transformation takes place. Art is absolutized, but at the same time it is rendered problematic. It is taken in an absolute sense, but without any obligation to achieve a grand and strict form or manifestation. (*Political Romanticism*, p. 15)

For Schmitt, the expansion and ultimate preeminence of the aesthetic precludes other forms of intellectual life, as well as decisive action in the political realm. He then offers a succinct definition of Romanticism, as "subjectified occasionalism": "the romantic subject treats the world as an occasion and an opportunity for his romantic productivity" (p. 17). This attitude is attractive because it allows the subject "to take any concrete point as a departure and stray into the infinite and the incomprehensible – either in an emotionally fervent fashion or in a demonically malicious fashion, depending upon the individuality of the particular romantic." Such an outlook on the world explains Romanticism's suggestive productivity: its adherents see a world full of occasions, of moments upon which to deploy a purely personal power of imagination, one that need never be brought to any test of reality. In essence, "A world that is ever new arises from ever new opportunities" (p. 19).

As such Schmitt's model addresses Romanticism in terms of a mood or perspective. But he is careful to connect this attitude with a specific historical situation:

In the liberal bourgeois world, the detached, isolated, and emancipated individual becomes the middle point, the court of last resort, the absolute . . . The subject always claimed, however, that his experience was the only thing of interest. This claim can only be realized in a bourgeois order based on rules. Otherwise the "external conditions" for the undisturbed occupation with one's own mood are not satisfied. Psychologically and historically, romanticism is a product of bourgeois security. (p. 99)

Such a connection between affect and determinate historical conditions gives Schmitt's model considerable power.

A quick look across the range of writers we have come to call Romantic shows both the strength and weakness of Schmitt's model. It cannot be fitted to the deeply conservative historical sense of Walter Scott's novels, nor can it address the revolutionary spirit of works such as Shelley's *Prometheus Unbound* or Blake's prophetic books. On the other hand, the concept of "subjective occasionalism" works very well for someone like Keats, whose negative capability closely approximates the attitude Schmitt proscribes so vigorously. Still other writers seem less, as Schmitt would have it, susceptible to "subjective occasionalism" than entangled with such an attitude in complicated ways. Coleridge, who, as Keats famously noted in his definition of negative capability, reached so irritably after fact and reason that he could not help but press "half-knowledge" into some system, castigates his own lapses into occasionalism with a vehemence like Schmitt's. In the opening lines of "Frost at Midnight" Coleridge disparages his "idling spirit," charging that its search for a "companionable form" makes "a Toy of thought," and one senses the same distrust in the decisive check his "pensive Sara" gives his airy speculation at the end of "The Aeolian Harp":

> Well hast thou said and holily disprais'd
> These shapings of an unregenerate mind:
> Bubbles that glitter as they rise and break
> On vain Philosophy's aye-babbling spring.

Byron's later work explores such moods with even greater intricacy and ironic self-awareness, as Manfred's complicated soliloquy on his false but momentarily fulfilling feelings of philosophic calm in *Manfred* III,i and *Don Juan*'s narrator's nostalgic yearning for the "illusion" of visionary freshness in Canto One amply demonstrate.[5] Schmitt's description does not do justice to the range and self-consciousness of English Romantic productivity, but it shrewdly isolates a tendency in some of the greater Romantics – a tendency that the *New Monthly* amplifies into a kind of Romanticism.

Schmitt's account makes much of the "external conditions" that enable the "subjectified occasionalism" of Romanticism to flourish. In an analysis of individual literary works and of particular subjects, like Schmitt's, these conditions have a kind of spectral existence: his discussion of Müller, for instance, shuttles between the specificities of individual poems or personal actions and general evocations of bourgeois consciousness. One of the virtues of studying Romanticism through literary magazines is that "external conditions," such as the "liberal bourgeois world" posited by Schmitt, leave more obvious traces in periodicals than in other modes of publication.

While the rules for *Blackwood's* and the *London* are largely political, or, in the case of the latter, ideological, those of the *New Monthly* are essentially economic. Its owner and publisher, Henry Colburn, was primarily a businessman, and his career leaves a record of astute adjustments to market forces and to the shifting demands of his audience. He began the *New Monthly* and *Universal Register* in February 1814, to capitalize on the apparent triumph of the Tories over Napoleon. His attack on Jacobinism begins as revolution ceases to be viable; what motivated

Colburn was an opportunity to compete with the old *Monthly Magazine*, which had supported Buonaparte and had, with many Whigs, opposed the peninsular campaign pursued by the Tories. Seven years later Colburn's sense of market again proved prescient, and he reorganized and renamed the magazine. The "New Series" of the *New Monthly and Literary Journal* appeared in January 1821 with the redoubtable Thomas Campbell as editor.[6]

An advertisement for the New Series in Colburn's popular weekly, the *Literary Gazette*, demonstrates the publisher's genius for puffing as well as the precision with which he can gauge the current wishes of the middle-class reader:

Aware that a taste for Literary Essays has long since increased far beyond the means of gratification afforded by the Old Magazines, they [the owners of the *New Monthly*] have enlarged their plan in order more fully to gratify the public curiosity, and have at the same time met the wishes of their subscribers by print-ing the original Essays in a large type, similar to those in the Quarterly and Edinburgh Reviews. They have also still further improved on the old plan by arranging the pages so that the Miscellaneous departments of the Magazine will form a distinct volume at the end of the year, thus combining in the same work the several characters of a Magazine, a Review, and an Annual Register.[7]

In addition to flattering potential readers and separating the new *New Monthly* from the old ways of its competitors, Colburn's notice provides three telling improvements. The use of large type – which implies single, rather than the economical but rebarbative double columns of other magazines – positions the magazine as a more elegant article of con-sumption. Large type also allows Colburn to associate the *New Monthly* with the more established and more intellectually respectable reviews and quarterlies. (At a price of three shillings and sixpence, a shilling more than either *Blackwood's* or the *London*, the magazine neared the four to six shilling price of the *Quarterly* or the *Edinburgh Review*.) Secondly, the separation, by a shrewd repagination, of the magazine into Original Essays and Miscellaneous Departments – a separation that could be rat-ified upon the completion of the year by separation into three volumes (two of Original Essays, one of the Miscellaneous Departments) – con-stitutes the typographical sign of the new spirit of the magazine, which divided the realm of the literary essay from that of current events and politics. Finally, the insistence on universality, despite the separation implicit in the new format, shows Colburn's talent for delivering "improvements" that are at once plausibly novel and comfortably familiar.

Most importantly, however, Colburn's advertisement raises one form, the literary essay, to preeminence in the magazine. By literary essay, Colburn means the flexible kind of personal essay, the play of reminiscence, fancy, and character that Lamb and Hazlitt had popularized in the *London* in the previous year. He does not seem to have in mind reviews of current literature, articles on individual authors, or literary analyses, as the pages of the *New Monthly* show conclusively. Nor does the magazine, in delivering these essays, provide the kind of subtle political inflection that we saw in Scott's *London*. Significantly, Colburn's *New Monthly* inverts the system employed in the *London*, where the Elia essays and Hazlitt's Table-Talk were woven into the larger scheme of the magazine. The literary essay in the *New Monthly* stands in a kind of isolation, neither a part of a larger representation nor absorbed into an ongoing "classical work."

This separation of literature and politics is echoed in the editor's "Preface" to the *New Monthly*.[8] Campbell cautiously allows that "political zeal," so long as it works "without outraging authority," is useful, but he insists on a sphere of cultural exchange secure from politics: "it does not follow, from the general utility of political discussion, that it should invariably pervade every species of literary compilation, or that there should be no calm spot in the world of periodical literature where minds of common charity and candour may meet without the asperities of party feeling" (*New Monthly* 2 [1821], v). Campbell's "calm spot" is as much a construction as the "stately pleasure dome" in "Kubla Khan," but during his tenure as editor of the *New Monthly*, Campbell largely stifles the "ancestral voices" of political struggle. As editor, his actions tend to be more negative and exclusionary than those of John Scott or the co-ideological band of *Blackwood's*. The articles in the *New Monthly* are shorter than those of its rivals, and they offer less argument. One rarely sees the defense of a delimited thesis or an exposition sustained over several installments of a series. One finds little of its rival publications' dialogic quality between and among the contributions, with the exception of a weakly ornamental tendency to the poetry, which often echoes some bland point in a preceding article. The poetry, almost always short, sentimental lyrics, functions more as a metrical respite between prose pieces than as an object of attention in its own right. Where *Blackwood's* is rural and the *London* urban, the *New Monthly* offers a suburban idyll,[9] a pleasant diversion from the cares of the middle-class life, and an intensification of its domestic and personal bias. Instead of the intellectual pleasures of a "conversation between friends" or the witty, self-conscious hilarity of Ambrose's tavern, it aspires to the coziness and warmth of a "rural villa at Hampstead" (*New Monthly* 7 [1823], 441). But while writers in the *New Monthly* indulge in the sentimental pleasures of the suburban retreat, they never forget the economic order that fueled the construction boom in Hampstead. While the essays put at a premium in the magazine exemplify and champion the "subjectified occasionalism" Schmitt finds characteristic of Romanticism, they also register the market capitalism that enables it.

The list of essayists who published in the *New Monthly* is a glittering one, but the earliest of Colburn's regulars, and in some ways the most typical, is Horatio (Horace) Smith. The son of a successful solicitor, Smith was born in London in 1779 and superbly educated at Chigwell. After training in a counting house, he went to work on the stock exchange. In 1820, he was able to retire. (Blamed for throwing away a fortune at the time, he congratulated himself on his good sense in the panic of 1825.) Smith had an enormous success in 1812 with *Rejected Addresses*, a collection of parodies of contemporary poets he wrote with his brother James. He wrote for the *London* until the spring of 1821, when he shifted to the *New Monthly*. He was so valuable a contributor that Colburn paid him £200 per year for whatever he wished to submit, and, judging by the number of articles and poems in the magazine attributed to Smith, Colburn got his money's worth. Much esteemed as sensible, conciliatory, and good-natured, Smith had a wide acquaintance among contemporary writers.

The bare facts of Smith's life are suggestive for the analysis proposed here, but even if we knew him only by the essays signed "H" in the *New Monthly*, he would exemplify the Romanticism described by Schmitt. In almost every essay, Smith explores the individual's ability, through the imagination, to produce emotional states that make up a world in themselves. In "The World," Smith notes that the world's beauty was wasted on the "bohemoths" that inhabited the earth before humans as well as on most men, who are careless of natural beauty as well. Unlike the "matter-of-course gentry," the man of an imaginative turn sees wonders everywhere: "For my own part, I thank Heaven that I can never step out into this glorious world, I can never look forth upon the flowery earth, and the glancing waters, and the blue sky, without feeling an intense and ever new delight; a physical pleasure that makes mere existence delicious" (*New Monthly* 4 [1822], 87). Smith presents himself as a kind of modern-day, London-based Jaques; like Shakespeare's character he moralizes the spectacle, and, significantly, takes great pleasure in the extension of his perception through repeated acts of imagination. From time to time he stretches his point further, finding the absence of nature more conducive to such flights of the imagination than presence. His essay "Winter" celebrates the trivialities on which the mind works: "more genuine Parnassian stimulus has emanated from a single chest of eight-shilling black tea, than from all the rills and founts of Arcady, Thessaly, and Boetia. I am even seriously inclined to doubt whether the singing of the nightingale has ever awakened so much enthusiasm, or dictated so many sonnets, as the singing of the tea-kettle" (*New Monthly* 1 [1821], 158). Later in the essay, Smith opts not for sonnets, but for enthusiasm, with which he builds, and defends, an ideal world:

Mine is an estate upon which I can reside all the year round, and laugh at the Radicals and Spenceans, while the bona fide landholders are only redeeming their acres from the grasp of those hungry philanthropists, that they may be devoured piece-meal by the more insatiable maw of the poor's-rates. Fortresses and bulwarks are not half so secure as my little mental domain . . . Is there a castle upon earth that has not, at some period, been taken; and did you ever know a castle in the air that was? As the traveller, when he beheld the Colisaeum in ruins, remarked that there was nothing stable and immutable at Rome except the river, which had been continually running away; so I maintain that no human possession is positive and steadfast, except that which is in its nature aerial and unembodied. (p. 160)

The complexities of such a passage are easy to miss, in part because the success of this kind of Romanticism has rendered its claims so familiar. Smith's "estate" is not simply a transitory daydream; it is a fantasy world that puts everyday existence into abeyance. In it, the conflicts of the real world are presented ironically: "bona fide landholders" are caught between radical movements and ruinous taxation. Ultimately, these conflicts are poetically transformed through comparison of the "estate" to the Tiber, a move which lifts them into the static and passive world of wisdom literature. By becoming the "traveller," Smith marks his removal from everyday life into a higher, emotionally satisfying harmony. There are, significantly, no causes for the political and economic forces that menace the estates of everyday life. Instead of social phenomena worthy of analysis, they are simply occasions for the work of the imagination.

In other essays, Smith gives such transcendence a distinctly middle-class turn. His series, "Walks in the Garden," entreats the reader to forget the large gardens of history and literature and to reduce his purview to "the paltry pretensions of a bare acre of ground scarcely out of the smoke of the city" (*New Monthly* 1 [1821], 517). For such suburban restraint, he rewards the reader with a roving account of various shrubs, trees, and flowers – much mythologized and at times painfully elegant. No real description of the plants is offered: each provides "H" the occasion for a variety of associations. At such moments, Smith is, as Schmitt puts it, "his own poet, his own priest, his own philosopher, his own master builder in the cathedral of personality" (*Political Romanticism*, p. 20).

Another series, "Journal of a Tourist," affords Smith abundant opportunities for the employment of aestheticism, irony, and poeticization typical of "subjectified occasionalism." Smith begins the series in October 1821 with a "saying" that admirably explains the basis of the "doings" that follow: "no man of ordinary observation, if he will give a faithful transcript of his mind, as he journeys through new scenes, can fail to produce something worthy of perusal" (*New Monthly* 2, 417). The terms proposed are exact. The traveler's mind, not the scenes through which he moves, forms the subject of the essay. The world exists as a spur to a Romantic productivity. We see this process at once: as the traveler proceeds to Dover, he sees the abundant fields of Kent on either side of the coach. This prompts thoughts of the agricultural crisis, and the "Tantalus-like fate of the cultivators" (p. 417). He further embroiders the situation with a Latin quotation and one from Tasso. The essayist then turns to the crisis in manufactures, which he connects through irony to the fate of the landed interest: "which classes can only be relieved at the expense of the other, thus keeping both, as an alliterative friend of mine expresses it, in a round robin of ruin, and a successive see-saw of starvation" (p. 418). Smith's disposition for poeticizing and the verbal facility of the "alliterative friend" transform troubling realities into something "worthy of perusal" in a literary magazine.

The third installment of "Journal of a Tourist" (January 1822) provides a memorable example of the "subjectified occasionalist" attitude. A visit to Paris and Versailles inevitably evokes considerations of the Revolution and the subsequent war, and the "faithful transcript" contains unusually rapid reversals of mood. Smith approaches the palace unsympathetically, speaking of the "impress of despotism" which the "vain and ostentatious Louis XIV" placed upon "this enormous mass of pompous extravagance" (*New Monthly* 4, 83). However, the "drudgery" (p. 84) of passing through rooms gives way to an imaginative description of the splendors of the pre-revolutionary court:

The Amours of the Gods, painted by Du Rameau, on the ceiling, could hardly suggest to the imagination scenes of more voluptuous enchantment than were once realized on the floor below, when, on the removal of a portion of the gilded columns, which were made hollow for that purpose, the whole arena was converted into a sumptuous ball-room; and the most splendid Court in Europe, in the height of its lustre, headed by Marie Antoinette in the zenith of her fascinations, mingling in the graceful dance, dazzled the spectator with the sight of beautiful and laughing faces, and sparkling diamonds, and nodding plumes, and gay colours, all reflected and multiplied a thousand times by the innumerable mirrors with which every box and every wall was completely pannelled. (p. 84)

Gone are the strictures against tyranny prompted by the signs of monarchal excess, as Smith indulges in a ecstatic vision of the court that seems innocent of any potential ironies in such phrases as "the height of its lustre." Smith then imagines another charged historical moment: "That lovely Queen, with her ill-fated husband, and a great portion of the beauty and chivalry of their court, all miserably slaughtered; the rest in exile, penury, and wretchedness; the palace devastated by an infuriate mob" (p. 85). Such passages, that recall the famous description by Burke in his *Reflections*, seem oblivious of the earlier, critical mood with which the visit to Versailles began. New occasions bring yet another reversal: Smith finds the grouping of statues that present Louis XIV and six mistresses as Apollo and attendant nymphs "fulsome and revolting," a combination of "unmanly vanity" and "crawling profligacy" (p. 87). This oscillation between "voluptuous enchantment" and "revulsion" (p. 87) ceases only with the visit, or, more properly, the essay. Later Smith reduces history to a series of opportunities for emotional response:

Could we trace that hidden relationship which sows in one age the seeds of the events that are to grow up in another, we might probably establish an unbroken connexion between the building of this palace and the destruction of the Bastille. These occurrences are action and re-action; cause and effect; and when certain writers lament (as they may well do) the outrages of the Revolution, it would be but fair to extend their sympathy a little farther back, and bewail those long-existing outrages of despotism by which it was generated. (p. 87)

The insidious work of a dubious "could we," the faint optimism of "probably," and the relativism of "as they well may do" preclude analysis. What remains for students of history are emotional states: to "lament," "bewail," and "extend their sympathy" to both oppressor and oppressed. In the "subjectified occasionist" mode, affect replaces cause and effect.

Taken out of context, Smith's facile, emotional responses and his insistence on the primacy of his own experience might be dismissed as an attenuated Byronism or Wordsworthianism. But publication in the *New Monthly* puts his work into a specific framework, providing what

Schmitt calls the "rules" that enable this kind of Romanticism. Other articles in the magazine are acutely aware of the domestic security necessary for such an intense preoccupation with one's ideal "estate," as Smith calls it. In a series of articles on economics the magazine lays down the plinth course of liberal bourgeois ideology on which its occasionalist Romanticism can run. Such articles address complicated economic problems and their social effects with the brisk efficiency of early capitalist theory: they cite restrictions on free trade, government intervention in business activity, excessive taxes, the poor laws, and the maintenance of a parasitical class of aristocrats by the crown as the causes of any economic difficulty.

T. C. Morgan, the husband of the flamboyant Lady Morgan and a materialist philosopher, sets out the *New Monthly*'s spare but powerful economic credo in the first number of the New Series. "Political Economy" begins with an account of the contemporary debate between Malthus and Say concerning population and the productive capacity of agriculture. Morgan dismisses both theorists, as well as the complexities of the argument, with a reductive claim that each economist is captive to his own experience: Say thinks too much on the immense development of French agriculture in his lifetime, and Malthus too much on the rapid industrialization of England. Morgan then warms to an extended attack on the unproductive classes, which has little to do with the claims of either Malthus or Say, and laments the injury done to both manufactures and agriculture by government intervention, absurd taxation, and commercial restraints. "Political Economy" exemplifies the pattern of economic discussion in the *New Monthly*, in which the commentators do not seek to convince or enlighten but to reassert economic ideas prevalent among the liberal bourgeoisie.

Other articles simply vary this formula. "The Science of Political Economy," published in three installments in the spring of 1821, is notable for the clarity with which it situates the discipline. According to the anonymous commentator, there was no rigor to political economy until Adam Smith, whose *Wealth of Nations* spawned a flurry of work exaggerating his principles, until happily corrected by Ricardo in 1817. Taking the most narrow reading of Ricardo possible, the article asserts the primacy of economics to politics and promises to examine the impact of the Corn Laws on rent, profit, and wages. In keeping with the propensity of the *New Monthly* for simplicity, the writer recommends free trade as a corrective in each case.

The lyrical praise of the productive power of capital, the single-minded championship of free trade, and the relentless assault on the unproductive aristocracy finds its place in other articles – even in those whose subjects seem far from the world of Malthus and Ricardo. The liberal bourgeois economic credo is not only present in the *New Monthly* but explicitly connected with other activities. In this early, expansive phase of capitalism, relations between base and superstructure are relatively transparent. The author of "Germany – Past and Present" (*New Monthly* 1 [1821], 294–304) is only too ready to cut the tangled skein of class privilege that constrains the emergent middle class in Germany. Particularly ruinous, at least in this writer's mind, is the separation of learning and commerce – "those great engines of political and moral advancement" (p. 298) – under feudalism. This has been reversed since the French Revolution, however, as "the nation of barons is daily imbibing more of the spirit of 'the nation of shopkeepers'" (p. 302): a new economic order, which has released "the spirit of improvement, and the activity of talent" (p. 295), will lead to "a mixed and middling class" of "important, independent, reasoning Germans, endowed with no arbitrary privileges, no prescriptive rights" (p. 302). The article eloquently describes the class struggle between the remnants of the aristocracy and the middle classes, but it carefully predicates it upon the inevitable conflicts of feudal and capitalist economic structures.

Occasionally, writers in the *New Monthly* invoke the bourgeois economic order to explain or to rationalize some of the more resistant sectors of the superstructure. In the January 1822 number, the author of "On the State and Improvement of the Fine Arts in England" recommends the establishment of a free market for artistic production. To raise the present low standard of British sculpture, public money should go to the best design, not to some coterie favorite. He advocates free trade in the art world as well: foreigners should be allowed to compete for public projects. Similarly, in the lead article of the August 1823 number, "New Society of Literature," Cyrus Redding attacks proposals for a Royal Society of Literature by contrasting the health of the current market for literature with the sickly operation of aristocratic literary circles. Authors, like the bourgeoisie, have been enfranchised, and they need to find a public, not a patron. Lest we assume that such recommendations are unconscious bits of dogmatizing, we might ponder the clarity with which the anonymous author of March 1821's "Collecting" repeatedly locates the pursuit of knowledge within the cash nexus. "In my mind," he writes, "money and knowledge stand to each other in the relation of cause and effect" (*New Monthly* 1, 360). Later in the article he is even more categorical: "In every department, in short, of research, the real distinction between the man of science and the ignoramus, between the adept and the sciolist, rests altogether in the power of purchase" (p. 360).

Such moments are, admittedly, extreme cases, but they demonstrate the *New Monthly*'s pervasive recourse to a specific set of economic principles. Far more characteristic of the magazine's representation of middle-class life is Smith's "Portrait of a Septuagenarian," which aetheticizes, ironizes, and ultimately poeticizes the realities of a market economy. This series, published in March, April, and May of 1822, offers the Septuagenarian's life story: his progress through a counting house, his slight but remunerative success as a writer for magazines, his retirement upon a modest competence at forty, and the subsequent thirty years spent in pleasant rustication. His bias, both as boy and man, was literary, but even upon modest success as a writer, he sticks to commercial pursuits: "education . . . and all the wise laws and modern instances of money-getting sages, had inspired me with such a horror of professional authorship" (*New Monthly* 4, 303). He loses everything in a crash, but manages over time to transform money earned with his pen – a "modest cargo" – into a sufficiency. His retirement allows him to "weed" his mind of the vices and bad temper developed in business, and much of the series is taken up with the Septuagenarian's happy, even rapturous recollections.

In addition to being an account (and a surprisingly prophetic one) of Smith's own life, the Septuagenarian's story is a particularly revealing middle-class fantasy, in which financial success is entwined, but never fused, with authorship. Smith begins the series with a self-deprecating restatement of the "subjectified occasionalist" mood – "If self-preservation be the first law of nature, self-description seems now to be the second" (*New Monthly* 4, 209) – and the Septuagenarian's last thirty years exemplify this attitude. In the context of the Septuagenarian's story and the *New Monthly*'s values, the rules of "self-preservation" are primarily those of bourgeois capitalism, and the form of "self-description" is a particular kind of Romanticism.

Versions of the Septuagenarian's happy post-commercial existence appear throughout the magazine. The anonymous "A London spring," which appeared in May 1823, is perhaps the most historically specific. Ostensibly an account of the poignance of spring for Londoners, the article becomes a hymn to suburban pleasures: "few of those who spend their lives in the midst of rural beauty know any thing of the deep delight that fills a Londoner's heart, and dances in his eye, when, after a week of ceaseless toil, he catches a glimpse of his rural villa at Hampstead" (*New Monthly* 7, 441). If this were *Blackwood's*, the idea of a "rural villa at Hampstead" would be a certain indication of some rough humor to follow: such words would evoke Leigh Hunt and the Cockney School, and the reader might anticipate yet another bullyragging of tea-drinking poetasters. But in the world of the *New Monthly*, the Hampstead villa represents a middle-class ideal.

The Septuagenarian's idyllic existence embodies Campbell's call for a "calm spot" in the "Preface" to the *New Monthly* in a particularly rich way, by incorporating the "external conditions" that allow it into the narrative. Other essays display a less easy balance between the "subjectified occasionalist" mood and the middle-class conditions that enable it. Both Smith and Cyrus Redding devote articles to the essential antagonism of means and ends, of bourgeois material circumstance and romantic productivity. Redding, in August 1822's "The Poetry of Life" seeks to sever the world from the life of the affections:

The poetry of life comprises our agreeable sensations, our tendernesses, our magical associations of thought, our spirit-stirring emotions, and our noblest enthusiasms. With the fatiguing realities of our being it has little connexion, but all that is just and generous belongs to it . . . it has little connexion with business, or trade, or traffic, with eating and drinking, or with any of the common occupations which we pursue. (*New Monthly* 5, 161)

In November 1822's "The Miseries of Reality," Smith, under his usual guise of "H," finds his garden and suburban villa insufficient for happiness: "It is a dull, plodding, scientific, money-getting, measuring, calculating, incredulous, cold, phlegmatic, physical age – a tangible world, limited to the proof of sense – a horrible æra of fact" (*New Monthly* 5, 391–2). He finds his only respite in dreams, to which he abandons himself, and, like Caliban, awakes crying to dream again.

Smith, in other essays, simply counsels withdrawal from the "ceaseless struggle of money-getting and money-spending" (*New Monthly* 7 [1823], 20); Redding finds modest relief in imaginative literature and reverie. Redding opens September 1823's "Writers of Imagination" by praising literature for its transformative potential, but he cannot sustain this belief through the essay. He repeats many of the usual apologies for literature – that writers have the power of "keeping the mind dissatisfied with common-place things" (*New Monthly* 8, 259), that they often "send us in search of better things than we already possess" (p. 261), and that their fictions, by touching our feelings and not our reason, are worth a thousand logical demonstrations – but his conclusion is tepid. For

Redding imaginative literature has outlived its early utility as the motive force behind human progress: it has done its work too well. What once inspired the vanguard of human progress now provides modest refreshment and relaxation for a tired middle class: "So far from valuing works of fancy less as we advance in civilization, we shall love them more, because we fly to them with more enjoyment from the fatigue of professional pursuits and the right-angled formalities of daily avocations, which multiply around us, as luxury increases our wants" (pp. 263–4). Characteristically, Redding's account of the experience of reading turns upon affect, not the power, knowledge, or vision invoked by other apologists. His conclusion, while recalling the traditional line set out by Plato, Sidney, and Shelley in their discussions of imaginative writing, resolutely turns toward Campbell's "calm spot": "we may visit scenes and beings of a purer world than our own; and when forced to return to every-day things, return to them with renovated spirits, and the hope that the delightful creations in which we have been revelling, may at some future time be realized to our senses, if not in this world, in another" (p. 264). Peacock, in "The Four Ages of Literature," likened poetry to "a rattle that awakened the attention of the intellect in the infancy of civil society" and considered its modern adherents to be as "absurd" as adults who "cry to be charmed to sleep by the jingle of silver bells."[10] Redding embraces the former proposition, and, if it is shorn of its deprecating rhetoric, he seems willing to grant the latter as well.

The occasionalist attitude taken up by Redding and Smith extends throughout the *New Monthly* – most notably in Patmore's fourteen part series, "British Galleries of Art," E. E. Crowe's travel essays, "Modern Pilgrimages," and John Carne's curious *mélange* of exoticism and religious quest, "Letters from the East." Schmitt's description of the kind of Romanticism these essays embody is a useful one, so long as one notes the clarity with which many of the writers articulate the relation between their "subjectified occasionalist" attitude and the external conditions that permit it. These writers are not, as Schmitt implies, oblivious of the historical circumstances that produce them. As often in the history of the literature we have come to call Romantic, the initiators of a kind of Romanticism show themselves well aware of aspects of their program occluded in the works of their successors. Writers who inaugurate a specific mode of expression, such as Smith and Redding, are usually aware of its relation to a historical moment; those who inherit such techniques, develop them, and ultimately define them for posterity pay more attention to formal concerns and to literary tradition.

At this point we are able to understand the paradoxical characterization of the *New Monthly* provided in the "Letter to the Editor" which leads the January 1823 number. In this oft-cited passage, the writer, *New Monthly* regular (and committed radical) T. C. Morgan, turns to politics: "The great merit of the publication is, that it does not meddle with politics; but – it is too decidedly a Tory work, the editor is a reputed Whig, and half the contributors downright Radicals" (*New Monthly* 7, 4). Such political heterogeneity can easily be incorporated into an occasionalist Romanticism in which a "liberal" like Horace Smith can by turns feel the tragedy of both tyrant and oppressed, and in which political antagonisms are aestheticized. It is not so much that the *New Monthly* eschews politics as subordinates them to other ends.

Given the *New Monthly*'s kind of Romanticism, one might ask what place a committed middle-class radical like Hazlitt found in it. We have seen the difficulties that Hazlitt had in the *London* with his editor John Scott and later with his publisher John Taylor. Yet Hazlitt published eleven Table-Talk essays and five chapters from his 1825 *Spirit of the Age* in Colburn's magazine between January 1822 and July 1824.[11] What made the *New Monthly* so congenial to Hazlitt when the *London* proved so constricting?

The case of Hazlitt proves one of the rules proposed in this book: that the meaning of a particular literary work is informed by the magazine. As in the case of Lamb's Elia essays, the meaning of Hazlitt's Table-Talk essays varies with the form of emergence. In book form, which encourages a reading of the essays in terms of each other, a political Hazlitt is very much evident. There, as John Scott puts it, Hazlitt introduces his politics "every where, and on all occasions" (*London Magazine* 1 [1820], 186). In this form one of the themes of the collection concerns his political disaffection – his weariness with what he called "Whig and Tory notches." In the politically inflected world of the *London*, this aspect of the Table-Talk essays was also prominent. In the *London* politics are not, as in the *New Monthly*, routinely aestheticized; the *London*'s Burkean–Coleridgean sensibility insistently connects the literature with politics while never confusing them. The *New Monthly*'s specific kind of Romanticism, however, emphasizes other aspects of the Table-Talk essays, producing a series of Table-Talks in line with the "subjectified occasionalism" of the magazine. Read in the light of essays by Smith, Redding, or Patmore, Hazlitt's politics have less claim on the reader. They have more to do with Hazlitt's personality than with any wider social concerns; they are occasions for the expansion of personality, not deep commitments. Hazlitt's intentions are, as in the case of Lamb's in the *London*, only part of the meaning of his work in the *New Monthly*.

Hazlitt's accommodation in the *New Monthly* can be seen in his first three Table-Talk essays. Because Hazlitt's first two essays turn largely upon the association of ideas, the magazine absorbs them easily. The first Table-Talk, "On Going a Journey," read in terms of the magazine, seems an occasionalist manifesto:

I am for the synthetical method on a journey, in preference to the analytical. I am content to lay in a stock of ideas then, and to examine them and anatomise them afterwards. I want to see my vague notions float like the down on the thistle before the breeze, and not to have them entangled in the briars and thorns of controversy. (*New Monthly* 4 [1822], 74)

One could hardly ask for a pithier description of the work of such writers as Smith and Patmore than "synthetical," and the celebration of "vague notions" conforms to the relaxed atmosphere of the magazine. Read in the context of Hazlitt's *London* Table-Talk, however, the pleasure described here would be less absolute: it could be read as the reflex of the intellectual struggle in which politics figures prominently. In such a context, the radical Hazlitt, having pushed for years the merits of a political case, relishes the momentary cessation of argument. There, Hazlitt appears not so much "content" as insistent on being content. Similarly, the opening of the February 1822 Table-Talk, "On Great and Little Things," admits of different constructions if read in different magazines: "The great and the little have, no doubt, a real existence in the nature of things but they both find pretty much the same level in the mind of man" (*New Monthly* 4, 127). In Colburn's magazine, this bold assertion of subjectivity squares with similar preferences by other contributors. Read in terms of the *London*, which foregrounded the political, and in which Scott lamented the loss of proportion in politics and in everyday life, it would become another measure of Hazlitt's frustration and dejection.

Perhaps the clearest indication of how an essay's form of emergence contributes to its meaning can be seen in the third Table-Talk, "On Milton's Sonnets." If viewed in terms of the *London*, it would appear a slashing attack on tergiversation and the degeneracy of patriotism. In the *New Monthly*, Milton's politics figure as the relativism of the subjectified occasionalist. As the meaning of the entire essay changes with the context, so do the charges given to particular passages, as in following example:

I do not pretend to defend the tone of Milton's political writings (which was borrowed from the style of controversial divinity) or to say that he was right in the
part he took: – I say that he was consistent in it, and did not convict himself of
error: he was consistent in it in spite of danger and obloquy, "on evil days
though fallen, and evil tongues," and therefore his character has the salt of
honesty about it. It does not offend in the nostrils of posterity. (*New Monthly* 4
[1822], 239–40)

The reader of the *New Monthly* would be familiar with this recourse to
the personal: in this context Milton is admirable for his consistency and
honor, not his cause. In the *London* such a passage would further exemplify the specificity of the political argument carried on by Hazlitt in
Scott's magazine, an arena in which precision was greatly valued and
political statements were carefully delimited. What reads as a disclaimer
of political intent in one context becomes a discrimination between
political claims in another. The protocols for interpretation developed
over time in the magazine determine the reading given the passage.[12]

While Hazlitt gives specific political resonance to many passages in
the remaining eight Table-Talks published in the *New Monthly*, the subjects and treatments for the most part comply with the occasionalist
Romanticism of the magazine. Indeed, Hazlitt at times seems to go out
of his way to avoid political controversy. August 1823's "On Londoners
and Country People" opens with a reference to the definition of the term
"cockney" in *Blackwood's* – which he names explicitly, a rare moment in
the *New Monthly*, which prefers allusion and innuendo: "He means by it
a person who has happened at any time to live in London, and who is
not a Tory – I mean by it, a person who has never lived out of London,
and who has got all his ideas from it" (*New Monthly* 8, 171). An opening
such as this in Scott's *London* would have immediately signaled a politically charged salvo to follow, but Hazlitt uncharacteristically forgoes the
opportunity. Here he follows the tendency of Colburn's magazine, conspicuously moving from the political to more general social commentary.

Hazlitt's next series in the *New Monthly* makes even fewer demands on
the magazine's absorptive capacities. Five installments from his 1825
Spirit of the Age – here entitled "Spirits of the Age" – appear from January
to July 1824. Because the coherence of the series, as well as the book
itself, lies more in Hazlitt's approach to his subjects than in some thesis
about the age itself, and since each portrait turns upon some inconsistency within or limitation to the character under scrutiny, in all cases
tracing any political feeling to character, not to principle, the series
exemplifies the "occasionalist" outlook of the *New Monthly*. Even the title

seems accommodating: the use of plural "Spirits" might well be considered a corollary to the preference for "synthetic" to "analytical" with which Hazlitt began his Table-Talk series earlier in the magazine. "Spirit" suggests analytic rigor; "spirits" a descriptive miscellany.

The first two installments, "Jeremy Bentham" and "Mr. Irving," steer clear of political entanglements altogether. In criticizing Bentham's excessive reliance on reason and abstraction, Hazlitt expatiates upon the importance of feeling:

> being as we are, our feelings evaporate in so large a space, we must draw the circle of our affections and duties somewhat closer, the heart hovers and fixes nearer home. It is true, the bands of private, or of local and natural affection, are often, nay in general, too tightly strained, so as frequently to do harm instead of good: but the present question is, whether we can, with safety and effect, be wholly emancipated from them? Whether we should shake them off at pleasure and without mercy, as the only bar to the triumph of truth and justice? Or whether benevolence, constructed upon a logical scale, would not be merely *nominal*, – whether duty, raised to too lofty a pitch of refinement, might not sink into callous indifference or hollow selfishness? (*New Monthly* 10 [1824], 72)

The even-handedness of this passage, as well as its promotion of feeling, echo many other moments in the *New Monthly*. As in the case of the Table-Talks, however, the context of the magazine contributes to the effect of the passage. If read in the context of Hazlitt's *London* Table-Talks, echoes of Burke in the passage become prominent, and we might relate it to Hazlitt's ongoing meditation on his relation to a figure who is at once his political opponent and a powerful influence on his thinking.

The third portrait, "The Late Mr. Horne Tooke," would seem destined to disturb Campbell's "calm spot." Horne Tooke, an associate of Paine tried for high treason during the conservative reaction following the French Revolution, would seem to require some consideration of politics. Hazlitt, however, traces everything to personality, not principle: "it was his delight to make mischief and spoil sport . . . Provided he could say a clever or a spiteful thing, he did not care whether it served or injured the cause. Spleen and the exercise of intellectual power was the motive of his patriotism, rather than principle" (p. 254). This is an occasionalism with a vengeance: Hazlitt implies that Tooke could have adopted nearly any political position so long as it allowed him opportunity for self-expression.

Hazlitt follows this approach in his next two portraits, Walter Scott and Lord Eldon. Scott, as Hazlitt well knew, was both openly and covertly partisan, an outspoken Tory apologist and a secret supporter of ministerial papers such as *John Bull*; Eldon, in his capacity as Lord Chancellor, was little more than a sturdy ministerial hack. Each of these portraits could easily turn political, yet Hazlitt again refuses to come up to scratch. The essay on Lord Eldon begins by asserting that the Chancellor is "good-natured," but proceeds to redefine this quality as an "indolent selfishness" borne of "indifference to the common feelings of humanity" (*New Monthly* 11 [1824], 17). Hazlitt insistently discovers the selfish motive under each of Eldon's superficially admirable qualities, and he ultimately traces his politics to self-interest. "The personal," writes Hazlitt, "always prevails over the intellectual, where the latter is not backed by strong feeling and principle" (p. 19).

A significant textual variation complicates consideration of the essay on Scott. The version of this essay included in *The Spirit of the Age*, which has become the standard text, culminates with a long paragraph containing a vitriolic denunciation of Scott's politics. This attack does not appear in the magazine, and while it is certain that Hazlitt had already written it,[13] the history of its suppression is a blank. It is likely that the ever vigilant Campbell would have cut it, if not his deputy editor Redding (or Colburn, for that matter), and we cannot, given his relatively subdued political voice in the magazine, rule out Hazlitt himself. The version that appears in the *New Monthly* provides a curiously unpolitical reading of the Scotch novels – "They are a relief to the mind, rarified as it has been with modern philosophy, and heated with ultra-radicalism" (*New Monthly* 10 [1824], 302) – and takes pains to show Scott as a reconciler of extremes and a clarifier of prejudices. Although Scott's bias is to "Legitimacy," Hazlitt notes that his defense of it is a curious one, as it often relies on heroes who are Jacobins or rebels. The picture that emerges is one of a writer whose genius is beyond his own comprehension, whose stated intentions as a Tory apologist cannot match his own performance. Without the suppressed (or canceled) final paragraph, the portrait of Scott, like the other "Spirits of the Age," exemplifies the strategies of aestheticization, irony, and poetization of the subjectified occasionalism that marks the *New Monthly*.

The *New Monthly*, despite its occasional professions to the contrary, has a coherent ideology. At decisive moments, as well as in unguarded ones, it follows the line of liberal bourgeois capitalism. It attacks the idle and ceremonial aristocracy, champions free trade, worries about popular unrest, advocates freedom of the press and the free exchange of ideas, and asserts selection by merit over connection or caste. In literature and the fine arts it unfailingly castigates the last century's patron–client relation, putting all its faith and reliance in booksellers and in the audience. Writers in the *New Monthly* are very conscious of the emergence of the middle class, the class that, as Redding writes, "gives a tone to public feeling, and the united opinion of which is irresistible" (*New Monthly* 10 [1824], 173).

The magazine's kind of Romanticism, its "subjectified occasionalism," is made possible by the circumstances of its middle-class readership. England, after the crisis years of 1818–21, enjoyed an expanding economy and relative political stability on the Continent. What *Blackwood's* attacked as "conciliation" in politics – overtures by from the Tories to the beaten and dispersed Whigs – was one manifestation of the relative calm of the era. Amidst moneymaking and general prosperity, the *New Monthly* sought to expand the personal world at the expense of larger political and social considerations.

By 1825 *Blackwood's* had settled into a less truculent, less experimental form. The *London*, after John Scott's death and years of weak management by John Taylor, had become irrelevant. As Redding notes in an 1846 recollection in the magazine, the *New Monthly* remained, at least throughout Campbell's editorship (until January 1831), "the widest circulated at the highest price of all works in its class."[14] The magazine consolidated its grip on the middle class market in January 1825 with the addition of Charles Lamb and Leigh Hunt, the latter of whom could be said to have brought the "subjectified occasionalism" of the magazine to its greatest pitch. The *New Monthly* establishes a kind of Romanticism, one that endures even today, and one that can, as in the case of Schmitt's critique, be mistaken for the entire movement. Romanticism, clearly, is so wide a movement that even its bitterest enemies, such as Schmitt, can prove partly correct in their attacks. For the student of the kinds of Romanticism, such opposition is indeed true friendship.

CHAPTER FIVE

Sartor Resartus *in* Fraser's
toward a dialectical politics

Sartor Resartus is, as Thomas Carlyle himself termed it, a "questionable little book."[1] Commentators have been sharply divided over its genre: one insisting that it is a novel, one that it is "a form of the persuasive essay," still others an anti-novel.[2] Its unity has been debated: one critic finding its last four chapters obtrusive ("a coda to the biography and the clothes philosophy, perhaps even marring the symmetry"); another contending that it is "a work of fragments: but it is a work, the whole somehow fused into unity."[3] Finally, *Sartor* has figured prominently in antithetical accounts of English Romanticism. M. H. Abrams, in a typically precise formulation, notes that Teufelsdröckh's life recalls "the familiar Romantic model of the self-formative educational journey, which moves through division, exile, and solitariness toward the goal of a recovered home and restored familial relationship,"[4] while Anne Mellor argues that *Sartor* "exhibit[s] a structure that is deliberately open-ended and inconclusive."[5] Questionable indeed.

This range of critical response can partly be attributed to the nature of *Sartor*. Carlyle had spent much of the 1820s introducing German literature and philosophy to the British reading public, and *Sartor* bristles with this learning. Hence it is reasonable to connect the book with this intellectual tradition as well as the native one. There is a strongly autobiographical element to *Sartor*, one seemingly authorized by Carlyle in subsequent statements,[6] which makes it reasonable to read the book in this context. The book presents shifting and conflicting centers of authority, as the editor by turns comments upon and quotes at length Teufelsdröckh's philosophical work, *Die Kleider*. Hence the editor of *Sartor* becomes a reliable guide for some critics, a shrewd expository device for others, and, for many, a humorous impediment to understanding the clothes philosophy. Finally, Carlyle affects what Elia termed "that most dangerous figure – irony,"[7] which adds to the instability of the performance.

Yet another part of this book's remarkable productivity lies in the tendency on the part of commentators to sever it from the material circumstances of its publication as a serial in a literary magazine. Begun as a two-part article for *Fraser's Magazine*, it grew into a book, failed to find a publisher, and emerged, much to Carlyle's chagrin, in the magazine. Notwithstanding its place in literary history as one of the characteristic texts of the early and middle Victorian period, *Sartor* has another, more specific time and place – in the pages of *Fraser's Magazine*. It stands there not only as the culmination of Carlyle's development as writer for magazines and periodicals, but also as the culmination of another development, that of the innovative and flexible essay fostered in the literary magazines of the 1820s. Its rejection there by the magazine's readers completes the first phase of British periodical literature in the nineteenth century.

Most importantly, however, a reading of *Sartor Resartus* in *Fraser's* permits the recovery of a singular meditation on politics – not simply the politics of parties, of voting, of bills, and of party loyalties, but politics in a larger sense, as a means of discussing and evaluating contemporary events without automatic recourse to the "Whig and Tory notches" that so exasperated Hazlitt. *Sartor* read in *Fraser's* concerns "the politics," that is, as the *Oxford English Dictionary* puts it, "public or social ethics, that branch of moral philosophy dealing with the state or the social organism as a whole." (That such a meaning of politics is, according to the most recent *Oxford English Dictionary*, "obsolete," is a pedantic bit of humor worthy of Teufelsdröckh himself.) Carlyle's odd masterpiece, read in its original serial form, presents a dialectical politics that contrasts sharply with the Burkean–Coleridgean political culture of the *London* under Scott, the rhetorically sophisticated Tory apologetics of *Blackwood's*, and the political Romanticism of the *New Monthly* – even as it owes something to each of them. *Sartor* was a failure in *Fraser's*, but it was a perfect fit for the magazine and a perfect culmination of the magazine tradition. Similarly, the dialectical politics that *Sartor* presents and *Fraser's* weakly echoes fails to find an audience in timid, post-Reform Bill England but nevertheless provides a culmination to the consideration of politics in the literary magazines of Romanticism.

"Narrative," wrote Carlyle in "On History," an 1830 essay for *Fraser's*, "is *linear*, Action is *solid*." The logic of this mathematical metaphor is exquisite: by it Carlyle intends that "actual events are nowise so simply related to each other as parent and offspring are" (*Fraser's* 2, 415) – that the action of cause and effect is more diffuse than historical narratives can possibly suggest. Carlyle's response to this representational impasse combines metaphysical nostalgia with shrewd practicality. He laments the absence of historians – really prophets – who can detect the workings of design in human action, who can rise above mechanical narratives to the illumination of teleological insight. Yet "On History" ends with a less ambitious plan for historical writing, which might "strive by running path after path, through the Impassable, in manifold directions and intersections, to secure for us some oversight of the Whole" (p. 418). Hence many narratives from a variety of perspectives might provide the "oversight" so elusive and so desirable.

Accounts of the genesis, composition, and emergence of *Sartor*, while generally agreeing on the events themselves, vary the relations of cause and effect considerably. I offer my account, one which emphasizes Carlyle's relations with *Fraser's Magazine*, less as corrective than in the spirit of a communal striving toward "oversight" of this complex action.[8]

Carlyle began *Sartor* in the fall of 1830 under conditions that were unpropitious. He had spent the previous decade establishing himself as a writer for magazines and periodicals, moving from piecework for the *Edinburgh Encyclopaedia*, to translations, to articles on German writers for magazines such as the *London* and later the *Foreign Review*, and finally to articles for the *Edinburgh Review*. This connection with the powerful Whig quarterly was especially gratifying to a writer who had struggled for a decade. In 1827 Francis Jeffrey had sought Carlyle out personally. Carlyle had, with typical bluntness, referred him to his recent work on German literature. Jeffrey commissioned an article on Richter, was delighted with its freshness and solid scholarship, and bespoke another on German literature for the fall. This was a valuable connection, one that might have been worked into a steady and substantial income, but Carlyle did not feel comfortable with the political stance of the *Edinburgh*. His 1829 "Signs of the Times" runs counter to the periodical's commitments to Enlightenment principles and to political economy. When MacVey Napier, who did not have Jeffrey's close personal relation to Carlyle, succeeded Jeffrey as editor in the fall of 1829, the connection grew tenuous. Meanwhile, the *Foreign Review*, a reliable source of money for Carlyle, seemed on the verge of collapse.

Prospects for literature in the early 1830s were generally poor. Political instability on the Continent, revolt by agricultural workers in Britain, and uncertainties in financial markets had depressed the book trade.

Moreover, the publishing business was changing rapidly, employing modern advertising techniques which required large amounts of capital. Publishers were mindful of the spectacular collapse of Constable in 1826, but they also noted the freewheeling, advertising-intensive success of Bentley & Co. Literature was particularly risky for publishers. Novels followed well-established – if not altogether exhausted – formulae: either as "tines" of the silver-fork school or as historical epics that weakly recalled Walter Scott. Poetry was cautious, if not moribund: early works by Tennyson and Browning failed, and activity centered on elegantly packaged poetic annuals and registers. This flat market would not improve greatly until the mid-thirties, when Chapman & Hall matched Dickens with the serial form for *The Pickwick Papers*.

The first number of *Fraser's Magazine* appeared in 1830. Edited by William Maginn, the venture was backed by (and named for) Hugh Fraser and published by James Fraser (no relation). Maginn, long a contributor to *Blackwood's* and the "Doctor" of "Noctes Ambrosianae," had recently found the magazine less friendly to him, and he sought a new venue partly in retaliation. *Fraser's* opened with verve, achieving quick success and a robust circulation of 8,700 by the end of the year.[9] The magazine positioned itself as a London version of Edinburgh's *Blackwood's*: just as Tory, but considerably less stuffy. It sought to recall the early days of the magazine, especially its attacks on personalities and cutting, occasionally cruel humor. Unlike *Blackwood's*, however, the politics of Maginn's new magazine are more self-conscious. Its description of itself as being "under the counsel of Coleridge and the countenance of Scott" suggests a sophistication beyond the "two or three principles . . . religion, loyalty, and the like" that Odoherty lauds in Christopher North, the fictive editor of *Blackwood's*.[10] Against the great quarterlies, *Fraser's* offered a more rapid response to political events, fiction, travel accounts, and personal essays as well as the quarterlies' stock in trade, the critical review essay.

The structure of *Fraser's* was straightforward: for each number Maginn usually provided two or three sheets (one sheet was sixteen pages out of the one hundred and twenty-eight that made up a number). He set the political tone of the magazine with what amounts to a series of position papers, and he acted as chief polemicist as well, applying these principles to specific issues as they arose from month to month.

Carlyle's first submissions to *Fraser's*, resuscitations of older unpublished material, were simply expedient. He needed money, and the magazine needed material. The relation of *Sartor* and *Fraser's* began in earnest when Carlyle received a packet of numbers in early September 1830. After considering the tenor of the magazine carefully, Carlyle began the first version of *Sartor*, tentatively entitled "Thoughts on Clothes," as an article for *Fraser's*. In a letter of 10 October to his mother Carlyle seems unsure whether it will be "a Book or a string of Magazine Articles,"[11] and in a letter to his brother shortly thereafter he describes it as "begun as an article for Fraser; then found too long (except it were divided into two)" (*Collected Letters*, vol. v, p. 175). His indecision about the length of the work persisted. In January 1831 he asked his brother John, then in London, to retrieve it from Fraser, and he spent March through August expanding the manuscript.

Having finished what he now considered to be a book, Carlyle borrowed £60 from Jeffrey and set off for London in search of a publisher. Murray dithered, Longmans declined outright, and James Fraser agreed to print only if Carlyle advanced him £150. Murray, despite Jeffrey's intervention on Carlyle's behalf, sent the manuscript to a reader and, the report being unfavorable, declined as well. Carlyle put the book aside and turned to other work. A year and a half later, Carlyle informs his brother in a letter that his "chief project for the summer is to cut Teufelsdreck into slips, and have it printed in Fraser's Magazine. . . .the Book-trade being still dead, – and as I reckon forever" (*Collected Letters*, vol. vi, p. 388). Ten days later Carlyle wrote a careful letter to James Fraser proposing serialization. He recalls the original circumstances of the book's rejection in 1831 and hazards that it was "perhaps better adapted" (*Collected Letters*, vol. vi, p. 395) for publication in a periodical and that to take it "a few chapters at a time is perhaps the most profitablest way of reading it" (p. 396). His description of the work deserves close attention:

It is put together in the fashion of a kind of Didactic Novel; but indeed properly *like* nothing yet extant. I used to characterize it briefly as a kind of "Satirical Extravaganza on Things in General"; it contains more of my opinions on Art, Politics, Religion, Heaven, Earth and Air, than all the things I have yet written. The Creed promulgated on all these things, as you may judge, is *mine* and firmly *believed*: for the rest, the main Actor in the business ("Editor of these sheets" as he often calls himself) assumes a kind of Conservative (tho' Antiquack) character; and would suit *Fraser* perhaps better than any other Magazine. The ultimate result, however, I need hardly premise, is a deep religious speculative-radicalism (so I call it for want of a better name), with which you are already well enough acquainted in me. (p. 396)

Fraser agreed to take *Sartor* in serial, and Carlyle worked from May to September, revising it for *Fraser's*.

The serial began in November of 1833 and ran until August of the following year. The reception of *Sartor* was hostile – one reader of *Fraser's* complaining violently at the publisher's office – and no reprint in book form materialized until, through Ralph Waldo Emerson's kind efforts, an American edition appeared in 1836. Despite the success of *The French Revolution* in 1837, the 1838 English appearance of *Sartor* was a small run of 500 on half profits. Carlyle read the proofs; in a letter of 14 July 1838 Carlyle states that "There is no change in *Teufk* from the genuine Fraser Copy" (*Collected Letters*, vol. x, p. 121). The second English edition, a run of 1000, was also proofed by Carlyle: "Him I print according to the printed copy, and correct only with pencil, a *comma* or so in the page" (*Collected Letters*, vol. xiii, p. 30). *Sartor* began to make money for its author in 1841, and it subsequently proved one of the greatest successes of the century.

It is apparent from this sketch that Carlyle's intentions varied. At times he was unsure just what form this work would take; at others the mode of the emergence was unclear. There are three versions of *Sartor*: the two-part article sent to Fraser in the fall of 1830, the manuscript intended as a book completed in the summer of 1831, and the manuscript sent to the printer in slips in the fall of 1833. It was begun for a magazine, specifically *Fraser's*, expanded for publication as a book, and revised for serial publication in *Fraser's*. Only the last version remains, which leaves the nature of the earlier two versions open to speculation. Evidence suggests that the first version roughly corresponds to the first book of *Sartor*, but, beyond the additions of passages directed to Oliver Yorke (the fictional editor of *Fraser's*), we do not know the nature of Carlyle's revisions as he prepared his manuscript for serialization. Carlyle's remarks in letters are not helpful: in a May letter to his brother he calls the revision his "chief project for the summer" (*Collected Letters*, vol. vi, p. 388), but in a June letter to his mother he speaks of the book as in need of "a very little sorting" (*Collected Letters*, vol. vi, p. 407). (That Carlyle chose not to revise *Sartor* yet again for the first or second English editions, which he proofread, is unsurprising, given the circumstances of the editions. The English editions over which he had some control followed American editions which had reproduced the magazine text. Moreover, seven years had passed since he had attempted to publish the book version of *Sartor*. Carlyle had begun other projects which fully engaged his attention.)

Therefore, when we read *Sartor* out of the *Fraser's* context, we honor Carlyle's fondest wishes (and as students of literary and intellectual history we repeat faithfully the reading experience of most Victorians), but we do not have the text of *Sartor* that embodies this authorial intention. What we have, in terms of Carlyle's ideal conception, is a compromise, the exact nature of which we can only guess at. However, in terms of his express intention when he produced what came to be the final version of *Sartor*, the serial in *Fraser's*, we have an excellent text. For Carlyle there was a difference, and, respecting his deep practicality, we might honor that as well.[12]

We can also make a positive case for a reading of *Sartor* in terms of the magazine. In a letter of January 1834 to John Stuart Mill, Carlyle explains that certain kinds of magazines provide advantages for persuasion:

I approve greatly of your purpose to discard Cant and Falsehood of all kinds: yet there is a kind of Fiction, which is not Falsehood, and has more effect in addressing men than many a Radical is aware of. This has struck me much of late years in considering *Blackwood* and *Fraser*: both these are furnished as it were with a kind of theatrical costume, with orchestra and stage-lights, and thereby alone have a wonderful advantage; perhaps almost their only advantage. For nothing was ever truer than this: *Ubi homines sunt modi sunt*; a maxim which grows with me in significance the longer I meditate it; modifying innumerable things in my Philosophy. The Radicals, as you may observe, appear universally *naked* (except so far as decency goes); and really have a most prosaic aspect. Barren, barren, as the Sahara sand is that Speculation of theirs (as for example, in *Tait*); almost more afflicting, only that it is *not* poisonous, than the putrid fermenting mud of *Fraser*! – The grand secret, I fancy, is that the Radicals as yet have almost no *genius* (tho' now not absolutely none); and so with prosaic *sense* and a vehement belief must do the best they can. (*Collected Letters*, vol. VII, p. 71–2)

Such advocacy, however cautious, is unusual for Carlyle: more typical, especially in his letters to Mill, are dismissive comments on magazines like *Fraser's*. The figural alignments within the passage are complex, but distinct, connecting the central image of *Sartor* – clothes – with germination and growth. In doing so, it points us back to the "putrid fermenting mud of *Fraser*" with a mixture of repulsion and admiration that is characteristic of Carlyle's attitude toward the magazine.

The fit between *Sartor* and *Fraser's*, like that between "Noctes Ambrosianae" and *Blackwood's*, is much more profound than those explored in other chapters of this study. Elia's relation to the *London* is largely crafted by John Scott, who saw a dimension in the essays that was congenial to the tone of the magazine and that could be made more prominent by careful presentation. In an act that is essentially critical,

Scott appropriates the Elia essays from the outside by providing a coherent reading for them. Similarly, Scott negotiates with Hazlitt for the production of a kind of personal essay amenable to the *London*'s Burkean–Coleridgean literary culture. Campbell's relation to his essayists takes the form of a straightforward prohibition: no politics disturb the "calm spot" of the *New Monthly*. *Sartor*, however, is shaped both internally and externally by *Fraser's*. If Lamb, Hazlitt, Redding, and Smith produced essays that were suitable for framing by magazines, Carlyle has produced an essay that has incorporated aspects of the frame. Hence an analysis must proceed on several levels at once. We need to look closely at the state of the manuscript that Carlyle delivered to the magazine, part by part, in order to see the unity and clarity of the individual installments. Moving outside the text, we need to examine the ways in which *Fraser's* tried to accommodate *Sartor*. Finally, the brilliance with which *Sartor* anticipates and internalizes the frame of the magazine deserves attention.

Critics typically lament the serialization of *Sartor*, finding the breaks in the text awkward and attributing the miserable initial reception of *Sartor* to the confusion this format caused its readers. Yet, upon examination, the cuts made by Carlyle in preparing the manuscript seem judicious. The individual installments of *Sartor* show as much unity and clarity as one finds in most individual numbers of the greatest Victorian serial novels.

One would be hard pressed to find awkwardness in the endings to each part of the serial. There are eight installments of *Sartor*, hence seven divisions. Two of these, the second and the fifth, fall at the ends of Books One and Two of the three into which Carlyle divides the text. The first installment (Book One, chapters 1–4) ends with the Editor's general remarks on *Die Kleider*, which provide a sense of closure. The third offers the first four chapters of Book Two, which concern Professor Teufelsdröckh's infancy and youth. The fourth begins with the romance with Blumine, which is narrated to its crisis, the sight of the carriage carrying Teufelsdröckh's friend Towgood and Blumine on their wedding journey in "The Everlasting No," and concludes with the devastation felt by Teufelsdröckh. The sixth installment (Book Three, chapters 1–5) culminates nicely in "The Phoenix," a chapter which begins by explicitly drawing the lesson of the previous four chapters. The seventh part, which closes with the rhapsodic discussion of "natural supernaturalism," ends roundly with a quotation from *The Tempest*.

Neat as these cuts are, the unity of the individual installments of *Sartor* is far more striking. The first installment demonstrates the level of coherence found within each part of the serial – both in terms of exposition and narrative. Chapter 1, "Preliminary," has a double function. It not only announces the stated subject of *Sartor*, the introduction of Diogenes Teufelsdröckh's *Die Kleider, ihr Werden und Wirken* (clothes, their origin and influence) to the English reader, but it also sets the vertiginous rhetorical mode of the serial, in which unusual, even grotesque metaphors are introduced and extended. Qualifications which unsettle the initial effect of the figure follow, and some figures are drawn out into lists which render their original force ambiguous.[13] Uncertainties about Teufelsdröckh's philosophy of clothes burgeon into uncertainties about the Professor himself, and this difficulty is registered by the disruption and distention of the figural language with which the Editor seeks to clarify these ambiguities. The second chapter in the installment, "Editorial Difficulties," examines the instabilities of the political and historical moment of *Sartor*, not neglecting their effects on literature and literary magazines. The next chapter, "Reminiscences," sketches the character of Teufelsdröckh: his mysterious political utterances (and disappearance), his night thoughts, and his silences. Emblematic of this chapter, notable for its whimsy and its juxtaposition of soaring transcendental thought with lower middle-class life, is the Editor's account of the last words he heard spoken by Teufelsdröckh. The Professor's toast – "The cause of the Poor, in the name of God and the Devil!" – made at a moment of political unrest, draws an ambiguous response from his audience at a coffee-house in Weissnichtwo, much as his philosophy perplexes the Editor. The final chapter of the installment, "Characteristics," considers Teufelsdröckh's prose style, thought, and morality. Their mixed character renders them ambiguous, as is the case with the Editor's account of the only time he heard the Professor laugh. The installment closes with the Editor's promise: "To bring what order we can out of this Chaos shall be part of our endeavour" (*Fraser's* 8 [1833], 592).

Such "cuts" leave little to be desired. The installment clearly sets out its topic, introduces the Editor and Professor Teufelsdröckh, and, through the Editor's attempts to bring order to the chaos of his subject's life and thoughts, provides an intriguing narrative tension. It prepares the reader for the more exacting exposition of the next installment, a detailed presentation of the clothes-philosophy. The installments which follow are equally attentive to the unity of the part.[14] It could easily be argued that the fitting of *Sartor* to *Fraser's*, insofar as the form of the work might have been affected, was no more of a disadvantage than serial publication was to many Victorian novels. In fact, given the difficulty of the text, it may well be an advantage to read it in the small, coherent parts of the serial.[15]

If Carlyle did his job in preparing the opening installment of *Sartor* for serial publication, so did Maginn, whose contributions to the November number help to introduce and reinforce the serial in a variety of ways. Writing with J. A. Heraud, Maginn reviews a recent republication of an apocryphal book in a style that recalls Teufelsdröckh himself:

Is the mind itself an inspiration? Is not man himself a revelation? Through what, save and except human agency, may news of the invisible world come to man? What reveals Nature to herself? Only to the Spirit in a human form has she a tale to tell – only to his questionings. And then answers she? Nay, but out of her silence it is that the Spirit shapes the responses – even as he will. What reveals she to him, in silence or eloquence – her silence the most eloquent of all things – what reveals she to him thus? Himself! (*Fraser's* 8 [1833], 12–13)

There is bombast enough here, but also a foreshadowing of some of *Sartor*'s most earnest assertions: that revelation is ongoing; that "responses" – that is, more or less provisional and more or less satisfactory revelations – are provided, and not absolute truth; that humans shape, or, as Carlyle will have it, "tailor," their beliefs; that silence, as will be seen in the figure of Teufelsdröckh, is a mysterious and blessed state. The review continues in a similar vein:

every one such is a poet, or a man inspired, an artist, or divine person. He it is who creates and turns to shape. The airy nothing? No; but the most substantial something – his own identical self! From that great whole of phenomena which fools call nature, but which the wise know to be only that of so many modifications of our own several being, he constructs a world and its hero, the Creator-creature, Author and Saviour, Demi-god and Man! (p. 513)

Not only is this a good approximation of Carlylese – right down to Carlyle's tic of half-invoking Shakespeare – but the anticipation of specific thematic concerns from *Sartor* is unmistakable.

To catch other resonances in the number, it is perhaps more convenient to work outwards from Carlyle's text. The opening paragraphs of *Sartor*, which situate the work amid the turbulence of political reform, find echo throughout the November number in articles by Maginn. The Editor, described by Carlyle in his letter to Fraser as "Conservative (tho' Antiquack)," reminds his reader that: "It is, after all, a blessing that, in these revolutionary times, there should be one country where abstract Thought can still take shelter; that while the din and frenzy of Catholic

Emancipation, and Rotten Boroughs, and Revolts of Paris, deafen every French and English ear, the German can stand peaceful on his scientific watchtower" (*Fraser's* 8 [1833], 581–2). This conservative perspective, in which any opposition to Tory principle becomes "din and frenzy," is seconded throughout the number by the strictures of "The First Session of the Reformed Parliament," by Maginn's attack on Harriet Martineau in the "Gallery of Literary Characters," and by Maginn's reply to economic analysis offered by the *Westminster Review* in "On National Economy." Later in the same chapter *Sartor*'s Editor clarifies his own politics:

he is animated with a true though perhaps a feeble attachment to the Institutions of our Ancestors; and minded to defend these, according to ability, at all hazards; nay, it was partly with a view to such defence that he engaged in this undertaking. To stem, or if that were impossible, profitably to divert the current of Innovation, such a Volume as Teufelsdröckh's, if cunningly planted down, were no despicable pile, or floodgate, in the logical wear. (p. 584)

This fear of innovation, which recalls the conservative diversionary tactics of Swift in *A Tale of a Tub*, animates the article that directly follows this installment of *Sartor*. The writer of "India and England" laments the change in John Bull, that conservative icon, whose "quaint but harmless prejudices" and "distinctive character among the nations" have been adulterated by "the motley robes of Liberalism." John Bull's innovations, his "mimetic follies," spoil him for the demanding role of imperialist governor, and they render him "a spectacle of pity for his friends, and of derision for his foes" (p. 595).

But perhaps the most effective bit of editorial framing lies in Maginn's inclusion of an admittedly questionable paper, "The Arcana of Freemasonry." Printed with a disclaimer (that *Fraser's* presents it for the subject, not the style), the article exceeds even Teufelsdröckh's rhetoric:

Now many a man, who hath well apprehended in the beginning the divine principles of truth, would have been overwhelmed by their abstract vastness, or perplexed by the complicate variety, or overthrown by their seeming opposition, but that he happily discovered in the character of some saint, or sage, or philosopher, a character so congenial to his own intrinsically and parallel circumstantiality, in which the truth he had well nigh despaired of was so finely imaged and exhibited, that the single recollection of that character in its vital unity did more to establish his own, and more to perfect it, than long seasons of metaphysical research, however sincere and anxious, could otherwise have achieved. (p. 569)

While such convoluted syntax lessens the apparent excesses of Teufelsdröckh's ruminations, it also should be noted that the idea here, that certain humans embody "the truth," parallels the Editor's soaring estimation of "a quite new human Individuality, an almost unexampled personal character, that, namely, of Professor Teufelsdröckh the Discloser" (p. 583). For both Carlyle and the author of "The Arcana of Freemasonry," exemplary men provide lesser humans access to the truth through their biographies. Later, "The Arcana of Freemasonry" sounds another note from *Sartor*: the Freemasons, like Teufelsdröckh himself, seek "the intimate relations existing between spiritual and material natures" (p. 575). The pomposity of the article renders the hyperbole of *Sartor* less singular.

Few readers of *Fraser's* would register all these echoes, which serve to foreground or to re-enforce particular thematic aspects of *Sartor*, but the sheer number of these resonances insures that some will be caught. One line of argument, however, could not fail to be traced in *Sartor* and in *Fraser's*: the attack on *laissez-faire* economics and on political economy generally. In a series of articles, one *Fraser's* contributor (probably Maginn himself), carries on a running argument about free trade with an author in the *Westminster Review*. In the November installment, "On National Economy. No. ix," the author meets particular arguments of his liberal opponent with a mixture of statistics and anecdotal evidence, but, as is his practice, he carefully connects his economic analysis to political principles. For the Tory propagandist, the recourse of the free-traders to the good of the "larger whole" repeatedly countenances the destruction of visible parts, and the consequences for the poor are cat-astrophic. The *Fraser's* writer summarizes (and not unfairly) one axiom of the liberal argument thus: "a man who has come honestly by his prop-erty, whether through his own labour or that of his parents, is under no obligation whatever to consider any person in the world, except himself and those who are his own, in the disposal of it" (*Fraser's* 8 [1833], 612). The *Fraser's* writer argues that Tory belief opposes (or should oppose) this narrow self-interest. He clearly outlines the difference between feudal and bourgeois social orders, insisting on the virtues of the older system's "relative duties" between rich and poor. Such nostalgia for feudal relations is prominent throughout *Sartor* in Teufelsdröckh's repeated attacks on "Utilitaria" and "Motive-Millwrights."

Compared to John Scott's editorial procedures, those of the November number of *Fraser's* are crude. Moreover, Maginn's efforts lack the consistency of those in the *London*. Maginn launched the opening installment of *Sartor* with considerable fanfare, but the quality and amount of framing varies in other numbers. Such inconsistency was characteristic of *Fraser's*: at times Maginn was capable of giving a focus and a clarity to a number that no review and few magazines could match. But other numbers are diffuse, at times as random as the "old series" of the *New Monthly*, which for several years had no editor at all. Nevertheless Carlyle shrewdly turns this inconsistency to advantage in fitting the text of *Sartor* to *Fraser's*. In the second chapter of the first installment, the Editor contemplates the difficulties of publication:

If, indeed, the whole Parties of the State could have been abolished, Whig, Tory and Radical, embracing in discrepant union; and the whole Journals of the Nation could have been jumbled into one Journal, and the Philosophy of Clothes poured forth in incessant torrents therefrom, the attempt had seemed possible. But, alas, what vehicle of that sort have we, except Fraser's Magazine? A vehicle all strewed (figuratively speaking) with the maddest Waterloo-Crackers, exploding distractively and destructively, wheresoever the mystified passenger stands or sits. (*Fraser's* 8 [1833], 583)

On one level such a passage stands as the typical cross-talk of literary magazines, asides which reassure readers of their status as knowing insiders. These self-referential gestures usually have no meaning whatsoever, aside from adding a patina of urbanity. Clearly this section of the text would not have been present in the book version Carlyle sought to publish in 1831. But by adding it for the serial version, Carlyle does more than mark his text as Fraserite. In describing the Editor's chosen "vehicle" as nationalist ("Waterloo-Crackers"), violent, and disorganized, Carlyle prepares his reader for the demanding character of the serial to follow. By insisting on the "mystified passengers" – the readers – he attempts to lessen *Sartor*'s strangeness. Finally, by describing the magazine as a place where party-divisions are "abolished," Carlyle shrewdly prepares for the complex political dialectic that the interplay of his conservative Editor and "speculative radical" Professor will set in motion.

This dialectic becomes evident as the Editor surveys Teufelsdröckh's book in the December installment of *Sartor*. As in the first part, *Sartor* suffers little from the form imposed by serialization. The installment has a straightforward structure: the first three chapters take up the origins of the clothes philosophy, the second three consider its influences, and the final chapter sets out the Editor's misgivings about the political and social ramifications of Teufelsdröckh's thought. In the initial three chapters of the installment, the Editor finds Teufelsdröckh's ideas congenial – that is, insofar as he finds them comprehensible at all. The conservative Editor affirms the Professor's attack on "Cause-and-Effect philosophy," for which human intelligences have little use. The Editor casually dismisses parts of Teufelsdröckh's historical treatment of clothes as he marvels at the surprising nature of the Professor's moral interjections. But as the clothes volume turns from "werden" to "wirken," the Editor grows nervous. In the chapter "Adamatism," he wonders at the "Sansculottist" sympathies apparent in Teufelsdröckh's deconstruction of the social hierarchy supported by clothes. The Editor's conservatism is shaken by the Professor's vision of a world in which "the Clothes fly-off the whole dramatic corps; and Dukes, Grandees, Bishops, Generals, Anointed Presence itself, every mother's son of them, stand straddling there, not a shirt on them; and I know not whether to laugh or weep" (p. 678). The Editor, with his "true though perhaps a feeble attachment to the Institutions of our Ancestors" (p. 584), is no match for Teufelsdröckh's apparent "Adamatism," his embrace and celebration of change. And herein lies the complexity of the relation between the Editor and Teufelsdröckh: however much the Editor, like the Professor, deplores the current state of society, he cannot bear to see the wrenching transformation that Teufelsdröckh's argument seems to encompass. In the final chapter of the second installment of *Sartor* the Editor articulates this difficulty in suitably Teufelsdröckhian rhetoric: "Is that a real Elysian brightness, cries many a timid wayfarer, or the reflex of Pandemonian lava? Is it of a truth leading us into beatific Asphodel meadows, or the yellow-burning marl of a Hell-on-Earth?" (p. 681). In other words, if "Society is founded on Cloth" – hence subject to wear and replacement – what makes a particular dispensation legitimate? If institutions, and even religious systems, are contingent, what force do they have?

The wary encounter between conservative and speculative radical made emphatic in the second part of *Sartor* is, seen from the present, a strange one. But Maginn sketches a similar rapprochement in "The State and the Prospects of Toryism," which appears in the following number of *Fraser's*. There Maginn divides the political world into two: Constitutionalists (by which he means the Tories) and Republicans (the Radicals). (Despite their current ascendency, the Whigs are simply trimmers and self-interested hypocrites.) Maginn's analysis of the situation, in which opposites find common ground, prefigures the relation of the Editor and Teufelsdröckh. Maginn recognizes, although he does not accept, the democratic position of the Radicals. Unlike the Whigs, they have principles and these deserve consideration. According to Maginn, the Radicals, despite their dislike of the monarchy, the aristocracy, and the House of Lords, know that abolishing them would lead to civil war. They may argue on principle that sensible men favor a republic, but it is clear that another position may be argued by experience, that of a limited monarchy. No republics have lasted, many monarchies have. Monarchies, he concludes, with their many checks, offer stability. Rudimentary (and self-interested) as this argument is, it is dialectical rather than dogmatic in its resolution of opposites by the introduction of a third term. Hence one of *Sartor*'s most unusual features, its complex dialectic between political opposites, is echoed in the pages of *Fraser's Magazine*. Moreover, while the specifics of Maginn's solution differ from that hinted at by Carlyle, the underlying principle – that of stability – is one that *Sartor* will eventually embrace.

Maginn concludes "The State and the Prospects of Toryism" with a restatement of Tory principles: nationalism, patriotism, reciprocal duties, paternalism, establishment of the Church of England, and resistance to the hegemony of manufacturing and commercial interests. But he seems to value them less in themselves than as ways of achieving stability in a rapidly changing world. *Sartor*'s Editor, in a similar fashion, will accept Teufelsdröckh's ideas only when he finds a mystical conservatism in them.

Before this acceptance, however, the Editor turns to the biographical material on Teufelsdröckh he has received from Herr Heuschreke. In book form, this material makes up Book Two of *Sartor*; as a serial, it forms three installments. As in the cases of November and December parts, these installments have considerable formal polish. The February installment recounts the Professor's formative years: from his arrival as foundling, through his idyllic childhood years and education at school, gymnasium, and university, and finally to the resistance he meets in his legal career. The pacing of the narrative is remarkable: the mystery of Teufelsdröckh's genealogy and the mythic resonances of his childhood give way to the constraints he endures under the present social order. The culmination of the part, Teufelsdröckh's mocking epitaph for a nobleman, neatly expresses his lack of direction and ironical bias. In the March installment, Teufelsdröckh falls in love, is jilted, and suffers a crisis of faith. The emblematic qualities of this narrative are clearly set out: Blumine, Teufelsdröckh's beloved, is presented as a sign of the "infinite"; hence romantic disappointment figures a more general loss of coherence, faith, and meaning. In a dramatic gesture that rivals the finish of a part in a work of serial fiction, the March installment concludes with a heroic flourish:

Thus, in spite of all Motive-grinders, and Mechanical Profit-and-Loss Philosophies, with the sick ophthalmia and hallucination they had brought on, was the infinite nature of Duty still dimly present to me: living without God in the world, of God's light was I not utterly bereft; if my as yet sealed eyes, with their unspeakable longing, could nowhere see Him, nevertheless in my heart He was present, and His heaven-written Law still stood legible and sacred there. (*Fraser's* 9 [1834], 312)

This manipulation of narrative tension continues in the next installment, which explores the consequences of Teufelsdröckh's defiant rejection of the "Everlasting No." This Romantic insistence of the self against the dead matter of the world brings about a visionary phase for the Professor, who, as he begins to trace the action of the spirit on matter, feels less alienated from the world. After this conversion, Teufelsdröckh casts about for the work particularly suited to his nature. Similarly, the Editor, while still ambivalent about the worth of the biographical documents he has organized, asserts that he has provided the "ultimate bent" (*Fraser's* 9, 455) of Teufelsdröckh's character and looks ahead to a systematic treatment of the clothes philosophy in the final book of *Sartor*.

Carlyle divided the third book of *Sartor* into three installments for *Fraser's*. Each serial part deftly clarifies a thematic concern within *Sartor* that finds echo in the magazine: the anxiety over the loss of social stability. Although Carlyle provides a complicated answer, the serial form makes it easier to grasp. Carlyle uses one of the oft-mentioned constraints of the serial – its divisions – as pauses to clarify his argument.

The June 1834 installment is perhaps the most perfect of the three. In it, the Editor succinctly renders the philosophy of clothes as he understands it and registers his uneasiness with its implications. By the close of the installment he has honed his misgivings into an objection – one that goes to the heart of *Sartor*'s difficult dialectic. The installment begins with the Editor's recognition of Teufelsdröckh's achievement:

Striking it was, amid all his perverse cloudiness, with what force of vision and of heart he pierced into the mystery of the World; recognising in the highest sensible phenomena, so far as Sense went, only fresh or faded Raiment; yet ever, under this, a celestial Essence thereby rendered visible: and while, on the one hand, he trod the old rags of Matter, with their tinsels, into the mire, he on the other everywhere exalted Spirit above all earthly principalities and powers, and worshipped it, though under the meanest shapes, with a true Platonic mysticism. (*Fraser's* 9, 664)

The difficulty for the Editor at this point is that the clothes philosophy seems to provoke as many difficulties as it solves. The doctrine seems to embrace change that is both revolutionary and unknown; the Editor's "feeble attachment to the Institutions of our Ancestors" finds this most disturbing. The rest of the installment cleverly prepares for the resolution of this difficulty.

The first chapter, "Incident in Modern History," presents Teufelsdröckh's thoughts on George Fox, the cobbler who founded Quakerism. The Professor, with typical whimsy, focuses less on Fox's ideas than on his manufacture of a "perennial suit of Leather." This confuses the Editor, who wonders whether the Professor has "his own deeper intention" and fears that Teufelsdröckh "laughs in his sleeve at our strictures and glosses" (p. 666). In the next chapter of *Sartor* the Editor addresses a "questionable" chapter in *Die Kleider*, one that concerns "Church-Clothes." His confusion, at least in this case, need not be shared by the reader, for whom the logic of this sequence becomes clear. Church-Clothes, according to Teufelsdröckh, are the various forms by which the religious principle is embodied in different ages. The present suit of Church-Clothes is worn out – that is, the religious impulse withdrawn from them for a generation and a half. This discussion makes the George Fox episode comprehensible: Fox's act of tailoring, however rough and unlovely, reminds the reader that the means of tailoring – that is, the visionary mode – needs no special preparation. The following chapter, "Symbols," reinforces this sequence: in it Carlyle encourages the reader to reconsider the significance of the George Fox episode. To see Fox's manufacture symbolically or, as Teufelsdröckh insists, as a combination of infinite and finite, is difficult at present. The work of "Motive-Millwrights," who have convinced humans that they are little more than a digestive apparatus, has all but precluded such a mode of vision. The attack on the "Genius of Mechanism" (p. 668) prepares for the fourth chapter, "Helotage." Teufelsdröckh's attack on Malthus is, read in terms of the doctrine of "Church-Clothes" or "Symbols," an attack on a particularly brutal aspect of the "Genius of Mechanism," the dominant philosophy of the present. The Professor's suggestion that the superabundant poor should, like Helots in Sparta, be hunted down and killed becomes a Swiftian reaction to Malthus's theory of population. The fifth chapter, "The Phoenix," culminates this line of development. Teufelsdröckh surveys the present to find the "Life-essence of Society," religion, "quite rent into shreds" and society itself "defunct" (p. 672). In this, he recalls the anxieties of the Editor and the bleaker outlook of Maginn and *Fraser's* generally. At this point the logic of Carlyle's unusual brand of conservative thought emerges. Teufelsdröckh counsels submission to "Utilitaria," a term which encompasses *laissez-faire* economics and Malthusian thought. But he does so in a negative dialectic: the embrace of the emerging capitalist economy will, according to Teufelsdröckh, hasten the destruction of an outmoded social order and usher in a vital one. The Professor's essential conservatism – in the sense of conservation of energy – abides even in this troubled and destructive phase. Viewed in terms of this complex dialectic, submission to the "Genius of Mechanism" provides a cure.

This brilliant and coherent exposition, perhaps the most perfect of the installments, prepares for the central sequence in *Sartor*, the July 1834 installment of the serial. There Teufelsdröckh's profound faith in tradition allays the Editor's misgivings. In the opening chapter of the part, "Old Clothes," the Editor muses over the Professor's deep attachment to the relics of outworn beliefs and institutions. The next chapter argues that such contemplation is not only nostalgic: as the old clothes are cast off, one discerns the new dispensation in what the Professor calls "organic filaments." Teufelsdröckh extends the figure (as the chapter on "Symbols" would lead us to expect) by insisting on the connection between generations:

nothing is completed, but ever completing. Newton has learned to see what Kepler saw; but there is also a fresh heaven-derived force in Newton; he must mount to still higher points of vision. So too the Hebrew Lawgiver is, in due time, followed by an Apostle of the Gentiles. In the business of Destruction, as this also is from time to time a necessary work, thou findest a like sequence and perseverance . . . Thus likewise, I note, the English Whig has, in the second generation, become an English Radical; who, in the third again, it is to be hoped, will become an English Rebuilder. (*Fraser's* 10, 80)

Hence the Professor's embrace of "Utilitaria," so disturbing to the Editor, becomes a necessary phase of a profound conservatism. Of course, the argument here, stripped of its figures and emotional language, depends on a stark appeal to faith. This attack on rationality culminates in the soaring spirituality of "Natural Supernaturalism" – in which custom is seen to blind humans to the miracle of everyday life and in which categories such as space or time preclude a fuller knowledge of the human condition.

The logic of the installment is cunning. Against the Editor's charges of "Adamitism" and "Sansculottism," Teufelsdröckh's ideas find persuasive form in the tripartite structure of the installment. The Professor appears in a nostalgic guise, which calms the Editor's fears; his conservative streak in "Organic Filaments" provides further comfort; and the mystical and prophetic strain of "Natural Supernaturalism" brings the Professor's persuasive appeal to a climax. By separating this sequence from the rest of Book Three of *Sartor*, serialization clarifies Carlyle's complex exposition.

Moreover, each of the three installments into which Book Three of *Sartor* was divided addresses a concern voiced in *Fraser's*. If Maginn's articles in the magazine set out certain social and economic concerns, then the June and July parts of *Sartor* reinforce or sharpen these views. Maginn insists that Malthusian analyses of poverty are flawed, and he often notes that the propagation of such ideas by factory owners is not disinterested. Teufelsdröckh's recommendation that the superfluous population be hunted emphasizes the point through satire. The Professor, who embraces "Utilitaria" only to speed the destruction of a worn-out social order, shares Maginn's detestation of political economy as well. However, Carlyle differs from the Editor of *Fraser's* in his understanding of the transformative force of capitalism. Like Marx and Engels in *The Communist Manifesto*, he shrewdly takes the measure of the system: like them, he sees its productive capacities as well as its pernicious tendencies; like them, he sees capitalism as inevitable; and like them, he sees it as a stage of social development. (Of course, unlike these other two thinkers, Carlyle envisions a very different kind of social order as the inevitable product of capitalism.) While Maginn's analysis of the contemporary social and economic upheaval is trenchant, his solution, a return to the conservative values of landed interests, is regressive. In Carlyle's dialectic, Maginn's position forms the thesis, and emerging bourgeois capitalism the antithesis: Tory and Radical oppositions merge in the mysticism of "Natural Supernaturalism."

After the soaring mysticism of "Natural Supernaturalism," one expects a drop as the next installment, the final one of the serial, begins. Critics have found its lapses more serious. G. B. Tennyson's complaints are typical: the last four chapters seem superfluous after the climax of "Natural Supernaturalism" and "perhaps even mar the symmetry" of the work.[16] Janice L. Haney finds that these chapters "collapse the imaginative donnée of the book," and she develops an emblematic reading for them, in which they trace Carlyle's journey from a Wordsworthian visionary Romanticism through a Germanic romantic irony to Victorian social concern.[17] Walter L. Reed, less inclined to see them as an interpretive crux, argues that the concluding chapters of *Sartor* "violate the imaginative pattern which informs the book."[18] Moreover the humor of Carlyle's division of society into Dandies and Tailors seems labored, and the relation of this practical inference to the argument of *Sartor* remains unclear. These strictures are compelling. The problem with them is that they apply to *Sartor* considered as a book, not a serial – to a text that we do not have, not to one that we possess. However inconsonant these

chapters seem when read in book form, they provide an excellent conclusion when read in the pages of *Fraser's Magazine*.

The structure of the last installment of *Sartor* is as unambiguous as
that of the previous parts. In the first chapter, "Circumspective," the
Editor, recalling the arduous nature of the journey so far, regrets the loss
of readers: some by impatience, some by engulfment in the chaos of
clothes philosophy. He briefly sets out the purpose of *Sartor*: "to Exhibit
the Wonder of daily life and common things; and to show that all Forms
are but Clothes, and temporary."[19] For readers who insist on utility, the
Editor promises to provide a practical application. An analysis of the
"Habilatory Class" of men – Dandies and Tailors – will follow.
Accordingly, the next two chapters are "The Dandiacal Body" and
"Tailors." In the first Teufelsdröckh reveals that the Dandy is "but a new
modification, adapted to the new time, of that primeval Superstition,
Self-worship" (*Fraser's* 10 [1834], 185). The splendor of this sect contrasts
with the self-denial of another, the Drudges. England is increasingly
composed of these two sects, one small and wealthy, the other enormous
and indigent. Their relation is unstable, and the Professor describes their
collision in apocalyptic terms. "Tailors" laments the low esteem in which
tailors are held and examines their metaphoric significance. In the final
chapter, "Farewell," the Editor registers "a mingled feeling of astonishment, gratitude, and disapproval" (p. 191) at Teufelsdröckh and his
clothes philosophy. He hints at the Professor's possible relations with revolutionary groups, ponders his disappearance, and reports rumors of his
presence in London. He concludes with a meditation that emphasizes
the serial basis of his relation to his audience: "Have we not, in the
course of Eternity, travelled some months of our Life-journey in partial
sight of one another; have we not existed together, though in a state of
quarrel?" (p. 193). With this questionable remark, the ten months of
Sartor's serialization end.

Given the Editor's assertion that "innumerable inferences of a practical nature may be drawn" from Teufelsdröckh's philosophy, we might
ponder the Editor's choice of "Dandies." On one level, such a move
seems purely capricious, especially viewed against the Editor's insistence
on "utility" in his demonstration. Of course, on another level, it cleverly
recalls the obsessional character of Teufelsdröckh, to whom no discussion of cloth is unwelcome. Read in these terms, *Sartor* finishes with more
of the ambiguous humor that appears throughout the work. Yet the
choice has additional significance for the reader of *Fraser's*. The magazine had targeted a contemporary dandy with great success in earlier

numbers: Edward Bulwer-Lytton. Bulwer had since become a convenient whipping-boy for *Fraser's*: an emblem of all that was cockney, presumptuous, tasteless, over-praised, and false. Carlyle's genius is to
reinterpret this familiar figure for the audience of *Fraser's* in a way that
exemplifies the dialectical method he pursues throughout *Sartor*. At such
moments as this, the "mud" of *Fraser's* – to return to Carlyle's description of the magazine quoted earlier – seems more "fermenting" than
"putrid."

No reader of *Fraser's* could have missed the specificity of the attack.
Maginn began the assault on Bulwer in a June 1830 article (one included
in the packet of numbers sent to Carlyle that may, in part, have sparked
Sartor). Articles in *Fraser's* bristle with sallies against Bulwer – at times
crudely obvious and at others oblique. Over time, disparagement of
Bulwer becomes one of the constituent features of the magazine.
Nowhere is Carlyle more overtly Fraserian than in his discussion of the
"Sacred Books" of the Dandiacal Sect. Teufelsdröckh's attempt to read
them recalls Maginn's professions of their incomprehensibility:

at the end of some short space, I was uniformly seized with not so much what
I can call a drumming in my ears, as a kind of infinite, insufferable, Jew's-
harping and scrannel-piping there; to which the fright-fullest species of
Magnetic Sleep soon supervened. And if I strove to shake this away, and absolutely would not yield, there came a hitherto unfelt sensation, as of *Delirium
Tremens*, and a melting into total deliquium: till at last, by order of the Doctor,
dreading ruin to my whole intellectual and bodily faculties, and a general break-
ing-up of my constitution, I reluctantly but determinedly forbore. (*Fraser's* 10
[1834], 185–6)

Such a passage could not fail to be interpreted in the context of other
attacks on the author of *Pelham*. In fact, if read simply as an extension of
a characteristic theme of *Fraser's*, "The Dandiacal Body" would provide
an amusing and fitting conclusion to *Sartor*: the "owlish purblindness" (p.
185) of the Professor would lead him at last to subjects familiar to the
audience, just as the final paragraphs of *Sartor* suggest that Teufelsdröckh
is "actually in London" (p. 193).

But if Elia's "jests scald like tears,"[20] Carlyle's parodies turn to par-
ables. He carefully interpellates his discussion of Dandies with material
that points beyond parody. The first passage from *Die Kleider* quoted by
the Editor links the appearance of dandies with the waning of religious
feeling: they are the product of a misdirected but powerful impulse
toward "some new Revelation" (p. 185). In this context, the Dandy's insistence that "you recognize his existence" (p. 184) and his "Self-worship"

(p. 185) powerfully recall Teufelsdröckh's protest against the Everlasting No: "and then it was that my whole ME stood up, in native God-created majesty, and with emphasis recorded its Protest" (*Fraser's* 9 [1834], 313). Neither assertion is religious, however much religiosity they contain, but they are critical steps in the process of tailoring the age's genuine Church-Clothes.

In itself, the rehabilitation of the Dandy would provide a finale worthy of *Sartor*. But it is in the imaginative extension of this figure that the profoundly dialectical cast of Carlyle's mind is evident. Having taken the measure of the Dandy, Carlyle turns from an analytical to a relational interpretive method. By putting the Dandy into play against a contrasting sect, the Drudges or Poor-Slaves, Carlyle manages to bring a social and political dimension to what has been largely a philosophical inquiry. The point by point comparison between the two sects is at once humorous and ominous, as its whimsy shifts to an examination of the gap between rich and poor. Teufelsdröckh's vision of apocalyptic destruction follows:

I could liken Dandyism and Drudgism to two bottomless boiling Whirlpools that had broken-out on opposite quarters of the firm land: as yet they appear only disquieted, foolishly bubbling wells, which man's art might cover-in; yet mark them, their diameter is daily widening: they are hollow Cones that boil-up from the infinite Deep, over which your firm land is but a thin crust or rind! (*Fraser's* 10 [1834], 189)

Carlyle is not coy about the agency here: in another figure, he presents the Dandy as the positive pole of an "Electric Machine," which "attracts hourly towards it and appropriates all the Positive Electricity of the nation (namely, the Money thereof)" (p. 189). Carlyle transforms the Dandy, once the object of scorn for the *Fraser's* reader, into an "organic filament," that is, a harbinger of the renovation of a worn-out society, and finally into an agent of destruction. Nowhere is the shaping force of the serial more evident than in the final part of *Sartor*. Carlyle turns his dialectic on an instance specifically fitted to the circumstances of his *Fraser's* readers, and in doing so he provides them with something very close to the lived experience of dialectical thought.

The ironies of Carlyle's meditation on politics are many. Through the vagaries of publication, *Sartor* emerges after the 1832 Reform Bill rather than in the anxious days before it, when Carlyle conceived and composed his work. Although its dialectical politics are a judgment on the concrete historical situation in which it arose, *Sartor* has, in the atmosphere of negotiation and compromise that the Bill ratifies, an oddly nostalgic feel. Its philosophical radicalism, its dynamic theories of class, and its insistence on conservation of energies rather than institutions have no place in the political settlement of the Reform Bill, which provides enfranchisement with all the mechanical and unfeeling pragmatism of a self-regulating cooling system.

That *Sartor* failed in its immediate purpose, as a reply to both the emerging liberal-bourgeois ideology and the intransigent conservatism of its day, is not surprising: its dialectic was much too complex for the purpose, and artistically it was too strange, even offensive, for its readers.[21] The shock of its complexity persisted until the standard Victorian reading of the book, which considered it largely as a spiritual biography, was developed. *Sartor* was fitted to an audience largely through the process of emphasizing Book Two, the biography of Teufelsdröckh, at the expense of its larger philosophical argument.[22]

What the *Fraser's* reader really wanted (and the publishing history demonstrates this clearly) was something like Francis Mahony's Prout papers. An examination of this successful series in *Fraser's* makes *Sartor*'s shortcomings obvious. The Prout papers first appeared in April 1834, when *Sartor* had run just over half its course in the magazine. Its success was immediate. Unlike *Sartor*, the first English edition of which appeared in 1838, almost four years after serialization, the *Prout Reliques* emerged in book form as soon as the serial had provided enough material.[23] The Prout series had much in common with *Sartor*. Father Prout, like Teufelsdröckh, is a man of staggering but erratic erudition given to flights of metaphor. Both are mysterious foundlings who live obscurely. Neither is the author of his series: each man has left papers that a puzzled editor arranges. Finally, both men are given to obscure explanations of society and history. For example, the first installment of the Prout papers reveals the "secret influences" (*Fraser's* 9 [1834], 494) that brought about the Reformation. According to Prout, Europe is divided racially into the Teutonics, the heavy feeders of the north, and the light-feeding Celts and Mediterraneans. The Protestant Reformation was a revolt against Lent – an attempt by Teutonics to return to continual heavy feeding.

But however much Prout recalls Teufelsdröckh, Mahony carefully smooths his sage's rough edges for the *Fraser's* reader. Prout's historical and social analyses never take more than a few pages to develop. The series is anecdotal; it is never necessary to recall a previous installment. More importantly, Mahony ensures that his audience knows how to respond to Prout's erudition. (Prout is in his own words "an Irish Potato seasoned with Attic salt.") Presented by themselves, his puns and witticisms, which assume a knowledge of Latin and Greek, would be heavy going even for classically trained readers. Mahony deftly accompanies these quips with unobtrusive translations and, at times, commentary, leaving little for the reader to do but enjoy Prout's eccentricity and facility. As is the case with Horace Smith's essays on aesthetics for the *London*, the readers of the Prout papers are not asked to evaluate or judge: they are told what to value and how to value it. Where Carlyle revels in the vertiginous and "questionable" effects produced by Teufelsdröckh, Mahony defines the role of his reader precisely, as in the following description of Prout's idiom:

The rubbish and dust of the schools with which his notions were sometimes encrusted did not alter their intrinsic worth; people only wondered how the diaphanous mind of Prout could be obscured by such common stuff: its brightness was still undiminished by the admixture, and like straws in amber, without deteriorating the substance, these matters only made manifest its transparency. (*Fraser's* 9 [1834], 539)

The comforts of "transparency" are never forgotten by Mahony. In one of the finest papers Father Prout seeks to prove that Tom Moore is a plagiarist. To do so, he provides several originals – that is, translations by Mahony of famous works by Moore into Greek or Latin. Even as he turns one of Moore's poems into an exquisite, and philologically correct, medieval Latin, Mahony makes it clear to his audience that they need not read it. The Latin poem is less a text than a relic that permits an elaborate joke. "Transparency" – or at least the illusion thereof – is the iron law of magazine success.

Taken together, the Prout papers and *Sartor* reveal the paradox of the magazine essayistic tradition. Partly because of the policy of anonymous contribution, novelty and personality are at a premium in magazines. In the pursuit of these qualities, magazines such as the *London*, *Blackwood's*, *Fraser's*, and, to some extent, the *New Monthly* permit considerable innovation in the essay – essays very different in form from that established by Addison and Steele and carried on by Goldsmith; more complex in tone than the earnest moralism of Johnson's moral essays or the clever impressionism of Leigh Hunt's work; and more personal and introspective than the straightforwardly informative and analytical review essay imported from the quarterlies. But in the long run, the insistence on immediate intelligibility reduces personality to a familiar procession of types. The literary magazine becomes a medium which, despite its claims and, at times, its practice, does not prize innovation or complexity.

Nevertheless, the dialectical politics of *Sartor*, which codify a similar but weaker tendency in *Fraser's*, make a fitting culmination to the consideration of politics that the study of literary magazines necessarily entails. John Scott was perhaps the most forthright in his connection of the literary magazine to politics. "Literature," he wrote, "has much to do with politics,"[24] and his brief tenure as editor of the *London* stands as a profound meditation on this carefully imprecise statement. His reconsideration of the legacies of Burke and the Enlightenment, mediated by Coleridge's dialectical turn of thought, offers a comprehensive assessment of and response to the politics of his day. The rivals to Scott's *London*, the far more successful *Blackwood's* and *New Monthly*, form instructive contrasts to this program: the one offering a tremendous expansion of the dialogic and rhetorical capacities of the literary magazine, but insistently promoting a far right, essentially feudal conservatism; the other, through the relentless maintenance of the editor's "calm spot" and the remorseless promotion of free market capitalism, putting into place the elements of what would later be called a political unconscious. In each case, literature and the discussion of literature and culture have much to do with politics, but in the pages of *Blackwood's* and the *New Monthly* these relations are simplified or suppressed. One magazine resists the transformation of society and culture attendant on capitalism with the intransigence of ignorance; the other capitulates uncritically. *Fraser's*, insomuch as it published *Sartor*, offers an alternative to the pragmatic solution of advocacy, either liberal or conservative: a dialectical politics that, like Scott's Burkean–Coleridgean culture, seeks a different kind of public conversation. Carlyle's Latin quip to Mill – *Ubi sunt homines, modi sunt* – clarifies his, and by extension Scott's, difference from the advocacies (both open and covert) of *Blackwood's* and the *New Monthly*: in the timeworn recognition that "where there are men, there are manners" are the beginnings of the critique that we have come to call historicism.

Conclusion

The growth of a market for literary magazines between 1820 and 1834 provided a window of opportunity for writers with a particular kind of talent or genius. Lamb, Hazlitt, the *Blackwood's* crew, and Carlyle, as well as other more distant figures such as Horace Smith, Cyrus Redding, and John Scott all flourished under what was, compared to the periodical industry of the mid century, a relatively unregulated system of publication. Their search, as both editors and writers, for an answerable form, that is, one that would satisfy individual readers as well as the market (or markets) they make up collectively, led to some conspicuous individual successes as well as what is more rare in the history of literature – collaborative successes. Early in the decade three magazines manage (albeit sometimes only momentarily) to coalesce, to form coherent and well articulated worlds: the *London* under Scott, *Blackwood's* from 1822 to 1825, and the *New Monthly* under Campbell. The later success of a fourth, *Fraser's*, whose program was explicitly nostalgic for the early days of *Blackwood's*, hints at the increasing economic rationalization of the medium and a concomitant reluctance to experiment with form.

By considering literary magazines as something like a genre, a fuller account of literary activity in the 1820s and 1830s emerges, one through which we can begin to see the continuities that persist in what we have come to call Romanticism. Indeed, the restless search for form that characterizes these periodicals finds parallels in the careers of many of the canonical Romantic poets, just as the intensity of their commitments to their particular political moment echoes the bias of more familiar figures. But as we learn to read – and in many cases, to re-imagine – literary magazines, we shall also find a strength in their articulation of politics, in their unvarnished and unabashed partisanship, in their frank explorations of the connections between literature and other discourses. As one of the era's preeminent forms, they offer a record of literary achievement as well as an astute, self-conscious meditation on that achievement.

Like the literature of sentiment and sensibility represented by the (then) conspicuous successes of Felicia Hemans and L.E.L., literary magazines have been disregarded and largely unread. Just as we have been unable to conceive of Hemans's work, we have been unable to think of the magazine as a genre, with its moments of triumph as well as its failures. As such, literary magazines stand as a challenge to current literary histories, providing more of the raw material that theories must work upon as they remind us of our over-reliance on poetry in our accounts of the period. A theory of literary history should, in principle, account for all the facts known. It must ultimately determine which facts are irrelevant and which are useful, but it must provide some basis for such decisions. Periodical literature, especially that of this period, stands as a large and relatively unknown body of empirical fact to which our current theories do not extend.

Notes

INTRODUCTION: THE STUDY OF LITERARY MAGAZINES

1 Donald H. Reiman (ed.) *The Romantics Reviewed; Contemporary Reviews of Romantic Writers*, 3 vols. (New York: Garland Publishing, 1972).

2 Michael Wolff, "Charting the Golden Stream: Thoughts on a Directory of Victorian Periodicals," *Victorian Periodicals Newsletter* 13 (1971), 27.

3 Walter E. Houghton (ed.), *The Wellesley Index to Victorian Periodicals*, 5 vols. (Toronto: University of Toronto Press, 1966–89).

4 William Hazlitt, "The Periodical Press," *Edinburgh Review* 76 (1823), 349–50.

5 The still classic formulation of this mood is Walter Jackson Bate's *The Burden of the Past and the English Poet* (New York: W. W. Norton, 1970), but see also Harold Bloom's splendid meditation on and extension of this phenomenon in *The Anxiety of Influence* (Oxford: Oxford University Press, 1973).

6 Given Hazlitt's penchant for glancing reference and slant quotation of Shakespeare, one might also catch a hint of Lear's scabrous "Let copulation thrive" speech in IV, vi. The reference would parallel the force of the quotation from the Duke Senior: in each case the exiled speaker reconciles himself to the turn of events by moralizing them.

7 James Mill, "Periodical Literature," *Westminster Review* 1 (1824), 206.

8 For a consideration of Mill's analysis that notes parallels with the poststructural strategies of Roland Barthes and Althusser's critique of ideology, see Lyn Pykett, "Reading the Periodical Press: Text and Context," *Victorian Periodicals Review* 22 (1989), 100–8.

9 See Jon Klancher, *The Making of English Reading Audiences, 1790–1832* (Madison: University of Wisconsin Press, 1987), especially chapter 2, "Reading the Social Text," and Peter T. Murphy, "Impersonation and Authorship in Romantic Britain," *English Literary History* 59 (1992), 625–49.

10 Raymond Williams, *Culture and Society, 1780–1950* (New York: Columbia University Press, 1983), p. xviii.

11 The continuation proposed by Hazlitt and John Stuart Mill's sequel to his father's article show these tendencies clearly. Hazlitt ends his article with jaunty personality, announcing his hope to continue the discussion and "to astonish our readers with a full and ingenuous account of our own merits and demerits, and those of our rivals" ("The Periodical Press," p. 378). In John Stuart Mill's "Periodical Literature," the son's use of the father's theoretical abstractions seems less a powerful demonstration than a way of man-

aging a relative dearth of information. See "Periodical Literature," *Westminster Review* 1 (1824), 505–41. (Mill was eighteen at the time, and had just begun what was to be an intense association with the "Philosophical Radicals" of the *Westminster Review*.)

12 Cited in "*The New Monthly Magazine*," in Houghton (ed.), *The Wellesley Index to Victorian Periodicals*, vol. 1, p. 163.

13 Perhaps the most luminous is John Scott's dissection of the concept of "Universal History" in "On Human Perfectability, and the Progress of Society," *London Magazine* 1 (1820), 269–71.

14 See Walter E. Houghton, "Periodical Literature and the Articulate Classes," in Joanne Shattock and Michael Wolff (eds.), *The Victorian Periodical Press: Samplings and Soundings* (Leicester University Press, 1982), pp. 3–27.

15 See Umberto Eco, *The Open Work*, Anna Concogni (trans.) (Cambridge, MA: Harvard University Press, 1989), especially "The Poetics of the Open Work," pp. 1–24.

16 M. M. Bakhtin, *The Dialogic Imagination*, Michael Holquist (ed.), Caryl Emerson and Michael Holquist (trans.), (Austin: University of Texas Press, 1981), pp. 262–3.

17 For instance, in the "Noctes Ambrosianae" of *Blackwood's Magazine*, the Ettrick Shepherd, the peasant-poet James Hogg, finds voice in all his vernacular splendor, but the dominant tendency of the representation is toward parody of and condescension toward him and his social world. The heteroglossia is constrained by the refusal to consider Hogg and Hogg's experience as full equals in the conversation. Only in the most sentimental moments of the series does the figure of Hogg establish any authority.

18 See Margaret Beetham, "Open and Closed: The Periodical as a Publishing Genre," *Victorian Periodicals Review* 22 (1989), 96–100, for a discussion of the paradoxical relation between closed and open form in periodicals.

19 See Eric J. Evans, *The Forging of the Modern State* (New York: Longman, 1983), p. 181.

20 *Ibid.*, pp. 181–9.

21 See Harold Perkin, *The Origins of Modern English Society: 1780–1880* (London: Routledge & Kegan Paul, 1972) for a nice summary of the oppositional view, and Evans for a restatement of the co-optational theory. But see also Lawrence Stone and Jeanne C. Fawtier Stone, *An Open Elite? England 1540–1880* (New York: Oxford University Press, 1986) for a reassessment of the oppositional view, with significant evidence drawn from surveys of movement between the middle ranks and the aristocracy in three counties over three hundred years.

22 See Perkin, *The Origins of Modern English Society*, chapter 7, "The Struggle Between the Ideals," pp. 218–70.

23 James Mill, in the article discussed above, has a similar moment of hesitation. In discussing the interests behind aristocratic political divisions, he insists that they are material in every case. Yet, when he turns to the interests of his own class, the "professional" class, his own position remains curiously resistant to the method he espouses.

24 Such fantasies figure in other Elia essays, such as "In Praise of Chimney Sweepers," in which Lamb recounts the familiar story of the chimney sweep who falls asleep in a great house and, upon waking, slickly takes up the role of aristocrat.

25 *Blackwood's* 14 (1823), 221. This familiar line of abuse broke out upon Hazlitt's publication of *Liber Amoris* in 1823. Lockhart and Maginn, predictably, are the culprits. But even before the renewed assault *Blackwood's* took great pleasure in reminding its readers of the former libel. Eyre Evans Crowe, in a review of *Table-Talk*, writes that Hazlitt is "one gaping sore of wounded and festering vanity" (*Blackwood's* 12 [1822], 157).

26 Scott makes this remark in his September 1820 review of "Poems by John Keats" (*London Magazine* 2, 315).

27 Stone, *An Open Elite?*, p. 291.

28 *Ibid.*, pp. 292.

29 Leonidas Jones, in perhaps the most complete and even-handed treatment of the Scott–Christie duel, hazards this guess. Murphy, in perhaps the most suggestive treatment of the episode, follows Jones and, to some extent, predicates his own argument on such a discovery. See Leonidas M. Jones, "The Scott–Christie Duel," *Texas Studies in Language and Literature* 12 (1971), 605–29.

30 A letter of 24 February 1821, from *The Letters of Sir Walter Scott*, H.J.C. Grierson (ed.), 12 vols. (London: Constable and Co., 1932–7), vol. VI, p. 363.

31 See *The Champion* 171 (14 April 1816), 118.

32 See Jones, "The Scott–Christie Duel," p. 608.

33 Quoted in Andrew Lang, *The Life and Letters of John Gibson Lockhart*, 2 vols. (New York: AMS Press, 1970), vol. I, p. 250.

34 Quoted in *ibid.*

35 Quoted in Jones, "The Scott–Christie Duel," 623.

36 Maginn does deserve some mention here for consistency. He coolly walked out in August 1836, with Grantley Berkeley, a dead shot, and stood two exchanges. See Miriam F. Thrall, *Rebellious Fraser's: Nol Yorke's Magazine in the Days of Maginn, Thackeray, and Carlyle* (New York: Columbia University Press, 1934), pp. 51–2 and 199–200.

37 Jones and, with some reservations, Murphy, hold to this view of the meaning of the duel.

38 Odoherty makes this claim in the fourth installment of the "Noctes Ambrosianae" (*Blackwood's* 12 [1822], 106).

39 Campbell makes this claim in the "Editor's Preface," (4 [1822], v).

40 See Scott's "Prospectus" to the *London Magazine* 1(1820), v.

I IDEOLOGY AND EDITING: THE POLITICAL CONTEXT OF THE ELIA ESSAYS

1 Mario Praz, *The Hero in Eclipse*, Angus Davidson (trans.), (Oxford: Oxford University Press, 1956), p. 65.

2 George Barnett, *The Evolution of Elia* (New York: Haskell House, 1973).

Robert Frank, *Don't Call Me Gentle Charles* (Corvallis: Oregon State University Press, 1976). Fred Randel, *The World of Elia* (Port Washington, NY: Kennikat Press, 1975). Gerald Monsman, *Confessions of a Prosaic Dreamer* (Durham, NC: Duke University Press, 1984).

3 Richard Haven, "The Romantic Art of Charles Lamb," *English Literary History* 30 (1963), 137–46. Donald Reiman, "Thematic Unity in Lamb's Familiar Essays," *Journal of English and Germanic Philology* 64 (1965), 470–8. Daniel Mulcahy, "Charles Lamb: The Antithetical Manner and the Two Planes," *Studies in English Literature* 3 (1963), 517–42.

4 William Flesch, "'Friendly and Judicious' Reading: Affect and Irony in the Works of Charles Lamb," *Studies in Romanticism* 23 (1984), 163–83. Thomas McFarland, *Romantic Cruxes* (Oxford: Clarendon Press, 1987), pp. 25–52.

5 See Carl Woodring, *Politics in English Romantic Poetry* (Cambridge, MA: Harvard University Press, 1970), pp. 74–7, for a short but astute assessment of Lamb's political views. Winifred Courteney's *Young Charles Lamb* (Hong Kong: Macmillan Press, 1982) contains a chapter on his politics.

6 Jerome McGann, *The Beauty of Inflections* (Oxford: Clarendon Press, 1985), p. 23.

7 Josephine Bauer, *The London Magazine, 1820–1829* (Copenhagen: Rosenkilde and Bagger, 1953), p. 94.

8 Walter Graham, *English Literary Periodicals* (New York: Thomas Nelson & Sons, 1930).

9 *The Writings and Speeches of Edmund Burke*, Paul Langford (ed.), 9 vols. (Oxford: Clarendon Press, 1981–), vol. VIII, p. 83. Burke has had some exceptional commentators, four of whom are particularly useful in the project of tracing the Burkean–Coleridgean tradition. Although I do not quote from Alfred Cobban's *Edmund Burke and the Revolt Against the Eighteenth Century* (New York: Barnes and Noble, 1929), I have, like the more recent critics of Burke I cite, relied on his lucid, brief account in forming my argument. It would be hard to improve on J. G. A. Pocock's terse summary of the "elementary Burke" in his pithy "Burke and the Ancient Constitution," in *Politics, Language, and Time* (New York: Atheneum, 1971), pp. 202–3: that an institution, the product of a number of "adjustments to the needs of circumstance" over time, could neither be "completely rationalized" nor comprehended by the individual; hence recourse to "first principles" or to "critical reason" was irrelevant and possibly dangerous. Also useful in tracing Burke's tradition is James Boulton's examination of "key-words" in *The Language of Politics* (London: Routledge & Kegan Paul, 1963), as well as his identification of key Burkean images, such as nature, the Bible, the noble house or castle, and the family. Friedrich Meinecke's claims in *Historicism*, J. E. Anderson (trans.) (London: Routledge & Kegan Paul, 1972) that Burke writes consciously against the rationalists, that his work represents "a counterblast to the Enlightenment," can also, with some modification, help in clarifying his currency in the late Regency. Finally, Seamus Deane's recent study, *The French Revolution and the Enlightenment in England* (Cambridge, MA: Harvard

University Press, 1988), esp. pp. 21–42, which stresses the deeply nationalistic thrust of Burke's writing and how this influenced the next generation, is a cogent reminder of the ubiquity of politics in Regency discourse. I refer here and throughout to the Clarendon edition of Burke.

10 *The Collected Works of Samuel Taylor Coleridge*, Kathleen Coburn (ed.), 14 vols. (Princeton: Princeton University Press, 1972), vol. VI, p. 9.

11 Perhaps the most concentrated display of Coleridge's debt to Burke's thought and expression is contained in the ecstatic paean to reason in Appendix C of *The Statesman's Manual*, where Coleridge follows Burke explicitly in associating the revolution with sexual license, cosmopolitanism, commerce, "the dissecting room," and chemistry. See *Collected Works*, vol. VI, pp. 73–7.

12 *Biographia Literaria*, James Engell and W. Jackson Bate (eds.), 2 vols. (Princeton: Princeton University Press, 1983), vol. I, p. 190.

13 It could be said to have preceded it, since the parts relevant to Burke are inserted with little or no revision from the 1809 and 1812 versions.

14 John Scott, "To Robert Baldwin, 9 November 1818," Holman Clippings, Houghton Library, Harvard University. One of six typescripts of Scott's correspondence with Baldwin.

15 Meinecke, *Historicism*, p. 228.

16 Scott, "To Robert Baldwin, 9 November 1819." Emphasis Scott's.

17 "To Robert Baldwin," 11 November 1819, in the *Collected Letters of Samuel Taylor Coleridge*, Earl Leslie Griggs (ed.), 6 vols. (Oxford: Oxford University Press, 1956–71), vol. IV, pp. 975–6.

18 *Biographia Literaria*, vol. I, p. 192.

19 Jerome McGann, *The Romantic Ideology* (Chicago: University of Chicago Press, 1983), p. 1.

20 Jon Klancher analyzes the ideology behind this typically bourgeois gesture of reading crowds as signs in *The Making of English Reading Audiences, 1790–1832* (Madison: University of Wisconsin Press, 1987), tracing it in the *New Monthly Magazine*, for which John Scott had worked. One might note the difference in Scott's interpretive practice, which, unlike Redding and others in the *New Monthly*, traces the meaning it finds in "signs of the times" to principles and ideas.

21 This portrait anticipates Dickens's Wemmick. Gordon Spence has studied some of Dickens's debts to Lamb in *Charles Dickens as a Familiar Essayist* (Salzburg: Institut für Englische Sprache und Literatur, Universität Salzburg, 1977).

22 McFarland makes this point in his chapter on Lamb in *Romantic Cruxes*.

23 See *ibid.*, p. 47.

24 See *ibid.*, p. 26.

25 The parallels between this social analysis and that of Wordsworth in his "Preface to *Lyrical Ballads*" are striking.

26 After Scott's death, the editorial duties were taken up by the new owner of the magazine, John Taylor. Although he had several well-qualified men at

hand – Hazlitt and Cary to name two – Taylor chose to edit the London himself. By the end of 1821 he had driven off many contributors, and the magazine never recovered (See Bauer, *The London Magazine*, pp. 80–91). With Scott's death, the elaborate coding of articles ended as well.

27 Janusz Sławiński, "Reading and Reader in the Literary Historical Process," *New Literary History* 19 (1988), 538.

28 Neither *Elia* nor the *Last Essays* sold particularly well. Lamb held that Southey's famous review, which claimed that the work "wanted a sounder religious feeling," had injured the sales. This seems feeble; I would argue that as their success in the *London* owed much to the inter-textual situation created by Scott, so did their relative failure in the 1823 and 1833 editions stem from their removal from this context. Later in the century audiences were prepared to read Lamb in the relentlessly auto-biographical and personal mode that the 1823 and 1833 texts encourage, and their popularity rose accordingly. (See *The Works of Charles and Mary Lamb*, E.V. Lucas [ed.], 5 vols. [New York: Putnam and Sons, 1903], vol. II, pp. 299 ff. for some remarks on the publishing history of *Elia* and *Last Essays*.)

29 Thomas Noon Talfourd (ed.), *The Letters of Charles Lamb, with a Sketch of His Life* (London: Moxon, 1837), p. 82.

30 Barry Cornwall (B. W. Proctor), *Charles Lamb: a Memoir* (London: Edward Moxon, 1866), p. 87.

31 Thomas De Quincey, "Recollections of Charles Lamb," *Tait's* 9 os, 5ns (April and June 1838), 242.

32 "Works of Charles Lamb," *Blackwood's* 3 (1818), 599.

33 "Gallery of Literary Characters. No. LVII. Charles Lamb, Esq.," *Fraser's Magazine* 11 (1835), 136.

34 H. N. Coleridge, "The Last Essays of Elia," *The Quarterly Review* 54 (1835), 58–77.

35 E. L. Bulwer, "Charles Lamb," *Westminster Review* 27 (1837), 296.

36 G. H. Lewes, "Charles Lamb – His Genius and Writings," *The British Quarterly Review* 7 (1848), 307.

37 William Henry Smith, "Charles Lamb," *Blackwood's* 66 (1849), 150.

38 Walter Pater, *Appreciations* (New York: The Macmillan Co., 1910), p. 109.

39 Thomas De Quincey, "Charles Lamb and His Friends," *North British Review* 6 (1848), 98.

40 R. Monckton Milnes, "Charles Lamb," *Edinburgh Review* 124 (1866), 261.

41 W. C. Hazlitt, "Charles Lamb: Gleanings after his Biographers," *Macmillan's Magazine* 15 (1866–1867), 473.

42 Augustine Birrell, "Charles Lamb," in *Obiter Dicta*, second series (London: Eliot Stock, 1887), pp. 222–35.

43 Pater, *Appreciations*, p. 112.

44 A. C. Ward, *The Frolic and the Gentle* (London: Methuen and Co., 1934), p. vii.

45 Denys Thompson, "Our Debt to Lamb," in F. R. Leavis (ed.), *Determinations* (London: Chatto and Windus, 1934), p. 205.

46 Graham Greene, "Lamb's Testimonials," *Spectator* 152 (30 March 1934), 512.
47 *The Works of Charles and Mary Lamb*, E.V. Lucas (ed.), vol. II, p. 152.

2 A CONVERSATION BETWEEN FRIENDS: HAZLITT AND THE *LONDON MAGAZINE*

1 *London Magazine* 2 (1820), 255.
2 "To Robert Baldwin, 18 January 1820," Holman Clippings, Houghton Library, Harvard University.
3 I refer throughout to *The Complete Works of William Hazlitt*, P. P. Howe (ed.), 21 vols. (London: Frank Cass & Company, 1967) for essays not in the *London Magazine*. This quotation vol. VII, p. 17.
4 For a general treatment of Hazlitt's debt to Burke, see Jonathan Cook, "Hazlitt: Criticism and Ideology," in David Aers, Jonathan Cook, and David Punter (eds.), *Romanticism and Ideology* (London: Routledge & Kegan Paul, 1981), especially pp. 137–54.
5 "To be attached to the subdivision, to love the little platoon we belong to in society, is the first principle (the germ as it were) of public affections. It is the first link in the series by which we proceed towards a love to our country and to mankind. The interests of that portion of social arrangement is a trust in the hands of all those who compose it; and as none but bad men would justify it in abuse, none but traitors would barter it away for their own personal advantage" (Edmund Burke, *The Writings and Speeches of Edmund Burke*, Paul Langford [ed.], 9 vols. [Oxford: Clarendon Press, 1981–], vol. VII, pp. 97–8.
6 Other than as records of historical performances, they only become interesting when he applies the principles of the first four numbers to a current performance. For example, the June entry, in taking up Kean's *Lear*, applies ideas from the February entry in criticizing Kean's method.
7 See Mark Schoenfield's "Voices Together: Lamb, Hazlitt, and the *London*," *Studies in Romanticism* 29 (1990), 57–72.
8 See Terry Eagleton's *The Function of Criticism* (Norfolk: Verso, 1984), pp. 7–26.
9 John Kinnaird's very readable book on Hazlitt is typical of this line of criticism. In his discussion of Hazlitt's turn from politics and its relation to his essays of the 1820s (pp. 268–71), Kinnaird emphasizes the process by which Hazlitt probes his private sense of loneliness and his public sense of political disillusion. Hazlitt's bleakest statements, such as in "On the Pleasure of Hating," are the reflex of a process of recovery of faith. The essays of 1820–3 allow Hazlitt "not only to confess but to confront, to understand, and master his pessimism, and thus ultimately to strengthen a faith that had been tested – and reshaped – in the crucible of self-doubt" (pp. 269–70). Kinnaird further remarks on the traditional orientation of Hazlitt's essays of 1820–3: how they have subject matter and interest akin to those of Bacon and Montaigne, to "the less celebrated Renaissance moralists in prose" who sought to impart *sapientia* and *prudentia*. Hazlitt's enduring concerns are "the

perennial problems of common experience and moral understanding – problems more interpersonal than personal, examined anew for his age in the light of a non-rationalistic psychology of the will" (p. 273). See his *William Hazlitt: Critic of Power* (New York: Columbia University Press, 1978).

10 Hazlitt laces his celebration of painting with allusions to and quotations of Wordsworth's poetry – a move which, as it seeks to defend the setting of painting over against writing, undermines it.

11 It is essentially irrelevant whether Scott or Hazlitt initiated this language. Scott uses it before Hazlitt in the pages of the magazine, but he might well have read the essay before he wrote the November "Historical and Critical Summary of Intelligence." The November "Lion's Head" comments on Hazlitt's forthcoming essay.

12 These effects are heightened considerably by other February contributions, notably Elia's "Mrs. Battle's Opinions" and Scott's "Signs of the Times" essay. See chapter 1 for a discussion of these two entries.

13 Edmund Blunden's assessment is typical: "For all ordinary purposes, only the *London* of Taylor & Hessey, 1821–1824, counts – and it counts a great deal in any survey of the finer periodical publications of this country." See his *Keats's Publisher: A Memoir of John Taylor* (London: Jonathan Cape, 1936 [reissued in the Life and Letters Series No. 97, 1940]), p. 130.

14 "I cannot but think the *London* drags heavily. I miss Janus. And O how it misses Hazlitt." See *The Letters of Charles and Mary Lamb*, ed. E. V. Lucas, 3 vols. (New Haven: Yale University Press, 1935), vol. II, p. 85.

15 This is not to say that eighteenth-century periodicals did not allow for readers with aspirations to "read up" – that is to use information supplied by the periodical to fashion a new self. One recalls Franklin's discussion of essays by Addison and Steele in his *Autobiography*. The difference is that where eighteenth-century periodicals provided a discussion of aesthetic principles, Smith provides prefabricated responses.

16 Clearly, the interim editor or editors were taken with Horace Smith's work: the second article in the March *London* is by him as well. An extremely sentimental essay, "Death – Posthumous Memorials – Children" (signed "A Father") is full of quasi-Victorian platitudes about the joys of hearth and children. Smith expatiates on the beauty of his daughter ("every articulation of the blue veins in her fair temple") and proceeds to explore his still fresh grief over his dead son. Smith appends a memorial poem, written by the child's mother, that is filled with what will become Victorian cliché: "cruel hand of death," "beauty's blossom," the hiding of the child's "trinkets, toys, and dresses," the "thrilling recollections" produced by the sight of other lovely children, and the inevitable finale, "Let us think with grateful hearts of the many that are left." The sentiment, like the aesthetic response in the previous essay, is prefabricated.

17 The essay ends with an anecdote embarrassing to the English clergy. A celebrated orientalist from Halle, Gesenius, visited Oxford to examine, copy, and publish a manuscript long held to be by St. Paul. Upon inspection, he

held this attribution to be mistaken. He was asked, however, not to publish his findings by "a certain society," lest his findings "tend to unsettle the belief of the multitude" (*London Magazine* 3 [1821], 303). He refuses; they offer him money. He still refuses, and leaves indignantly. Croly concludes with a tart remark on this incident as an indication of the purblind, dogmatic turn of this assembly.

18 Walter E. Houghton, "Periodical Literature and the Articulate Classes," in Joanne Shattock and Michael Wolff (eds.), *The Victorian Periodical Press: Samplings and Soundings* (Leicester University Press, 1982 [simultaneous printing, Toronto: University of Toronto Press, 1982]), pp. 3–27.

19 The *London*, like other periodicals, regularly ran features it thought prominent first in the number.

20 Mark Schoenfield's recent study of the intertextual relation between "On Antiquity" and Lamb's "The Old and New Schoolmaster" remarks upon the tonic qualities of Hazlitt's essay in a reading of Lamb's nostalgic and evasive essay. But his reading entails a flattening of the equivocal nature of Hazlitt's point: the truth cannot set the reader free; the Enlightenment master-narrative has limits. The inextricable coil of "reason and fancy" that Hazlitt presents cannot debunk Lamb's play of nostalgia and displacement. See Schoenfield, "Voices Together," pp. 57–72.

21 Perhaps the most winning aspect of Hazlitt's ruminations on his "ridiculous" position is his unwillingness to revert to irony as a resolution of these contradictions.

22 See David Bromwich, *Hazlitt: The Mind of a Critic* (New York, Oxford University Press, 1983), pp. 335–6, for a discussion of the unusual metaphor of property in Hazlitt's essay.

23 In 1823 and 1824 Hazlitt published some essays on art collections which became *Sketches*. These pieces are remarkably illuminating about the holdings they describe, but they lack the verve and epigrammatic flair of Hazlitt's other essays.

24 The last two Table-Talk essays for the *London*, while interesting in the context of the magazine, were not subsumed into any collection.

25 John Sutherland, "Henry Colburn Publisher," *Publishing History* 19 (1986), 59–84.

26 See Blunden, *Keats's Publisher*, pp. 137–8.

27 Leigh Hunt was nominally in charge, but he was busy contemplating a new periodical in Italy with Shelley. Hunt's last editorial column was on October 21; he was off to Italy on November 15. His brother John was in prison again for libel of the House of Commons. "Guy Faux" appeared in the *Examiner* on 11, 18, and 25 November 1821.

28 The essay is full of such indirect hits. Clearly Hazlitt enjoys recalling Southey's hot, radical youth in this context. Part of the invective, of course, is directed at Hazlitt himself.

29 The Constitutional Association was formed in 1820 by those on the ministerial side as a response to what they considered unpunished libels in the

anti-government press. About forty bishops and peers contributed money to fund the prosecutions it undertook. It was widely perceived as an abuse of power, as a way of allowing the ministerial party to harass the anti-government press while preserving the fiction of neutrality. See A. Aspinall, *Politics and the Press c. 1780–1850* (London: Home & Van Thal Ltd., 1949), pp. 63–5.

30 Reynolds's early association with Scott on the *Champion* is telling. In an essay of 13 October 1816, "Popular Poetry – Periodical Criticism, & C.," Reynolds contrasts popularity and genius in a way that sheds light on his political sensibilities. The two chains of association presented by Reynolds have an unmistakable tendency: genius/the gold system/the past/the few/moated castles/epics/"the romantic and prodigious" versus popularity/paper currency/modern times/the many/"country houses and shooting boxes"/Magazines and Reviews/"the convenient." Such a network of associations suggests the turn of Reynolds's liberalism – one that apparently puts him very much in the recessive frame of mind evoked by Scott in his essays for the *London*. Reynolds's biographer, Leonidas Jones, sounds the proper note when he suggests that "in print he was moderate and prudent in declaring his views." See Leonidas Jones, *The Life of John Hamilton Reynolds* (Hanover, NH: University Press of New England, 1984), p. 288.

31 Alan Lang Strout, "Knights of the Burning Epistle," *Studia Neophilologica* 26 (1953–4), 85.

32 See Jones, *Life*, p. 196.

33 See also his 6 October 1818 contribution to *The Alfred*, in which he defends Lady Morgan's patriotism against the abuses heaped on her by the *Quarterly*.

34 See Schoenfield, "Voices Together," for a consideration of the intertextual relation between "On Antiquity" and the essay by Lamb in the same number.

35 This part of the footnote is not reprinted in the first edition of *Table-Talk*.

36 See Richard Verdi's "Hazlitt and Poussin," *The Keats–Shelley Memorial Bulletin* 32 (1981), 1–18. Verdi treats Hazlitt's essay in terms of Romantic and neoclassical views of Poussin. The political linkage with which the essay ends is not at issue. Verdi is concerned with vindicating Hazlitt's surprisingly modern insights about a neglected quality of Poussin's work.

37 The first quotation is from *The New Times* of Friday, 20 July 1821; the second from the 19 July 1821 *Courier*. Opposition papers, of course, carried a different account, and more even-handed papers, such as the *Times*, provided detailed coverage of the Queen's rebuff: "Every where, indeed, the only topic of interest and of conversation was the situation of her Majesty the Queen." The *London Times* of Friday, 20 July 1821, takes a different view of the coronation: "We have now to describe a coronation, unproductive, at least in its outset, of any of that enthusiasm by which transactions of this kind were formerly distinguished." The account makes frequent mention of the lack of enthusiasm in the lower and middling classes, which it attributes to the King's "want of sensibility to the absence of a Queen, hitherto

deemed a principal figure in the piece." Further details continue the criticism of the ceremony: pugilists stalk about keeping order; there is quite a bustle upon the Queen's application to be admitted; the King's poor health is emphasized – he is unable to descend steps and distressed to the point of fainting; the horsed "Champion" is described in satiric detail, replete with quotation from Boiardo's *Orlando*.

38 Reynolds's account of the coronation nicely traces the difficulties attendant on making George a plausible monarch. The description of the King's descent from the throne is perhaps ambiguous: Reynolds notes that he needs assistance to step down. His progress is also watched closely: "He walked slowly, and with a sort of balanced precision, not from any immediate weariness, but as though he were husbanding his powers for the labours of the afterday. He certainly looked well, and much younger than I expected to find him" (*London Magazine* 4 [1821], 187). Apparently the intent here is to moderate the widespread fears about the King's health. Reynolds argues that he looks better than expected, and this is a kind of victory. Other descriptions are laced with appeals to sincerity: "Do not think that I speak extravagantly here. It was all enchantment" (p. 188). Perhaps the equivocal nature of Reynolds's statements owes to the difficulty of getting such positive descriptions over – the audience is skeptical. If this is the case, the frame of the story – writer as foppish sophisticate – is a clever attempt to legitimate the coronation: if a fool finds it unexpectedly splendid and moving, even to the point of leaving off his foolishness, then perhaps the more skeptical may approve as well.

Given Reynolds's generally liberal politics and his penchant for satire, one is inclined to wonder whether he writes ironically here. Hood's notice of this coronation essay in the July "Lion's Head" does not settle the issue, at least not at once. It seems more directed at the dandyism of either Reynolds himself or the persona of Reynolds's essay: "Lion's Head is not a Dandy-lion, but its mane will be carefully cut and turned for the occasion; and it will go ruffled, like a true British Lion. The readers of the *London Magazine*, in fine, may rest assured, that the Lion's Head will, on that day, seek its own food, and not trust to the established Jackalls of the diurnal press" (*London Magazine* 4 [1821], 3). But Reynolds's remarks in his drama contribution, which follows his account of the coronation, make such an ironic reading difficult. There he seems earnest about the ceremony, noting that the coronation allows the populace to be "dutiful and wise," unlike the theater, which allows for "merry and wise" (p. 197). The coronation is "the great imposing marvel of the season" (p. 197).

39 Jones, *Life*, pp. 291–3.

40 The arguments are several: (1) he does not yet know his own country; (2) there are so many foreigners in London ("we have them all in epitome") that travel is unnecessary; (3) human nature is common, "different nations . . . are only compounds of the same ingredients, but in varied proportions"; (4) the differences arise in the influences of education, laws, and religion.

Hence the "immeasurable distances between the minds of men" (*London Magazine* 4 [1821], 508).

41 See Jon Klancher's "Reading the Social Text" in *The Making of English Reading Audiences, 1790–1832* (Madison: University of Wisconsin Press, 1987), pp. 47–75. The attitude taken up by Hood's persona has a remarkable durability. *Blackwood's* includes a similarly oriented essay, "London," in October of 1899 (*Blackwood's* 166, 460–83).

42 The attribution in *The Wellesley Index* is uncertain but reasonable. The article is not unlike other contributions known to be by Phillips. Walter Houghton (ed.), *The Wellesley Index to Victorian Periodicals*, 5 vols. (Toronto: University of Toronto Press, 1966–89).

43 Much is made in the penultimate paragraph of Hölty's piety, and, oddly, of the disposition of a gift of fifty dollars sent him near the end of his life by a benevolent lady. Phillips painstakingly traces the money into the hands of Hölty's brother. This is a telling juxtaposition – religious feeling, though not fervor, and proper accounting procedures. There is no hint of irony involved; Phillips seems to appreciate the interest in financial matters that his audience might have.

44 Perhaps more relevant to this conjunction of Hölty and Keats is the fact that Taylor and Hessey had published Keats's *Isabella* and *Lamia*. It serves, to some extent, as a kind of advertisement for current stock. To support such a claim, one need only turn to a much more direct bit of marketing in the November number, Taylor's "A Visit To John Clare, with a Notice of his New Poems." In part a sampling of the recent volume of Clare's poems published by Taylor & Hessey, most of the article is taken up with comparative accounts of Taylor's visits to some of the sites described by Clare. The first, Lolham Brigs, is as unpropitious a spot as can be imagined:

> to me, the triumph of true genius seemed never more conspicuous, than in the construction of so interesting a poem out of such common-place materials. With your own eyes you see nothing but a dull line of ponds, or rather one continued marsh, over which a succession of arches carries the narrow highway: look again, with the poem in your mind, and the wand of a necromancy seems to have been employed in conjuring up a host of beautiful accompaniments, making the whole waste populous with life, and shedding all around the rich lustre of a grand and appropriate sentiment. Imagination . . . hath done wonders here. (*London Magazine* 4 [1821], 540)

One might think, upon reading Taylor's account, that Clare has given value to the worthless, that imagination turns the useless to, with some luck, the saleable. Taylor's account sounds a bit like land speculation. He emphasizes the value that Clare's genius has added, not the beauties that Clare has celebrated or rendered in nature. The entire poetic experience is painstakingly and cleverly constructed as a way of authenticating that absolute barometer of poetic genius – imagination.

Taylor's analysis tends toward the sociological; Clare's poetry is a healthy but endangered reaction to the age:

Clare is highly commendable for not affecting a language, and it is a proof of the originality of his genius. Style at second-hand is unfelt, unnatural, and common-place, a parrot-like repetition of words, whose individual weight is never esteemed, – a cluster-language framed and cast into set forms, in the most approved models, and adapted for all occasions, – an expedient, in fact, to give an appearance of think-ing, without "the insupportable fatigue of thought." It suits the age, for we abound with machinery, invented to supersede man's labour; and it is in repute, for it "is adapted to the meanest capacities"; but there never was a great poet, or grand orig-inal thinker in prose, who did not compose his phraseology for himself; words must be placed in order with great care, and put into combinations which have been unknown before, if the things which he is solicitous to express, have not been discov-ered and expressed before. In poetry, especially, you may estimate the originality of the thoughts by that of the language; but this is a canon to which our approved critics will not subscribe: they allow of no phrase which has not received the sanction of authority, no expression for which, in the sense used, you cannot plead a precedent. They would fetter the English poet as much as they circumscribe the maker of Latin verses, and yet they complain that our modern poets want originality! (pp. 544–5)

Taylor presents poetry as a kind of oppositional force to the machine age, which glories in repetition and standardization. Yet what he celebrates in Clare's work, his originality of expression, has other, less disinterested impli-cations: it presumes a revolution in taste and a concomitant renovation of market share. If new things are not said in new language, the business of publishing might languish. Critics who too stringently police a tradition are a clog to trade. The article constitutes the commodity text *par excellence* – a meta-commodity text.

45 This frame allows for a virtual advertisement of the attractions to come in the series:

I have now a double pleasure in witnessing the various scenes which make up the great drama of life in this metropolis, from a knowledge of the gratification I shall have in describing them, and the interest you will feel in hearing them described. You know my restless and unappeasable hunger of mind, after all that is either curious or instructive in this world, – not regarding personal comfort, or even per-sonal safety, in the attainment of any interesting object, and ever disciplining my temper and my mind to meet and mingle with all descriptions of persons, in order to the observing of their habits, their pleasures, or their peculiarities. (*London Magazine* 4 [1821], 527)

46 The passage deserves quotation:

Mr. Morton, the father, is one of those gentle and silent characters, which are rather spirits of the household, than active and common mortal portions of it: – never min-gling in the petty strifes and light joys of the moment, – but softening and quieting the former with a bland and pleasant placidity, and heightening the latter by a cheer-ful and generous regard. His age I should guess to be about fifty-six; you may per-ceive that Time is beginning to write a few faint lines upon his forehead, and that his eye begins to show that patient wisdom which only comes of the light of many years. His hair (which Mrs. Morton tells me was a raven black "when they were married," and of which she has one precious lock, neatly folded in fragrant paper, and kept in the inner-most recess of her pocket book) is just dashed with a glossy white, which seems to light upon him more like the glory than the waste of age, and brightens, if possible, the serene sweetness of his forehead. He speaks very little, but he looks as if his thoughts ran on with the radiant solemnity of a river. His observations, indeed, when they do come forth, are remarkable only for their simplicity and humane gentleness; – you feel convinced that they are, as the old play hath it, killed with kindness. His thoughts remain with him, but his feelings come forth and speak, and you may ever perceive that his mind discourses silently and with itself, while his heart is the active and eloquent minister to his tongue. I wish, Russell, you could see him sitting at his table, or at his fireside, and lighting the conversation with his pleasant looks. All customs, all pleasures, all regulations, take their exactness from his presence, and I never saw order wear so attractive a garb as that in which Mr. Morton clothes her. He has the most precise and quiet mode of taking his seat, or reading the newspaper (and quiet as he naturally is, he is yet deeply interested in the political agitations which disturb the heart of his country), or stirring the fire, or putting on his spectacles. He goes to an office somewhere in the city daily, but I do not see that his merchant-life distracts his home comforts, or molests his morning thoughts; whether it be that his peculiar temperament places all commercial fluctuation in a mild and softening atmosphere, or that he meets not with those temporary difficulties and perplexities which call daily at the most obscure and dusty dens of business, and afflict the nerves of the oldest and most staid merchant, I know not; but the rise and fall of stocks – the intricacies of the markets – the uncertainties and dangers of the shipping – the more polished difficulties, and changes, and higher mysteries of the court, abide not with Mr. Morton. He hears the din of the nation, and it stuns him not: – he sees the great game of the world played, and heeds not its rogueries, its ruin, or its fascinations. His heart is in his home, and in his family, and he does not ever look to the winners and the losers elsewhere. Such is Mr. Morton. To me he is unusually loquacious, which is a sure mark of his regarding me kindly; – and the other evening he took particular joy, during our rubber, in always having a king for my queen, and laughed outright in detecting a revoke which I committed; which was the most gratifying sign. – He, in general, pities the objects of his triumphs, and silently pines over his own success, which he ever thinks "runs too much on one side". (*London Magazine* 4 [1821], 528–9)

3 THE BURIAL OF ROMANTICISM: THE FIRST TWENTY INSTALLMENTS OF "NOCTES AMBROSIANAE"

1 Margaret Oliphant, *Annals of a Publishing House: William Blackwood and His Sons*, 3 vols. (Edinburgh: William Blackwood and Sons, 1897), vol. 1, p. 94.
2 This pattern of mystification is also evident in the advice which follows this passage. Murray quickly leaves the pursuit of "higher duties" to themselves to urge that Blackwood be mindful of profits to be made in joint ventures between their Edinburgh and London houses.
3 Blackwood's own account of the success of the magazine blends the elements of class, market competition, and politics that swirl around literary magazines. In a 23 June 1821 letter to J. W. Croker Blackwood writes:

At the time when I began it [the Magazine], the Edinburgh Review, and Edinburgh Whigs were entirely predominant here. Not to belong to their coterie at once stamped a man to be fool or rogue, or both. All the Talents, as well as all the honesty were with Jeffrey and his friends. This tyranny had been long felt, but no one ventured here to make head against it, or attempt to throw off the yoke. After I had begun my Magazine I found I had gathered some friends around me who were fit for greater things, and were able to turn the laugh against those who had so long sat in the Chair of the Scorner. They very soon entered into my views, and you know what has been the result. The laugh is now as much against the Whigs, as it formerly was with them, and therefore their rage has known no bounds. Upon my devoted head have they poured the vials of their wrath, and God only knows what I have suffered in one way or another. I need not say that it is not my Magazine alone that has wrought all this change here, for the folly and baseness of the party have done it, but this without vanity I may say that the papers in my Magazine opened the eyes of our young men, and have quite turned the tide among the lawyers who were formerly so devoted to the little despot of the Edinburgh Review. (MS 30969, Blackwood Papers, National Library of Scotland)

4 See Oliphant, *Blackwood and Sons*, vol. 1, p. 133: "we are obliged to allow that it was an attack for which there is no word to be said, and which can only arouse our astonishment and dismay that the hand of a gentleman could have produced it, not to speak of a critic."

5 Blackwood, in a letter to "delta" (D.M. Moir) of 15 August 1820, speaks of the market for books of poetry in much the same way:

I was above all however glad that you wished the Poems to appear in the Magazine for much as I admire them, yet a volume of Poems is always somewhat of a hazardous experiment. Not that the mere expense would be so very great but that volumes of poetry often are never heard of, and die almost still born. Now in the Magazine, a poem is read by thousands at once and its merits are properly appreciated. (MS 30304, Blackwood Papers, National Library of Scotland)

6 See George Croly's December 1823 review, "The Graces, or Literary Souvenir" (*Blackwood's* vol. 13, pp. 669–72) or John Wilson's January 1825 review of Alaric Watt's *The Literary Souvenir* (*Blackwood's* vol. 17, pp. 94–101).

7 See Richard Altick, *The English Common Reader* (Chicago: University of Chicago Press, 1957), pp. 392–3.

8 Oliphant, *Blackwood and Sons*, vol. 1, p. 350. The copy of this letter in the Blackwood Papers reads somewhat differently: "the Mag. is now too serious a concern to be trifled. It has got quite above the attacks and malignities of these two low creatures [meaning Pringle and Cleghorn]." See MS 30305, Blackwood Papers, National Library of Scotland. Many of the letters in the Blackwood Papers (including the later) are copies; perhaps Oliphant had access to an autograph copy.

9 Francis Jeffrey, "Secondary Scotch Novelists," *Edinburgh Review* 39 (1823), 158–96.

10 Oliphant, *Blackwood and Sons*, vol. 1, p. 125.

11 See the numerous (but undated) letters from Lockhart to Blackwood in Oliphant, *Blackwood and Sons*, vol. 1, pp. 200–10. Various letters in the Blackwood Papers thank Watts, Doubleday, Gifford, and Croker for anecdotes and hints that were taken up into "Noctes." In a 22 March 1822 letter

to Alaric Watts (with whom Blackwood keeps up a chatty epistolary relation, always eager for gossip and information on the London rival periodicals) Blackwood writes: "You will see that in the Noctes Ambrosianae we
have made good use of your precious dispatches and this too will give good
matter for another No. – with what I expect you will favour us with in good
time" (MS 30305). In a letter to Croker of 19 October 1821 Blackwood
acknowledges "interesting accompaniments of a letter of the 13th" and
writes: "I have the pleasure of telling you that they have not suffered by
being made use of by North and Tickler in the Noctes. In this way the Blue
& Yellow is much better shewn up than if had in a formal article" (MS
30969, Blackwood Papers). He later writes to Doubleday on 23 October
1823: "I hope you will be pleased at seeing your sentiments, and indeed your
very words adopted. I hope that whenever you can spare a quarter of an
hour you will write me and give me your ideas, remarks, news, or any thing
that occurs to you, for anything from you may often give us good subject
matter for the Noctes." He goes on to assure Doubleday of his discretion in
the use of such material: "nothing you say to me is known to any one" (MS
30306, Blackwood Papers).

12   The question of editorial control in *Blackwood's* is a vexed one. Blackwood
typically refers to his editor in any dealing with outsiders, such as potential litigants (often when it suits his interests). When rejecting submissions,
he often uses the phrase "Christopher's imprimatur" to soften the blow,
again shifting the responsibility. And it is clear that Lockhart and Wilson
did much of the editorial work from time to time. Yet the Blackwood
Papers contains numerous letters in which Blackwood tries to elicit
certain kinds of articles, urges revisions to accepted material, or informs
contributors of substantial cuts. Letters to Maginn in 1825 show pretty
clearly that he is in editorial control of the magazine. Possibly the most
revealing moment in the letters comes in a 3 November 1820 rejection
notice to Charles Lloyd: "It is a pity you did not write to me at once
instead of writing to Prof. Wilson, for much as I respect the Professor's
opinion, I do not on many accounts wish to trouble him or any one but I
wish always myself to be the medium of communication between my
Editor and Contributors." The complex and ambiguous relation of
"medium" seems to cover Blackwood's activities here nicely, although the
statement still maintains the fiction of a single, relatively autonomous
editor (MS 30304, Blackwood Papers). The evidence is sketchy, but it
tends to support the idea of a trusted individual (like Lockwood or Wilson)
taking the role of editor but accepting the interventions of the publisher
rather freely.

13   See Peter Murphy's "Impersonation and Authorship in Romantic Britain,"
English Literary History 59 (1992), 625–49, for a discussion of the use of
pseudonyms in *Blackwood's*.

14   See H. Aram Vesser (ed.), *New Historicism Reader* (New York: Routledge,
1994), p. 2.

15 As Eyre Evans Crowe puts it in a review of La Martine's poetry: "The great axiom of association is, that the mind cannot pass from an *insensible* idea to another *insensible*, but through the intervention of a *sensible* one. Every object in the sphere of reflection is single, isolate, and unconnected even with its opposite, except through the sensible matters that are substituted for it – these are *words*, uttered words" (*Blackwood's* 15 [1824], 258).

16 S. T. Coleridge, *A Lay Sermon*, in *Biographia Literaria*, James Engell and W. Jackson Bate (eds.), 2 vols. (Princeton: Princeton University Press, 1983), vol. I, p. 121.

17 See Vesser (ed.), *New Historicism Reader*, p. 2.

18 The pagination of this *Noctes* runs from 369 to 376 and then from *359 to *371.

19 The denial also echoes Byron's letter to Douglas Kinnaird of 26 October, 1819 concerning *Don Juan*: "it may be profligate – but is it not *life*, is it not *the thing?*" *Byron's Letters and Journals*, ed. Leslie Marchand, 12 vols. (London: John Murray, 1972–83), vol. VI, p. 232.

20 Vesser (ed.), *New Historicism Reader*, p. 2.

21 Byron was thirty-four, but the "Noctes" crew consistently add to his age, probably to allow themselves the flash of alliteration – "fat and forty."

22 See "Public Affairs" (*Blackwood's* [1823] 13, 43–50).

23 See John Wilson's "Heaven and Earth, a Mystery" (*Blackwood's* [1823] 13, 72–7) and "The Candid. No. II" (*Blackwood's* [1823] 13, 261–75).

24 Wilson in "The Age of Bronze" (*Blackwood's* [1823] 13, 457–60).

25 See Alan Lang Strout's useful edition, *John Bull's Letter to Lord Byron* (Norman, OK: University of Oklahoma Press, 1947). Strout provides an informative sketch of the *Edinburgh*, the *Quarterly*, and *Blackwood's*, and he gives an overview of *Blackwood's* criticism of Byron in an appendix.

26 This new dispensation is taken up in January 1825 by John Wilson in a review of Alaric Watt's *Literary Souvenir*:

> We cannot help thinking, that poetry like this . . . awakens a much deeper feeling than that sort of poetry, which, dealing in troubled and sinful passions, might be supposed to have been groaned out to the Muse in auricular confession. There is something sickening in your assiduous poetical sinner, who sees nothing grand but guilt – thinks life dull unless it be devilish, and is oppressed with ennui, if forced for a season to have recourse to some honest employment. (*Blackwood's* 17, 98)

27 But hinted at much earlier in *Blackwood's*. Wilson, in his July 1818 "Essays on the Lake School of Poetry," sets Scott, Byron, and Wordsworth at the head of current poets.

28 The autobiography was later destroyed at the behest of the family and executors.

29 Murray had given Maginn all the materials in his possession. The two decided the timing was poor, however, and the work was eventually executed by Thomas Moore.

30 Which is not to say that the intensity of focus insured by Jeffrey's method does not have its advantages. Jeffrey's consideration of individual works is another matter entirely.

31 See Vesser (ed.), *New Historicism Reader*, p. 2.
32 A letter of 23 August 1821 shows the cruelty and duplicity of Blackwood's treatment of Hogg. Blackwood urges Hogg to dismiss the magazine's many jokes on him and to consider them a kind of tribute: "In short if you take the whole thing as a joke, it can do you not a particle of harm but rather the reverse." Fantastically, he intimates that he published one particularly objectionable article to *protect* Hogg: the writer was bent on publication, and rather than see it in its original "objectionable" state, Blackwood's accepted it in order to "get it softened and make as little offensive to you as possible." Characteristically, Blackwood also maintains that he is the victim: he complains of Hogg allowing himself to be used as a tool by "these precious fellows of the Scotsman" (MS 30301, Blackwood Papers).
33 The reviewer of Landor's book is not certain, but it is most probably John Wilson. See the entry in Walter Houghton (ed.), *The Wellesley Index to Victorian Periodicals*, 5 vols. (Toronto: University of Toronto Press, 1966–89).
34 Blackwood's tone changes greatly in letters to Maginn in the first half of 1825. They increasingly disagree in their estimation of work for the magazine, and Blackwood frequently rejects material from Maginn. Over and over Blackwood alludes to what's good for the magazine – as opposed to what's good for Maginn himself – in his remarks to Maginn. Recriminations over a review of Hook's *Sayings and Doings* take up several letters (Blackwood Papers, MS 30308).
35 Ferrier begins with *Noctes* 19. He notes that the American edition, by Mackenzie, is "encumbered with that *plethora* of alien matter which is cleared off in the present impression." See *Noctes Ambrosianae*, J. H. Ferrier (ed.), 4 vols. (Edinburgh: Blackwood and Sons, 1864), vol. I, p. ix.
36 Letter to Douglas Kinnaird, 26 October 1819, in *Byron's Letters and Journals*, ed. Marchand, vol. VI, 232.

4 MAGAZINE ROMANTICISM: THE *NEW MONTHLY*, 1821–1825

1 John Scott, "To Robert Baldwin, 9 November 1818," Holman Clippings, Houghton Library, Harvard University. One of six typescripts of Scott's correspondence with Baldwin.
2 See Fredric Jameson, *The Political Unconscious: Narrative as Socially Symbolic Act* (Ithaca, NY: Cornell University Press, 1982), especially pp. 74–83. See also my article, "The End of Emma," *Journal of English and Germanic Philology*, 91 (1992), 344–59, for a consideration of the "political unconscious" in Austen.
3 Carl Schmitt, *Political Romanticism*, Guy Oakes (trans.), (Cambridge, MA: MIT Press, 1986).
4 Schmitt uses this term repeatedly, and he is fond of such absolute phrasing as "the core of an intellectual movement must be clear and precisely defined if we are to pass judgment on it and make up our minds about it" (*ibid.*, p. 7). I make no claims about the fitness of Schmitt's definition for German Romantic writers.

5　See *Manfred* III, i, 6–18 and *Don Juan* I, stanzas 214 and 215.

6　Campbell's contract provided for a sub-editor. Edward DuBois, after one number, proved obnoxious to Campbell, and he was replaced with the indefatigable Cyrus Redding. See Walter Houghton (ed.), *The Wellesley Index to Victorian Periodicals*, 5 vols. (Toronto: University of Toronto Press, 1966–89), vol. III, p. 163.

7　*Literary Gazette*, 3 February 1821, p. 79. Cited in *ibid.*, vol. III, p. 163.

8　Cambell's "Preface" was published with the December 1821 number, but it is often bound up with the January–June 1822 volume.

9　Although the use of the term "suburban" might appear anachronistic, F.M.L. Thompson uses the term to describe building activity in Hampstead in the first quarter of the nineteenth century. He notes that the object of this speculation "was to create a series of residential estates, each house set in its few acres of park-like grounds and surrounded by its own paddocks and meadows to give the perfect impression of a country estate in miniature; a rural illusion which was yet, in the early years of the nineteenth century, more than a half truth, and one which was in the reach of the successful business or professional man whose affairs did not demand an excessively punctilious attendance at the office." See *Hampstead: Building a Borough, 1650–1964* (London: Routledge & Kegan Paul, 1974), especially pp. 84–110; this quotation pp. 91–2.

10　In David Perkins (ed.), *English Romantic Writers* (Fort Worth, TX: Harcourt Brace and Company, 1995), p. 832.

11　Hazlitt's Table-Talk essays in the *New Monthly* did not all go into his volumes of *Table-Talk*; some emerged in the 1826 *Plain Speaker*. (Further complicating the matter is the fact that some emerged in the 1825 Paris edition of *Table-Talk* before they appeared in *Plain Speaker*.)

12　One can easily extend this consideration of the relation of form of emergence and meaning to the book that "On Milton's Sonnets" appeared in, volume II of *Table-Talk*. There the essay followed on the heels of the more overtly political "On the Landscape of Nicholas Poussin" (discussed above). In that context a political emphasis seems unavoidable.

13　See Howe's discussion of this passage in *The Complete Works of William Hazlitt*, P. P. Howe (ed.), 21 vols. (London: Frank Cass & Company, 1967), vol. XI, p. 335.

14　Cited in Richard Altick, *The English Common Reader* (Chicago: University of Chicago Press, 1957), p. 319.

5　*SARTOR RESARTUS* IN *FRASER'S*: TOWARD A DIALECTICAL POLITICS

1　Carlyle uses this phrase in the "Testimonies of Authors" which he included in the first English edition of *Sartor*. See the edition by Charles Frederick Harrold, *Sartor Resartus* (Garden City, NJ: Doubleday, Doran & Co., 1937).

2　These claims are made by G.B. Tennyson in *Sartor Called Resartus* (Princeton:

Princeton University Press, 1965) and Gerry H. Brookes in *The Rhetorical Form of Carlyle's Sartor Resartus* (London: University of California Press, 1972).

3 Tennyson, *Sartor Called Resartus*, p. 302, and Jerome Beaty in "All Victoria's Horses and All Victoria's Men," *New Literary History* I (1970), 285.

4 M.H. Abrams, *Natural Supernaturalism* (New York: W. W. Norton and Company, 1971), p. 309.

5 Anne Mellor, *English Romantic Irony* (Cambridge, MA: Harvard University Press, 1980), p. 6.

6 The mystical conversion of the Leith Walk episode, to which Carlyle often referred, is crucial to such reading. Tennyson's appraisal is typical: "*Sartor Resartus* is in a real sense the outcome of the period introduced by the incident in Leith Walk" (*Sartor Called Resartus*, p. 14).

7 Charles and Mary Lamb, *The Works of Charles and Mary Lamb*, E. V. Lucas (ed.), 5 vols. (New York: Putnam and Sons, 1903), vol. II, p. 152.

8 See also Emory Neff's *Carlyle* (London: George Allen and Unwin, 1932), especially the chapter "Romanticism in the Machine Age," and Tennyson, *Sartor Called Resartus*, pp. 126–56.

9 See Miriam M. H. Thrall, *Rebellious Fraser's: Nol Yorke's Magazine in the Days of Maginn, Thackeray, and Carlyle* (New York: Columbia University Press, 1934), p. 14.

10 See *Ibid.*, p. 8 and chapter 3 of this study, page 120.

11 *The Collected Letters of Thomas and Jane Welsh Carlyle*, Charles Richard Saunders an Kenneth J. Fielding (eds.), 21 vols. (Durham, NC: Duke University Press, 1970–), vol. V, p. 171.

12 Even critics who draw on Carlyle's relations with Fraser do not respect the difference between versions. Tennyson gives a painstaking account of Carlyle's "apprenticeship" as a magazine writer, but this genetic account has little relation to his main argument, that *Sartor* is a novel, and to the stylistic analysis that makes up the bulk of his book. Brookes, in arguing that *Sartor* is "a kind of persuasive essay," refers to *Fraser's* and the magazine world generally, but only to clarify Carlyle's formal intentions. Thrall considers the relation between Maginn and Carlyle in *Fraser's* very carefully, but only in an attempt to discern which writer influenced the other. See Tennyson, *Sartor Called Resartus*, pp. 126–56; Brookes, *Rhetorical Form*, pp. 16–47; and Thrall, *Rebellious Fraser's*, pp. 88–94 and 120–8.

13 The opening paragraph of *Sartor* exemplifies this ambiguous use of figural language:

> Considering our present advanced state of culture, and how the Torch of Science has been brandished and borne about, with more or less effect, for five-thousand years and upwards; how in these times especially, not only the Torch still burns, and perhaps more fiercely than ever, but innumerable Rushlights, and Sulphur-matches, kindled thereat, are also glancing in every direction, so that not the smallest cranny or doghole in Nature or Art can remain unilluminated.

> A little below this, the grotesque description of the "Creation of the World" as "little more mysterious than the cooking of a dumpling" is further distended by the Editor's query of "How the apples were got in."

14 Brookes argues that "*Sartor* was not well adapted for serial publication" (*Rhetorical Form*, p. 38). In particular, he echoes Richard Garnett's reservations, that "intervening distractions . . . obscure Carlyle's drift," notes that "The Centre of Indifference" and "The Everlasting Yea" were separated from "The Everlasting No," and points out that the opening of "The Centre of Indifference" is poorly suited for the beginning of an installment. The arguments for this position are based on one particular division, between the fourth and fifth installment, and upon the judgments of two readers, Garnett and, later in Brookes's account, Emerson.

15 Harrold seems to appreciate this reading technique: "Carlyle's book is best read in appropriate moods, a little at a time, not continuously from beginning to end" (*Sartor Resartus*, Harrold [ed.], p. xxxiii).

16 Tennyson, *Sartor Called Resartus*, p. 302.

17 See Janice L. Haney, "'Shadow-Hunting': Romantic Irony, *Sartor Resartus*, and Victorian Romanticism," *Studies in Romanticism* 17 (1978), 327.

18 Walter L. Reed, "The Pattern of Conversion in *Sartor Resartus*," *English Literary History* 38 (1971), 427.

19 This is Carlyle's formulation, from the headings he wrote for the first English edition.

20 This is Hazlitt's description of Lamb's conversation in one of his Table-Talk essays for the *London Magazine* (2 [1820], 257). Characteristically, Hazlitt reworks a famous passage from King Lear – "But I am bound / Upon a wheel of fire, that mine own tears / Do scald like molten lead" – to forge a relation between Lamb's often manic congeniality and the tragedies of his personal life.

21 Abrams, with his characteristic combination of accuracy and felicity, terms it "so blatantly eccentric that it is readily misestimated as a freak in the history of prose narrative." See *Natural Supernaturalism*, p. 129.

22 This persists today, in anthologies that reprint the central sequence of Book Two – the "Everlasting No," "Centre of Indifference," and "Everlasting Yea" – with Book Three's "Natural Supernaturalism," which completes the pattern. See William Buckler (ed.), *Prose of the Victorian Period* (Boston: Houghton Mifflin Company, 1958) and, of course, *The Norton Anthology of English Literature*. This emphasis has been enforced by M.H. Abrams's powerful account of Romanticism, *Natural Supernaturalism*.

23 *The Reliques of Father Prout* (London: J. Fraser, 1836) had the signal dignity of being reviewed by the author in *Fraser's Magazine* as well.

24 John Scott, "To Robert Baldwin, 9 November 1818," Holman Clippings, Hougton Library, Harvard University.

Bibliography

Abrams, M. H., *Natural Supernaturalism*, New York: W. W. Norton and Company, 1971.

Alexander, J. H., "*Blackwood's*: Magazine as Romantic Form," *Wordsworth Circle* 15 (1984), 57–67.

Alexander, J. H. (ed.), *The Tavern Sages: Selections from the Noctes Ambrosianae*, Aberdeen: The Association for Scottish Literary Studies, 1992.

Allen, Michael, *Poe and the British Magazine Tradition*, New York: Oxford University Press, 1969.

Richard Altick, *The English Common Reader*, Chicago: University of Chicago Press, 1957.

Aspinall, A., *Politics and the Press c. 1780–1850*, London: Home & Van Thal Ltd., 1949.

Bakhtin, M. M., *The Dialogic Imagination*, Michael Holquist (ed.), Caryl Emerson and Michael Holquist (trans.), Austin: University of Texas Press, 1981.

Barnett, George, *The Evolution of Elia*, New York: Haskell House, 1973.

Bate, Walter Jackson, *The Burden of the Past and the English Poet*, New York: W. W. Norton, 1970.

Josephine Bauer, *The London Magazine, 1820–1829*, Copenhagen: Rosenkilde and Bagger, 1953.

Beaty, Jerome, "All Victoria's Horses and All Victoria's Men," *New Literary History* 1 (1970), 271–92.

Beetham, Margaret, "Open and Closed: the Periodical as a Publishing Genre," *Victorian Periodicals Review* 22 (1989), 96–100.

Birrell, Augustine, "Charles Lamb," in *Obiter Dicta*, second series, London: Eliot Stock, 1887, pp. 222–35.

Blackwood Papers, National Library of Scotland.

Bloom, Harold, *The Anxiety of Influence*, Oxford: Oxford University Press, 1973.

Blunden, Edmund, *Keats's Publisher: A Memoir of John Taylor*, London: Jonathan Cape, 1936 (reissued in the Life and Letters Series No. 97, 1940).

Bromwich, David, *Hazlitt: The Mind of a Critic*, New York: Oxford University Press, 1983.

Bulwer, E. L., "Charles Lamb," *Westminster Review* 27 (1837), 294–302.

Boulton, James, *The Language of Politics*, London: Routledge & Kegan Paul, 1963.

Brookes, Gerry H., *The Rhetorical Form of Carlyle's Sartor Resartus*, London: University of California Press, 1972.

Burke, Edmund, *The Writings and Speeches of Edmund Burke*, Paul Langford (ed.), 9 vols., Oxford: Clarendon Press, 1981–.

Butler, Marilyn, "Culture's Medium: the Role of the Review," in Stuart Curran (ed.), *The Cambridge Companion to British Romanticism*, Cambridge: Cambridge University Press, 1993, pp. 120–47.

Carlyle, Thomas, *Sartor Resartus*, Charles Frederick Harrold (ed.), Garden City, NJ: Doubleday, Doran & Co., 1937.

Carlyle, Thomas and Jane, *The Collected Letters of Thomas and Jane Welsh Carlyle*, Charles Richard Sanders and Kenneth J. Fielding (eds.), 21 vols., Durham, NC: Duke University Press, 1970–.

Cobban, Alfred, *Edmund Burke and the Revolt Against the Eighteenth Century*, New York: Barnes and Noble, 1929.

Coleridge, H. N., "The Last Essays of Elia," *The Quarterly Review* 54 (1835), 58–77.

Coleridge, Samuel Taylor, *The Collected Works of Samuel Taylor Coleridge*, Kathleen Coburn (ed.), 14 vols., Princeton: Princeton University Press, 1972.

   Biographia Literaria, James Engell and W. Jackson Bate (eds.), 2 vols., Princeton: Princeton University Press, 1983.

   Collected Letters of Samuel Taylor Coleridge, Earl Leslie Griggs (ed.), 6 vols., Oxford: Oxford University Press, 1956–71.

Cook, Jonathan, "Hazlitt: Criticism and Ideology," in David Aers, Jonathan Cook, and David Punter (eds.), *Romanticism and Ideology*, London: Routledge & Kegan Paul, 1981, pp. 137–54.

Cornwall, Barry (B. W. Proctor), *Charles Lamb: a Memoir*, London: Edward Moxon, 1866.

Courteney, Winifred, *Young Charles Lamb*, Hong Kong: Macmillan Press, 1982.

Deane, Seamus, *The French Revolution and the Enlightenment in England*, Cambridge, MA: Harvard University Press, 1988.

De Quincey, Thomas, "Recollections of Charles Lamb," *Tait's* 9 os, 5 ns (April and June 1838), 227–47 and 355–66.

   "Charles Lamb and His Friends," *North British Review* 6 (1848), 97–116.

Eagleton, Terry, *The Function of Criticism*, Norfolk: Verso, 1984.

Eco, Umberto, *The Open Work*, Anna Concogni (trans.), Cambridge, MA: Harvard University Press, 1989.

Erickson, Lee, *The Economy of Literary Form*, Baltimore: Johns Hopkins University Press, 1996.

Evans, Eric J., *The Forging of the Modern State*, New York: Longman, 1983.

Ferrier, J. H. (ed.) *Noctes Ambrosianae*, 4 vols., Edinburgh: Blackwood and Sons, 1864.

Flesch, William, "'Friendly and Judicious' Reading: Affect and Irony in the Works of Charles Lamb," *Studies in Romanticism* 23 (1984), 163–83.

Frank, Robert, *Don't Call Me Gentle Charles*, Corvallis: Oregon State University Press, 1976.

Graham, Walter, *English Literary Periodicals*, New York: Thomas Nelson & Sons, 1930.

Greene, Graham, "Lamb's Testimonials," *Spectator* 152 (30 March 1934), 512–13.

Haney, Janice L., "'Shadow-Hunting': Romantic Irony, *Sartor Resartus*, and Victorian Romanticism," *Studies in Romanticism* 17 (1978), 307–33.

Haven, Richard, "The Romantic Art of Charles Lamb," *English Literary History* 30 (1963), 137–46.

Hazlitt, William, *The Complete Works of William Hazlitt*, P. P. Howe (ed.), 21 vols., London: Frank Cass & Company, 1967.

"The Periodical Press," *Edinburgh Review* 76 (May 1823), 349–78.

Hazlitt, W. C., "Charles Lamb: Gleanings after his Biographers," *Macmillan's Magazine* 15 (1866–1867), 473–83.

Houghton, Walter E., "Periodical Literature and the Articulate Classes," in Joanne Shattock and Michael Wolff (eds.), *The Victorian Periodical Press: Samplings and Soundings*, Leicester University Press, 1982, pp. 3–27.

Houghton, Walter (ed.), *The Wellesley Index to Victorian Periodicals*, 5 vols., Toronto: University of Toronto Press, 1966–89.

James, Louis, "The Trouble with Betsy: Periodicals and the Common Reader in Mid-Nineteenth-Century England," in *The Victorian Periodical Press: Samplings and Soundings*, Leicester University Press, 1982, pp. 349–66.

Jameson, Fredric, *The Political Unconscious: Narrative as Socially Symbolic Act*, Ithaca, NY: Cornell University Press, 1982.

Jeffrey, Francis, "Secondary Scotch Novelists," *Edinburgh Review* 39 (1823), 158–96.

Jones, Leonidas M., "The Scott–Christie Duel," *Texas Studies in Language and Literature* 12 (1971), 605–29.

The Life of John Hamilton Reynolds, Hanover, NH: University Press of New England, 1984.

Kinnaird, John, *William Hazlitt: Critic of Power*, New York: Columbia University Press, 1978.

Klancher, Jon, *The Making of English Reading Audiences, 1790–1832*, Madison: University of Wisconsin Press, 1987.

Lamb, Charles and Mary, *The Works of Charles and Mary Lamb*, E.V. Lucas (ed.), 5 vols., New York: Putnam and Sons, 1903.

Lang, Andrew, *The Life and Letters of John Gibson Lockhart*, 2 vols., New York: AMS Press, 1970.

Latané, David, "The Birth of the Author in the Victorian Archive," *Victorian Periodicals Review* 22 (1989), 109–17.

Lewes, G. H., "Charles Lamb – His Genius and Writings," *The British Quarterly Review* 7 (1848), 292–311.

The London Magazine, 10 vols., London: Baldwin, Cradock, & Joy, 1820–5.

McFarland, Thomas, *Romantic Cruxes*, Oxford: Clarendon Press, 1987.

McGann, Jerome, *The Beauty of Inflections*, Oxford: Clarendon Press, 1985.

The Romantic Ideology, Chicago: University of Chicago Press, 1983.

Meinecke, Frederich, *Historicism*, J. E. Anderson (trans.), London: Routledge & Kegan Paul, 1972.

Mellor, Anne, *English Romantic Irony*, Cambridge, MA: Harvard University Press, 1980.

Mill, James, "Periodical Literature," *Westminster Review* 1 (1824), 206–49.

Mill, John Stuart, "Periodical Literature," *Westminster Review* 1 (1824), 505–41.

Milnes, R. Monckton, "Charles Lamb," *Edinburgh Review* 124 (1866), 133–40.

Monsman, Gerald, *Confessions of a Prosaic Dreamer*, Durham, NC: Duke University Press, 1984.

Mulcahy, Daniel, "Charles Lamb: The Antithetical Manner and the Two Planes," *Studies in English Literature* 3 (1963), 517–42.

Murphy, Peter T., "Impersonation and Authorship in Romantic Britain," *English Literary History* 59 (1992), 625–49.

Neff, Emory, *Carlyle*, London: George Allen and Unwin, 1932.

O'Leary, Patrick, *Regency Editor: Life of John Scott*, Aberdeen: Aberdeen University Press, 1983.

Oliphant, Margaret, *Annals of a Publishing House: William Blackwood and His Sons*, 3 vols., Edinburgh: William Blackwood and Sons, 1897.

Parker, Mark, "The End of Emma," *Journal of English and Germanic Philology* 91 (1992), 344–59.

Pater, Walter, *Appreciations*, New York: The Macmillan Co., 1910.

Perkin, Harold, *The Origins of Modern English Society: 1780–1880*, London: Routledge & Kegan Paul, 1972.

Pocock, J. G. A., "Burke and the Ancient Constitution," in *Politics, Language, and Time*, New York: Atheneum, 1971.

Praz, Mario, *The Hero in Eclipse*, Angus Davidson (trans.), Oxford: Oxford University Press, 1956.

Pykett, Lyn, "Reading the Periodical Press: Text and Context," *Victorian Periodicals Review* 22 (1989), 100–8.

Randel, Fred, *The World of Elia*, Port Washington, NY: Kennikat Press, 1975.

Reed, Walter L., "The Pattern of Conversion in *Sartor Resartus*," *English Literary History* 38 (1971), 411–31.

Reiman, Donald, "Thematic Unity in Lamb's Familiar Essays," *Journal of English and Germanic Philology* 64 (1965), 470–8.

Schmitt, Carl, *Political Romanticism*, Guy Oakes (trans.), Cambridge, MA: MIT Press, 1986.

Schoenfield, Mark, "Voices Together: Lamb, Hazlitt, and the *London*," *Studies in Romanticism* 29 (1990), 57–72.

Scott, John, "To Robert Baldwin, 9 November 1818," Holman Clippings, Houghton Library, Harvard University. (One of six letters from Scott to Baldwin copied by Holman.)

Scott, Walter, *The Letters of Sir Walter Scott*, H. J. C. Grierson (ed.), 12 vols., London: Constable and Co., 1932–7.

Sławiński, Janusz, "Reading and Reader in the Literary Historical Process," *New Literary History* 19 (1988), 521–39.

Smith, William Henry, "Charles Lamb," *Blackwood's* 66 (1849), 133–50.

Stone, Lawrence and Jeanne C. Fawtier, *An Open Elite? England 1540–1880*, New York: Oxford University Press, 1986.

Strout, Alan Lang, *John Bull's Letter to Lord Byron*, Norman, OK: University of Oklahoma Press, 1947.

"Knights of the Burning Epistle," *Studia Neophilologica* 26 (1953–4), 77–98.

A Bibliography of Articles in "Blackwood's Magazine": 1817–1825, Library Bulletin No. 5, Texas Technological College, 1959.

"Concerning the 'Noctes Ambrosianae,'" *Modern Language Notes* 51 (1936), 493–504.

Sullivan, Alvin (ed.), *British Literary Magazines*, 2 vols., Westport, CT: Greenwood Press, 1983.

Sutherland, John, "Henry Colburn Publisher," *Publishing History* 19 (1986), 59–84.

Victorian Novelists and Publishers, London: The Athlone Press, 1976.

Talfourd, Thomas Noon (ed.), *The Letters of Charles Lamb, with a Sketch of His Life*, London: Moxon, 1837.

Tennyson, G. B., *Sartor Called Resartus*, Princeton: Princeton University Press, 1965.

Thompson, Denys, "Our Debt to Lamb," in F. R. Leavis (ed.), *Determinations*, London: Chatto and Windus, 1934.

Thompson, F. M. L., *Hampstead: Building a Borough, 1650–1964*, London: Routledge & Kegan Paul, 1974.

Thrall, Miriam F., *Rebellious Fraser's: Nol Yorke's Magazine in the Days of Maginn, Thackeray, and Carlyle*, New York: Columbia University Press, 1934.

Verdi, Richard, "Hazlitt and Poussin," *The Keats–Shelley Memorial Bulletin* 32 (1981), 1–18.

Ward, A. C., *The Frolic and the Gentle*, London: Methuen and Co., 1934.

Wheatley, Kim, "The *Blackwood's* Attacks on Leigh Hunt," *Nineteenth Century Literature* 47 (1992), 1–31.

Williams, Raymond, *Culture and Society, 1780–1950*, New York: Columbia University Press, 1983.

Wolff, Michael, "Charting the Golden Stream: Thoughts on a Directory of Victorian Periodicals," *Victorian Periodicals Newsletter* 13 (1971), 23–38.

Woodring, Carl, *Politics in English Romantic Poetry*, Cambridge, MA: Harvard University Press, 1970.

Zietlin, Jacob, "The Editor of the *London Magazine*," *Journal of English and Germanic Philology* 20 (1921), 340–54.

Index

gentility, 60; and Godwin, 36–7, 44–5; and
Hazlitt's politics, 62; on Keats, 37;
challenged by Lockhart, 21–7; contrasted
with Maginn, 168–9; and Peterloo, 35;
politics of, 35–7, 90–1; program in the
London, 135–6; and Walter Scott, 39–40, 47;
and Shelley, 40–1; and Table-Talk, 65–72;
"Historical and Critical Summary of
Intelligence," 38; "On Human Perfectibility,"
64–5; "The Signs of the Times," 48–9; *see
also Burkean–Coleridgean literary culture*
Scott, Walter, 26, 47
Shakespeare, salient quotation of, 6, 19, 22, 27
Shelley, P. B., 40–1
Six Acts, 16
Sławiński, Janusz, 51
Smith, Horace, in *London*, 74–6, 191n.16; in
New Monthly, 142–6; "Journal of a Tourist,"
144–5; "Portrait of a Septuagenarian,"
148–9; "Walks in the Garden," 143–4;
"Winter," 143; "The World," 142–3

Smith, W. H., 54
Spence, Gordon, 180n.21
Stone, Lawrence and Jeanne C. Fawtier,
18–19, 185n.21
Strout, Alan Lang, 193n.31, 200n.25
Sutherland, John, 192n.25

Taylor, Arthur, 39
Taylor, John, and Clare, 195n.44
Tennyson, G. B., 157, 175, 202n.2, 202n.3
Thackeray, William, 53, 58
Thompson, Denys, 57
Thompson, F. M. L., 202n.9
Thrall, Miriam F., 186n.36, 203n.9

Ward, A. C., 57
Wellesley Index to Victorian Periodicals, 4
Williams, Raymond, 11
Wolff, Michael, 3, 184n.2
Woodring, Carl, 187n.5

CAMBRIDGE STUDIES IN ROMANTICISM

General editors
MARILYN BUTLER,
University of Oxford
JAMES CHANDLER,
University of Chicago